Ventures
in
Worship 3

Edited by
David James Randolph

Published by Abingdon Press
Nashville and New York

Ventures in Worship 3

Scripture quotations noted RSV are from the Revised Standard Version of the Bible, copyrighted 1946 and 1952 by the Division of Christian Education, National Council of Churches, and are used by permission.

Scripture quotations noted NEB are from The New English Bible © the Delegates of the Oxford University Press and the Syndics of the Cambridge University Press 1961, 1970.

Scripture quotations noted TEV are from the Today's English Version of the New Testament. Copyright © American Bible Society 1966.

Scripture quotations noted Phillips are from The New Testament in Modern English, copyright 1958 by J.B. Phillips.

ISBN 0-687-43689-3

MANUFACTURED BY THE PARTHENON PRESS AT
NASHVILLE, TENNESSEE, UNITED STATES OF AMERICA

Contents

To
Lance Webb and William Frederick Dunkle, Jr.
President and Vice President
of The Commission on Worship
1968—1972
and
Lovers of Liturgy and Fathers of Faith

Foreword

It is the time of the breaking of many waters
                              and of the shaking of foundations
It is the day of blood on the moon
                              and other unbearable calamities
It is the hour when brother strikes brother
                              and the generations are set on edge

All things are at an end
Or a beginning
Corpsed
Or struggling to be born
It is a time for God
Let the people gather
And let us worship
Sing
And bow down
Praise
And pray
Let what is to be
Begin

—John Killinger

Introduction

"Worship is not only recollection of the past,
but creation of a future."

I have often felt like a thirsty man finding a spring of water as I looked over material submitted to the Project on Worship. From creative local churches and individuals have come materials for worship so refreshing and substantial that I could hardly wait to share them with others. Thus, an inspiration for *Ventures in Worship 3*.

When the Project on Worship began there were some who felt that its publications would be limited, if any appeared at all. Some felt that there might be one sampling of "contemporary" material, and that would be it. Soon after the publication of *Ventures in Worship*, however, it became clear that creativity is a process which once set in motion becomes endless in its range and productivity. The *Ventures* series has helped to stimulate some of this creativity and provide a means of sharing, and confirms the hope of those who began the project. Once congregations get into the act of developing worship which is real for them, there is no turning back and endless avenues of exploration open up.

There is evidence of maturation, as well as creativity, in the materials collected here. One of the most encouraging signs to me is evidence that the more persons work with liturgy the better they become at it. This is due in part to the kind of practical field testing that goes on as congregations seek to find their own liturgical voice, keeping the elements that speak for them and discarding those which do not. Also, persons refine and develop as they work harder at their liturgical responsibilities.

The dialogue with scholars also encourages hope. The *Ventures* series from the beginning has sought to combine scholarly reflection with actual parish explorations. One of the purposes of the *Ventures* publications has been to make emperical data on contemporary worship available to scholars. References such as that by Paul W. Hoon, in his masterwork, *The Integrity of Worship*, (Nashville: Abingdon, 1971), demonstrates that that purpose is being fulfilled, at least to some degree. Two papers included in *Ventures 3* also advance the necessary dialogue between what is going on in the parishes and what is going on among the professional scholars. The phenomenological analysis of The Lord's Supper, by Gary Barbaree, and the analysis of *Ventures 2* by Professor Louis Bloede, I think, advance this dialogue. Moreover, the scholars have offered us helpful suggestions for the future as well as careful analyses of our present situation.

This dialogue comes at a time when it is especially needed. The criteria for meaningful Christian worship and the process by which it may be developed become increasingly important as creativity increases. The Project on Worship and the *Ventures* publications have been concerned about creativity and criteria from the beginning. When the goals and objectives of the 1968-1972 quadrennium were set by the Commission on Worship, research and the theology of practice at the local level was primary. In the report to the General Conference which met at Dallas in 1968, a paragraph I submitted said that "Worship is not only recollection of the past, but creation of a future, and the Commission is most interested in emerging, as well as established patterns of worship. . . . Folk music and other art forms on the one hand are media which communicate the Gospel to people who would not listen otherwise (particularly youth), and on the other hand these media help express more of the fullness of the reality of the Gospel. The biblical and theological dimensions are thus at the heart of this research."

The Project on Worship was created to carry out this research. The project is designed to collect, evaluate, share, stimulate, and create resources for contemporary worship. Since its creation in 1968 as a joint venture of the General Commission on Worship and the General Board of Evangelism, significant progress has been made in fulfilling the design.

1. *Collecting.* Essays, questionnaires, elements of worship, orders of Holy Communion, Baptism, Morning Worship, Weddings, Funerals, plus banners, photographic slides, audio tapes, video tapes, and other data have been collected from all over America and from other countries. Most, but not all, of the materials are from parish churches. Knowledgeable people have estimated that this is perhaps the largest collection of its kind.

2. *Evaluation.* Evaluation is carried out by the Committee on Resources for Worship (which advises the project), the director, consultants, and indirectly by the Board itself.

3. *Sharing.* Sharing from the project has been in the form of correspondence, interviews, workshops, and notably publications. *Ventures in Worship* is a selection of material from the project edited by the director and published by Abingdon Press in April, 1969. A swift and wide acceptance prompted *Ventures in Worship 2*, which appeared in October, 1970. *Ventures in Song* was published in February of 1972.

4. *Stimulation and Creation.* Ventures is designed to stimulate questing for more vital worship, rather than to substitute for it. One of the most striking signs of effectiveness at this point is that *Ventures 3* is made up in large part of materials submitted under the stimulus of the earlier *Ventures.* One person commented that *Ventures* had given them "the courage to create." Those directly related to the project have constantly been involved with creating new materials as well as commenting on the work of others, especially in the area of mixed media communications.

My approach to the question of criteria has been to establish a framework in which materials submitted to the project could be evaluated without establishing rigid regulations about what was or was not "proper" worship. Philosophically speaking, I have taken a phenomenological approach; that is, I have tried to let the materials submitted speak for themselves. Within the general framework set forth in the introduction to *Ventures in Worship*, I have sought to develop the criteria in dialogue with material actually submitted and with the traditional worship which we have inherited and with the theology of worship currently being developed by professional scholars. A full scale report of this analysis, and what we have learned in the project, along with guidelines for the future, is now in preparation. In the present volume the article by Professor Louis Bloede is especially helpful on this point.

Simply to suggest the kind of criteria which have emerged out of the study and to offer some guidelines for material submitted to the project, we can say that our quest is for *meaningful* Christian worship, worship that has a basis, that adds up and makes sense, and that is consistent with the Christian revelation. Meaningful Christian worship, and, by implication, materials sought for the *Ventures* publication is:

a. theologically discerning
b. biblically based
c. historically conscious
d. missionally sensitive
e. personally authentic
f. liturgically whole

Two further comments: First, the most significant thing I observe in the current worship explosion lies not in mod liturgies, jazz masses, and new music in themselves, but in the way in which liturgy is becoming the work of the people in the preparation of, as well as the presentation of, worship. In the virtually unprecedented fashion in which the people are helping to develop the resources with which they praise God lies the key to the dramatic revolution in worship in our time.

Second, the Project on Worship would not be remotely possible without the interest, support, and hard work of many people. It is itself a work of the people, and to all of them I am deeply grateful. The names of many of them are on record in the publications and elsewhere in this report, and I salute them.

As these words are being written we are nearing the conclusion of one quadrennium on the calendar and are in the beginning of a new quadrennium in actuality. The Commission on Worship and the Board of Evangelism which collaborated to create the Project on Worship are now part of the Board of Discipleship of The United Methodist Church. Those of us connected with this project feel that this offers a greater opportunity than ever to develop the potential for meaningful worship. As we look to the future we are hopeful that advances can be made upon the past. We hope that there are ways that we can improve the service and ways in which we can improve upon what we have been doing. We are not yet clear at the moment of just what forms our future publications will take, but we are sure that this area is one of the greatest importance. We are sure, also, that we will want to continue to collect materials from across the country and around the world which express the church's worship in this day. Therefore, we encourage the submission of further material.

Don McLean, in his album *American Pie*, seems to say farewell to a way of life that's passing. It's a sad song, in a way, about growing up and leaving behind James Dean's jacket, rock and roll, marching bands and cheerleaders, pink carnations, and pickup trucks. But the more one listens to the title song and "Vincent," the more you realize that McLean is also saying hello to a new way of life, to a new future. *Ventures in Worship* has been like that—a kind of saying goodbye to some things we thought were indispensable and a joyous saying hello to a new way to worship. Ironically, we haven't been saying goodbye to tradition or to the grandeur of the past, but to some limitations of that which we took for the original. The real exuberance lies with the way in which that which was true yesterday and will be true tomorrow becomes true today in our worship.

One closing note: "Cross roads" is another number in that album, and the cross symbolism is not accidental. It's about how we end up walking all the roads, no matter what we plan. In editing *Ventures* I have come to know a lot of people I have never met. There is a genuine community that has represented a coming together on these pages. To read something and to realize that somebody has walked a road that I thought I traveled by myself, and to see this experience transformed and elevated into praise of God has been a great reward. Thanks.

DAVID JAMES RANDOLPH

Acknowledgments

To all who have made this publication possible we are deeply grateful, especially to those who have contributed their work. Thanks go to Bishop Lance Webb and his colleagues on the former General Commission on Worship, for whom this work was edited. Vice-Chairman, Dr. William F. Dunkle, Jr., and Executive Secretary, the Rev. Hoyt Hickman have been especially helpful. The Committee on Resources for Worship was chaired by the Rev. Eugene Holmes and was made up of Mrs. Wilbur Longstreth, Paul M. Davis, Robert Hoffelt, and the Rev. Joe Harding. Their judgment and suggestions were invaluable.

Thanks are extended to the Rev. Joseph H. Yeakel, formerly General Secretary of the General Board of Evangelism and now Bishop of the Syracuse Area. Dr. Ira Gallaway has offered welcome stimulus and support as this work continues, as has the Rev. Edward Duncan.

We express thanks to the following people who typed the manuscript—Mrs. Ursa Worthy, Mrs. Linnea Carter, Mrs. Frances Johnson, and Miss Gail Ratzloff.

Genuine thanks are extended with acknowledgments to the following who have contributed to this volume:

Ms. Daisy Ann Baar
Mason United Methodist Church
Tacoma, Washington

Gary W. Barbaree
Rt. 4, Box 298
El Dorado, Arkansas 71730

The Rev. Daniel T. Benedict, Jr.
Covina United Methodist Church
512 S. Avington
W. Covina, California 91722

The Rev. Louis Bloede
15 South Wright Street
Naperville, Illinois 60540

The Rev. Thomas Blowers
The Community Church
Schroon Lake, New York 12870

Eight Groups at Calvary United
   Methodist Church
3701 Hillsboro Road
Nashville, Tennessee 37215
The Rev. Doyle Masters, pastor

The Rev. Dennis Camp
St. Andrews United Methodist Church
Killeen, Texas 76541

The Rev. Norton Campbell, Jr.
Powers Ferry United Methodist Church
135 Hamby Road, S.E.
Marietta, Georgia 30060

The Rev. Don Collins
United Ministry in Higher Education
Wisconsin State University
Oshkosh, Wisconsin 54901

The Rev. Richard Collman
43 W. Schlieman Avenue
Appleton, Minnesota 56208

The Rev. John H. Curtis
P.O. Box 113
Thomasville, Georgia 31792

Mrs. Kathryn Rogers Deering
1116 West Washington Street
Ann Arbor, Michigan 48103

The Rev. James Edward Doty
Baker University
Baldwin City, Kansas 66006

The Rev. William F. Dunkle, Jr.
The Northern Illinois Conference
1024 Lake Avenue
Wilmette, Illinois 60091

The Rev. George C. Engelhardt
34 Harrison Street
New Haven, Connecticut 06515

The Rev. Ray Fife
8100 N.W. 9th Avenue
Vancouver, Washington 98665

Ms. Cindy Fridley
c/o Rev. G. A. Zimmerman
The United Methodist Church
170 N. Main Street
Liberty, N.Y. 12754

O. Allen Gianniny, Jr.
c/o Wesley United Methodist Church
Charlottesville, Virginia 22903

Confirmation Class of
First United Methodist Church
Centre and S. Aiken Avenues
Pittsburgh, Pennsylvania 15232
The Rev. William B. Grove, pastor

The Rev. Myron M. Hall
820 Jefferson, N.E.
Salem, Oregon 97303

The Rev. Hoyt L. Hickman
1908 Grand Avenue
Nashville, Tennessee

Hamline United Methodist Church
1514 Englewood
St. Paul, Minnesota 55104

The Rev. Larry Dan Hollon
Aldersgate United Methodist Church
3617 Greene Avenue
Omaha, Nebraska 68147

The Rev. Dr. Grantas E. Hoopert
1525 Grampian Blvd.
Williamsport, Pa. 17701

Ms. Janet Joyce
c/o Rev. Frank Wooldridge
First United Methodist Church
912 W. Chestnut Street
Centralia, Washington 87531

Kansas East Conference
Baldwin City, Kansas
Sent by The Rev. E. Merris Brady

Dr. John Killinger
Vanderbilt Divinity School
Vanderbilt University
Nashville, Tennessee 37203

Mrs. John H. Landrum
13200 East Bagley Road
Parma Heights, Ohio 44130

Dr. William G. Law
Hamline United Methodist Church
1514 Englewood
St. Paul, Minnesota 55104

The Rev. W. Harold Loyd
First United Methodist Church
201 West North Street
Decatur, Illinois 62521

The Rev. Kenneth D. McCaw
South United Methodist Church
4500 S. Division Street
Grand Rapids, Michigan 49508

The Rev. Leon A. McCleary
Grace United Methodist Church
370 S. Yale Street
York, Pennsylvania 17403

The Rev. James Evans McReynolds
1401 Lant Circle
Evansville, Indiana 47714

The Rev. Charles Merritt
West End United Methodist Church
2130 West End Avenue
Nashville, Tennessee 37203

The Rev. David G. Pease
1700 South River Road
Janesville, Wisconsin 53545

The Rev. Randall Phillips
Wilshire United Methodist Church
711 S. Plymouth Boulevard
Los Angeles, California 90005

The Rev. Philip E. Pierce
100 S. Main Street
Ellsworth, Illinois 61737

Ms. Jeanne Audrey Powers
Room 1373
475 Riverside Drive
New York, N.Y. 10027

The Rev. W. Benjamin Pratt
Good Shepherd United Methodist Church
3043 N. Ashdale Avenue
Woodbridge, Virginia 22191

From *The Interpreter*
September 1972, p. 29
(Division of Interpretation,
Program Council,
The United Methodist Church)
Adapted for responsive reading by
Dr. David James Randolph

Dr. James L. Ray
First United Methodist Church
601 Main Street
Mt. Vernon, Indiana 47620

The Rev. Carl B. Rife
Brook Hill United Methodist Church
Rt. 7, Indian Springs Road
Frederick, Maryland 21701

The Rev. James D. Righter
1171 Kirby Road
McLean, Virginia 22101

The Rev. William A. Ritter
36500 Ann Arbor Terrace
Livonia, Michigan 48150

The Rev. David L. Semrad
Fort Hays State College
6th and Elm
Hays, Kansas 67601

The Rev. John J. Shaffer
123 Fourth Street
Juneau, Alaska 99801

The Rev. Donald Slover
The United Methodist Church of
    Green Trails
12501 Starspur Lane
Saint Louis, Missouri 63141

Ms. Susan Staff
1708 Hobart Street, N.W.
Washington, D. C. 20009

The Rev. Dr. John N. Strout
The United Methodist Church
2394 Erringer Road at Cochran Street
Simi Valley, California 93065

The Rev. Wesley D. Taylor
1115 W. 28th Avenue
Albany, Oregon 97321

Ms. Pamela Terkerson
1225 Nipomo Avenue
Los Osos, California 93401

The Rev. Don Vroon
637 Banner Avenue
Brooklyn, New York 11235

Dr. Don Wardlaw
Professor of Homiletics
Columbia Theological Seminary
Decatur, Georgia 30030

Washington Square United Methodist
    Church
133 W. 4th Street
New York, N.Y. 10012
The Rev. George Hill (pastor who
    submitted the material)
The Rev. Bonnie Jones-Goldstein,
    (present pastor)

The Rev. Charles E. Weigel, Jr.
208 S. Queen Street
Lancaster, Pennsylvania 16703

The Rev. Frank M. Witman
The United Methodist Church
2394 Erringer at Cochran
Simi, California 93065

The Rev. Ted R. Witt, Sr.
St. Paul United Methodist Church
4014 Garden Drive
Knoxville, Tennessee 37918

The Rev. Scott Wood
Mt. Comfort United Methodist Church
RR 2, Box 326
Greenfield, Indiana 46140

The Rev. Frank Wooldridge
First United Methodist Church
912 W. Chestnut Street
Centralia, Washington 98531

On the basis of our past experience, it seems both wise and necessary to refine the procedures by which materials are submitted to the Project on Worship.

1. Material for which permission cannot be granted is not useful as far as publication is concerned. Such material is welcomed to the Project, however, although it cannot be printed.

2. Material submitted for possible publication should be typed (double-space) on white paper with the name, address, and church of the person (minister or lay person) contributing in the left-hand lower corner. Note that the person who should be credited with authorship is not always the one who submits material to the Project.

3. A reproduction of the following permission sheet should be made in triplicate and signed and submitted with materials for publication:

Assignment

This document is an assignment of publishing rights between the Author,

_____, and the Division of Evangelism, Worship, and Stewardship of the Board of Discipleship of The United Methodist Church, which is seeking to make available additional resources for worship.

The Author hereby grants and assigns to the Division of Evangelism, Worship, and Stewardship, during the full term of copyright and renewals thereof, the right to publish or cause to be published in all forms and all languages material presently entitled _____

_____ .

The Author guarantees that he is the sole proprietor of this work, that he has full power and authority to make this assignment, and that the work does not infringe upon proprietary right at common law or any statutory copyright of any other person.

Witness my signature this the _____ day of _____ .

_____
Author

Material should be submitted to:

Dr. David James Randolph
Project on Worship
1908 Grand Avenue
Nashville, Tennessee 37203

Profiles

1.

Order For Morning Worship

Prepared and led by the Youth of the Church, a part of the Youth Summer Program
Mason United Methodist Church
Tacoma, Washington

The End   Variation on "Braint" by *William Mathias*   Leslie Doerner

The Parade (people stand)   "Hymn to Joy"   Hymnal, No. 38

The Call

Act I

The Act of Recognition

Call to Recognition

Leader: We are here

People: **In the name of Jesus Christ. We are here because we are men—but we deny our humanity. We are stubborn fools and liars to ourselves. We do not love others. We war against life. We hurt each other. We are sorry for it and know we are sick from it. We seek new life.**

Leader: Giver of life, heal us and free us to be men.

People: **Holy Spirit, speak to us. Help us to listen for we are very deaf. Come, fill this moment.**

The Act of Silence

The Act of Assurance

The Lord's Prayer

The Anthem   "Who Am I?"   Country Joe and the Fish

Act II

The Act of Not Playing God
(Man's witness to the Word)

The Psalter (people stand)   Psalm 96   Hymnal, No. 583

The Statement of Commitment (affirmation of faith—people stand)

We believe in a God whom we cannot categorize, or express the reality of, in our own words. But we are convinced that in the life and death of Jesus Christ he has made his purpose known. We are terrified and frightened by the demand of that purpose, and yet we know that it is the fulfillment of life. And so we commit ourselves to that purpose which is love, for we know that we live in the last times, and the proclamation of the Word is urgent. Amen.

The Gloria Patri

(When the congregation stands to sing, children in the first-third grades may go the back of the sanctuary to meet the adults who will supervise their activity during the remainder of the service.)

The Word

Old Testament Lesson   I Chronicles 29:10-18
New Testament Lesson   Luke 18:9-14

The Witness to the Word

"Sounds of Silence"

Ray Fife
Simon and Garfunkle

Act III

The Act of Community Concern

The Announcements

The Confrontation of Chaos Through the Offering of Our Substance

The Offertory

The Doxology (people stand)

The Hymn (people stand)　"Old 107th"　　　　　　　　　　　　Hymnal, No. 468

Act IV

The Sending

The Offering of the Peace

The Beginning　Prelude on "Hyfrydol" by Ralph Vaughn Williams

Editor's Note: Ray Fife was a summer youth worker at Mason Church when this service was developed. He acknowledges his indebtedness to Glide Church, San Francisco, for the outline of the service.

2.

the celebration of the gospel at . . .

First United Methodist Church, 201 West North Street
Decatur, Illinois 62521
The Rev. W. Harold Loyd, pastor

An Order for Worship: the GATHERING of God's people in a spirit of true Christian JOY, expressing HONESTY about ourselves, our CONCERN for others, an OPENNESS of mind and heart, and finally SCATTERING into the community and world to practice what we have said and learned on the occasion of consecrating the sanctuary.

Joy

Call to Worship

Hymn of Joy　"Let All the World in Every Corner Sing"　　　　Hymnal, No. 10
　　　　　　　　　　　　　(people stand)

Call to Awareness (people stand)

Honesty

Litany of Confession and Affirmation

O God, we know ourselves as those who violate your creation.

WE LIVE THE "NO!"

We speak loudly of wanting our lives to count for something.

AND YET, WE DRIFT SO SOFTLY INTO AN ENDLESS PROCESSION OF EASY TOMORROWS.

We want to give of ourselves.

BUT WE FEAR TO RECEIVE ANOTHER INTO OUR LIVES.

We decry the breakdown in communication.

YET KNOW THAT, REALLY, WE PREFER NOT TO LISTEN.

We wince at the disparity of rich and poor in the world.

BUT WE CLING TO OUR POSSESSIONS, LEST IN LOSING THEM, WE LOSE A PORTION OF OURSELVES.

Turn us about this day in the neatly
beveled rut we have worn!

THE "NO" IN LIFE IS NOT ENOUGH!

Christ the wayshower spoke of life. . .

TURN US ON TO LIVE AT THE DEPTHS OF OUR TIME!

Christ the servant spoke of hope. . .

TURN US INTO BEARERS OF HOPE WHERE OTHERS SEE ONLY DESPAIR!

Christ the open one spoke of love. . .

TURN US ON TO LOVE WHEN THOSE ABOUT US ARE LEAST LOVABLE!

Christ the man for others spoke of joy. . .

LET OUR JOY BE FULL THIS DAY AS WE TAKE HOLD OF OUR LIFE TOGETHER AS A FORGIVEN AND FORGIVING COMMUNITY!

Words of Renewal (in unison)

Into your hands we commend our spirit, O Lord.
Into your hands we commend our hearts.
For we must die to ourselves in loving you.
Into your hands we commend our love.

Concern

Greetings

Pastoral Prayer

The Offering

Music of Celebration

"Alleluia"
"Lauda Anima!"

Dedication of the Offering

Hymn of Concern (people stand) "O Holy City, Seen of John"   Hymnal, No. 481

Openness

The Word

> Gospel Matthew 9:35-38 (Good News for Modern Man TEV)
> Epistle: Ephesians 3:1-13 (Good News for Modern Man TEV)

The Interpretation: What Is Normal?   Dr. Loyd

Song of Dedication (people stand)   "O Master, Let Me Walk with Thee"   Hymnal, No. 170

The Act of Gathering

As we arrive, let us prepare to worship. This is a time to be aware of others, but not a time for visiting or conversation. Let us wait with expectancy. Read the texts of the hymns in order to sing them understandingly. Let the carillon and organ music be the beginning of our worship experience. Let each one prayerfully and openly participate throughout this hour.

Organ   Variations on the Chorale "Our Father in Heaven"   Dietrich Buxtehude

Call to Recognition and Awareness (people stand)

Hymn   "O For a Thousand Tongues to Sing"   Hymnal, No. 1

The Act of Evaluation

Call for Self-Evaluation and Confession (Minister)

Silent Prayer and Meditation

Prayer (Minister and people)

> **O gracious God, help us now to see our lives illuminated by thee. Shine upon our sins. Too easily we deceive ourselves concerning them and with vain excuses cover them. Help us to see clearly what our tempers and selfishness, our cherished grudges and vindictiveness, our mean ambitions and smallness, signify to other lives than ours. Set us against the white background of the Cross that we may be ashamed of the things that are shameful and may love the things that are lovely. Amen.**

Response Free me, release me

Anthems

> I. "Surely the Lord is in this Place"   Carl F. Mueller
> (Wesley Choir)

> II. "Litany" Irish melody, setting by Lloyd Pfautsch
> (Crusader and Sanctuary Choirs)

Greetings

The Act of Stewardship

> Bell Anthems   "Built on the rock the church doth stand"
> Tintinnabulation   Theodore W. Ripper

The Prayer of Dedication (people stand)

The Act of Praise

Hymn of Praise "How Lovely Is Thy Dwelling Place"   Hymnal, No. 295

Act of Praise (people stand)   Psalm 150:   Hymnal, No. 606

Minister: O Praise the Lord.

People: **O Praise God in his holy place,**
           Praise him in the vault of heaven, the vault of
           his power:
           Praise him for his mighty works,

Minister: Praise Him for his immeasurable greatness.

People: **Praise him with fanfares on the trumpet,**

Minister: Praise him upon lute and harp;

People: **Praise him with tambourines and dancing,**

Minister: Praise him with flute and strings;

People: **Praise him with the clash of cymbals,**

Minister: Praise him with triumphant cymbals;

People: **Let everything that has breath praise the lord!**

Minister: O praise the Lord.

The Gloria Patri   Hymnal, No. 794

Anthems

I. "Earth and all Stars" (Chapel Choir)   David N. Johnson

II. "O How Amiable" (Sanctuary Choir)   Ralph Vaughn Williams

Hearing the Word

The Scriptures Speak Today
        Old Testament: Isaiah 65:8-12, 1-3a, 17-25.
          Response: GOD HAS SPOKEN! MAN HAS WRITTEN!
        New Testament: I Corinthians 12:12-15, 27-31.

The Contemporary Word "The Church Beautiful and Enduring"   Bishop Lance Webb

The Act of Consecration
(people stand)

Bishop: To the glory and praise of the living God;

People: WE CONSECRATE THIS SANCTUARY.

Bishop: For worship that encounters God through music, the Word, the Sacraments;

People: WE CONSECRATE THIS SANCTUARY.

Bishop: To be a place of quietness, reflection, direction, and dedication;

People: WE CONSECRATE THIS SANCTUARY.

Bishop: In the confidence of recovery from our sins, and true direction for our lives;

People: WE CONSECRATE THIS SANCTUARY.

Bishop: As a place to accept the covenant of marriage, and the celebration of eternal
           life at death;

People: WE CONSECRATE THIS SANCTUARY.

All: LET US BE GLAD TO COME INTO THE HOUSE OF OUR GOD, AND MAY THE REALITY OF HIS PRESENCE THROUGH JESUS CHRIST OUR LORD ALWAYS BE CELEBRATED IN THIS HOLY PLACE.

Bishop: The Prayer of Consecration.

Hymn of Consecration   "Glorious Things of Thee Are Spoken"   Hymnal, No. 293

The Act of Going Out

Charge and Benediction

Response by the choir "O Spirit of the Living God"   Hymnal, No. 136

A Moment for Meditation

We have spent this hour in this sanctuary. Worship is response to God, and this service is to help me to respond. Its meaning, the message received, and the challenge depend upon my openness and response. The test is in the direction my life will take as I go out into the world.

Organ

3.

Order of Worship

Wilshire United Methodist Church
Los Angeles, California
Randall Phillips, pastor

The Gathering

Silent Preparation

Christians gather for worship as the forgiven ones, the thankful ones, the dedicated ones. Thus the structure of our worship is three-fold: (1.) confession and pardon (man's need); (2.) Word and witness (God's action); and (3). dedication to mission (man's response). These three divisions, like the three acts of a great drama, reflect the life of the individual before God: separation, reconciliation, and responsible service; or, in Pauline terms: death, resurrection, and new life.

Organ Voluntary   Passion Chorales J.S. Bach

"See the Lord of Life and Light,"   "O Man, Bewail Thy Grievous Fall"

Choral Introit

Call to Worship

Hymn "Holy, Holy, Holy! Lord God Almighty"   Hymnal, No. 26

Act I: Man's Need

Call to Confession

Minister: If we would honestly seek renewal in order to serve God, we must begin by being honest about our past failures.

People: Can any of us deny that our lack of vision, our self-interest and pride have separated us from those who stand in need?

Minister: All of us have been guilty of postponing good words and actions until the time for saying and doing was past.

People: Let us honestly confess before God the things that we have done or failed to do which have caused us to be less effective servants.

Prayer of Confession (in unison)

Our Father, whom we so quickly and easily call Lord; forgive us for failure to understand and accept the great demands placed upon us by your lordship. We enlist in your causes, but find ourselves losing interest. We promise to be courageous, but find ourselves afraid. We want to be sensitive, but find ourselves hard and callous. We are confronted with great opportunities, but fail to take advantage of them. Forgive us, Father; Take our limitations and turn them into possibilities for service. Have mercy on us and grant us this grace. Amen.

Personal Confession

Words of Assurance

The Lord's Prayer

Act II: God's Action

Canticle of Praise "Praise God in His Sanctuary"   Hymnal No. 606

Gloria Patri

The Anthem: "Go, Congregation, Go!"   John Antes

God's Creative Word (the New Testament Lesson)   Matthew 5:1-16

The Affirmation of Faith (people stand)

Minister: Let us recall our faith as God's people.

People: We believe that God, Creator, Redeemer, and Life Giver, summons the Church to mission in the world:

Minister: To witness by word and deed to his revelation in Christ and the acts of love by which he reconciles men to himself;

People: To evoke in men the personal response of repentance and faith through which, by God's grace, they may find newness of life in loving relationships with him and with their fellowmen;

Minister: To bring men together into a Christian community of worship and fellowship, and to send men into the world as servants in the struggle for meaning and justice;

People: And to move men to live in awareness of the life-giving power of God's presence, in acknowledgment of his rule over history, and in confident expectation of the ultimate consummation of his purpose. Amen.

Hymn of Praise and Thanksgiving   "Fairest Lord Jesus"   Hymnal, No. 79

A Contemporary Witness to the World (sermon)

"Shaking the Salt"

Act III: Man's Response

Prayers of Petition and Intercession

Minister: Realizing that we are responsible for the world, we lift up our concerns and prayers for the structures of society and for those who find no place within those structures: We pray for the family and the home,

People: **And for those who are lonely and forgotten.**

Minister: We pray for our system of law and order,

People: **And for those who suffer injustice.**

Minister: We pray for the Church universal,

People: **And for those bound by superstition.**

Minister: We pray for colleges and universities,

People: **And for those denied an education.**

Minister: We pray for the world of business and labor,

People: **And for those who are poverty stricken.**

Minister: We pray for all nations and for world peace,

People: **And for those who suffer the effects of war. Amen.**

Commitment to Our Mission of Work, Study, and Witness
  (registration and announcements)

The Offering of Our Gifts and Ourselves

The Doxology

Offertory Anthem   "Go Not Far From Me, O God"   Zingarelli

Confirmation and Reception into the Church   Hymnal, No. 829

Closing Hymn   "Blest Be the Tie That Binds"   Hymnal, No. 306

Benediction

Choral Response

Postlude

Invocations

4.

Lord, we remember that Jesus made a big thing out of right motives, the attitudes inside us that guide our actions. We have a suspicious feeling that we haven't yet become all that he was and wanted us to be. So speak to us now, through your Holy Spirit, and direct us toward what we should be. Amen.

—James L. Ray

5.

We find ourselves in a world we did not plan or make, a world weary of war and desperate for acts of mercy and brotherhood, O God. But we stand bewildered, not knowing how to change dull old patterns into glorious new ways. We are even confused as to what our duty is and what Christian character should lead us to do in these times. As we brood over the world and seek your divine purpose, may the Holy Spirit direct us to what we can do for peace. Amen.

—James L. Ray

6.

If we have taken your gifts for granted, forgive us, Lord. As we are gathered here before your altar, bring to our minds the full awareness of the truth of our blessedness. Teach us how to enjoy what we have and be grateful, and save us from envy and greed. Amen.

—James L. Ray

7.

God of grace and glory, we praise your great name and worship you as maker and ruler of all. We pray now for eternal light to illumine our time—bound minds. Through our biases and prejudices, O God, help us to recognize the truth that judges our biases and prejudices. Beyond the custom of this place and time in history, help us to see the truth that is never dated and knows no bounds. Help us to shake off the terrestrial fears and affections that bind, and hold out hospitality to the highest—the ideals and hopes which you alone inspire in us. Amen.

—James L. Ray

8.

Father of our Lord Jesus Christ, and our Father, we confess our reservation in accepting Jesus and what he says to us. Like the religious people of another day, neither do we want our status quo disturbed. But teach us now that being in tune with the Eternal Spirit is the treasure that lasts. Make us free to respond to Christ and his truth for our age. Amen.

—James L. Ray

9.

Spirit of Truth and Wisdom of the Universe, we seek your blessing today. We fall into the sins of arrogance and pride, but we shall never unlock the secrets of life until you reveal them. Conditions today tempt us to doubt your designing purpose in this world and to think that much of life is accidental. But give us today the spiritual discernment to know that we are here for a purpose and that life is a challenge to know and honor you. Amen.

—James L. Ray

10.

O God, Power that brought forth the unfathomable universe, we look at the lives of great men and are humbled to know that we are but beginners in your school of truth. Bring us closer today to the truth toward which all history moves. Keep our feet on the path toward the higher life that is your goal for us. Open us to the love that was in Christ and make us channels of love to people who need its blessing. Amen.

—James L. Ray

11.

O God, Will above all wills and Mind behind our minds, we come to receive your blessing for our souls. Even the crumbs from your bountiful supply can nourish our spirits. While we are made to love, we are still weak in it. We need the transfusion of your own Spirit to make us love as we ought. Give us, we pray, the bread from heaven which is the true bread of life. Amen.

—James L. Ray

12.

God our Father, you are versatile beyond our understanding. You make the giant stars and the tiny atom. You make the galaxy to turn and the flower to bloom. And we confess that we often are unsure of what our purpose is in this mysterious creation, so we pray for light. Help us now to see our individual call to a purpose you have ordained. Amen.

—James L. Ray

13.

O God, living Spirit of truth and righteousness, we have heard all our lives that we should be truthful, and we have prided ourselves on being honest. But when we place our lives against the ideal of Jesus Christ we know that there are limits to our truthfulness, even blindness to what it is. So illumine us and sanctify us as we commit ourselves once again to walking in the way of Christ our Lord. Amen.

—James L. Ray

Calls to Worship

14.

It almost goes without saying that Jesus was a revolutionary. He started a revolution based on God's love, and we are being called to volunteer as troops in that revolution. We are being called to become *revolutionaries.* A revolutionary is one who is so intent in his purpose that he is willing to sacrifice his reputation, his livelihood, his friends, and maybe even his life. The problem is that half of us don't even *hear* the Lord's call—we're half-asleep or something. And if we sleep through *this* revolution, we may never wake up.

Let us worship the One who calls us, and listen to what he has to say to us

—Kathryn Rogers Deering

15.

The Order of Worship

The Second Sunday after Easter

Prelude

Call to Worship

Leader: "Behold, I stand at the door and knock. . . ."

People: HOW WAS THAT AGAIN?

Leader: "Behold, I stand at the door and knock. . . ."

People: WHAT IS THAT SUPPOSED TO MEAN?

Leader: It means that God is always seeking us.

People: AND IF HE IS SEEKING US, AND HAS FOUND US, WHAT THEN?

Leader: We are the objects of God's search—but we are persons—not things. We must respond. God does not force us.

People: THE FIRST STEP, THEN IS FROM GOD, AND THE RESPONSE IS OUR RESPONSIBILITY?

Leader: Right! And this is what worship is about. To open doors through which the spirit of God may move, and we can respond.

People: SO BE IT!

—Frank M. Witman

16.

The Order of Worship

The Third Sunday in Epiphany

Declaration of Joy (People standing)

Leader: We have been directed to search;

People: TO SEARCH DILIGENTLY FOR THE CHILD.

Leader: The trouble is we have wanted to find just the *Child!*

People: OR TO LET OUR FAITH BE WHAT IT WAS WHEN WE WERE CHILDREN.

Leader: It is great to follow new directions;

People: IN RESPONSE TO GOD'S GUIDING

Leader: And to rejoice with great joy when we discover the place.

People: WHAT PLACE?

Leader: The place where we can experience the birth of Christ in our lives.

People: AND THEN WE CAN WORSHIP.

Leader: We can bring the full gift of our lives to God, in thanksgiving for what he has done for us.

People: HALLELUJAH! AMEN!

—Frank M. Witman

17.

The Order of Worship
The Fourth Sunday of Advent

Introit

Invocation

Carol (Standing)   "Angels We Have Heard on High"   Hymnal, No. 374

Call to Worship

Advent   *(Note that the Leader here is other than the minister)*

Leader: People of Simi Valley, you have heard on high.

People: WHO HAS HEARD?

Leader: That's right! People of Simi Valley!

People: WE HAVE HEARD ON WHAT?

Leader: That God has become a part of human life in Jesus.

Minister: Hallelujah!

Leader: That God loves us so much that he gave his only Son!

People: HALLELUJAH!

Leader: That whoever believes in him will have life.

Minister: Hallelujah!

Leader: People of Simi Valley, you have heard!

People: WE HAVE; WE COME TO THE BETHLEHEM OF OUR LIVES TO SEE, TO BELIEVE, AND TO ACCEPT THE LOVE GOD HAS FOR US.

Minister: Hallelujah!

People: AMEN!

—Frank M. Witman

18.

Leader: We would like to see better who Jesus is.

People: BUT SOMETIMES OUR SMALLNESS PREVENTS THIS.

Leader: We are like Zacchaeus, who needed to add to his stature in order to see.

People: AND WE NEED TO ADD TO OUR STATURE BY SELF-EXAMINATION, AND BY RECOGNIZING OUR LIMITATIONS.

Leader: How can we do this?

People: WE CAN BEGIN BY PRAISING GOD, AND OPENING OURSELVES TO THE INFINITENESS OF HIS LOVE.

Leader: OK, let's do it!

—Frank M. Witman

19.

Leader: The experience called "conversion" represents a radical change for each person who would call himself "Christian."

People: CHANGE. CHANGE. CHANGE. THAT IS ALL WE SEEM TO HEAR ABOUT TODAY.

Leader: But that is what life is—change; and we need to respond to change not just react to it.

People: I SEE THE DIFFERENCE: TO RESPOND TO CHANGE MEANS THAT I WILL WORK WITH IT AND TRY TO ACCEPT IT; WHILE TO REACT OFTEN MEANS REJECTION ON MY PART.

Leader: The experience of conversion calls for response not reaction.

People: I WILL BE OPEN TO ALL POSSIBILITIES! AMEN!

—Frank M. Witman

20.

Leader: Do you recognize that sometimes in a group of people you are uncomfortable, and want to reach out, but can't?

People: YES! AND WE FIND THAT EVEN IN CHURCH.

Leader: Yet, one of the chief ways that the church is described is as a fellowship.

People: FOR FELLOWSHIP TO BE, WE MUST BECOME ACQUAINTED. WHILE IT IS HARD TO DO, WE WILL MAKE EVERY EFFORT TO SPEAK TO ONE PERSON THIS MORNING WHOM WE DO NOT RECOGNIZE.

Leader: Great!

People: AMEN!

—Frank M. Witman

21.

Thanksgiving

Leader: Have you ever stopped to think about what it means to be thankful?

People: IT HAS TO DO WITH "THANK," "THANKS," TO BE "FULL OF THANKS."

Leader: The last phrase says it: full of thanks.

People: NOT ONLY DO WE ASK OURSELVES WHAT THANKFUL IS, BUT WE ALSO WONDER IF WE ARE REALLY FULL OF THANKS

Leader: As we worship today let us think about the meaning of "thankful" to us and see when we really are.

People: O.K.!

—Frank M. Witman

22.

Leader: Serving can be fun or drudgery.

People: SOMETIMES WE HAVE WONDERED ABOUT THE ROLE OF A CHRISTIAN AS A SERVANT.

Leader: What do you mean?

People: WE MEAN THAT THE ROLE OF SERVANT HAS REALLY NOT BEEN INTERPRETED IN A WAY THAT IS MEANINGFUL.

Leader: Let us think it through today, to see in what way God has called us.

All: Amen.

—Frank M. Witman

23.

Festival of the Christian Home

Leader: Welcome to this celebration of the Festival of the Christian Home!

People: WHAT HAPPENED TO MOTHER'S DAY?

Leader: Nothing has happened to it. We are simply trying to see the family as a whole.

People: YOU MEAN INSTEAD OF OBSERVING CHILDREN'S DAY AND FATHER'S DAY AND . . . .?

Leader: Yes, there is enough artificial division of the important, without the church contributing to it.

People: WE SEE THE FAMILY AS A WHOLE, AND FAMILY MEMBERS AS CONTRIBUTORS TO THE WHOLENESS OF THE FAMILY.

Leader: And don't forget our relationship to the total family of man, under the fatherhood of God.

People: IT IS IN THIS SPIRIT THAT WE WORSHIP—AWARE OF ONE ANOTHER, AWARE OF ALL GOD'S FAMILY, WITH AN OPENNESS TO GOD.

All: **Amen!**

—Frank M. Witman

24.

Leader: Good news is not something we hear of a great deal.

People: YOU'RE RIGHT! MORE OFTEN THAN NOT, WHAT WE HEAR (AND SOMETIMES TALK ABOUT) DOESN'T REALLY CONTRIBUTE MUCH.

Leader: But yet the Good News we possess as Christians, ought to be an experience which we share with others.

People: FROM WHAT WE RECEIVE IN WORSHIP, WE SHALL TRY TO BE MORE EFFECTIVE WITH THE GOOD NEWS.

—Frank M. Witman

25.

Leader: O God, it is good to continue to be in your presence;

People: AND TO BE INVOLVED WITH ONE ANOTHER IN YOUR WORSHIP.

Leader: We recognize the common bond of our humanity;

People: AND GIVE THANKS FOR YOUR ACCEPTANCE OF EACH OF US.

Leader: Let us worship out of thanksgiving to God;

People: AND MOVE INTO SERVICE OUT OF OUR CONCERN AND LOVE FOR ONE ANOTHER. AMEN!

—Frank M. Witman

26.

Leader: It is good to give thanks to God!

People: AND TO SHARE EXPERIENCES WHICH DEEPEN OUR GRATITUDE.

Leader: Let this worship service be a place where God may know our thankful hearts;

People: AND LET US LIVE THANKFULLY SO THAT OTHERS MAY SEE WHAT GOD HAS DONE FOR US! AMEN!

—Frank M. Witman

27.

Leader: In our most independent (and sometimes stubborn) moments, we find ourselves saying, "I don't need others!"

People: YES, WE HAVE THOUGHT OR SAID THAT ON OCCASION.

Leader: And, it is good to be able to be independent.

People: BUT, IT IS EVEN BETTER TO RECOGNIZE OUR INTERDEPENDENCE, AND WE DO THAT NOW AS WE WORSHIP. SO BE IT!

—Frank M. Witman

28.

Leader: We do not lose heart!

People: THOSE ARE SEEMINGLY EASY WORDS TO SAY OR TO WRITE.

Leader: But it becomes another thing to put them into the perspective of living.

People: TO BE ABLE TO SENSE THAT LIGHT WHICH SHINES OUT OF DARKNESS.

Leader: Let us work together in doing that.

All: AMEN!

—Frank M. Witman

29.

Leader: The Great Commission tells us to "Go therefore and make disciples of all nations" (Matt. 28:19 RSV).

People: WE SEE THAT, BUT DOESN'T SOMETHING ELSE HAVE TO TAKE PLACE FIRST?

Leader: Yes. This word of Jesus came following his appearance to the disciples, after his resurrection. It came after *recognition of doubt* on the part of some of them.

People: SO WE NEED TO CONFRONT OUR OWN DOUBTS IN WORSHIP—IS THIS WHAT YOU ARE SAYING?

Leader: Yes. Each of us needs to do this with an awareness that change can take place.

People: LET US EXPECTANTLY WORSHIP GOD IN SPIRIT AND IN TRUTH. AMEN!

Hymns: "All Hail the Power of Jesus' Name" Hymnal, No. 73
"God of Our Fathers" Hymnal, No. 552

—Frank M. Witman

30.

The Order of Worship

Eighth Sunday of Kingdomtide

Leader: In the Sermon on the Mount, we read "Blessed are the peacemakers" (Matt. 5:9a).

People: THOSE WHO MAKE PEACE SHALL BE CALLED SONS AND DAUGHTERS OF GOD.

Leader: This places us in the position of responsibility with God,

People: TO FIND AVENUES OF PEACE—BEGINNING WITH OURSELVES—

Leader: And extending through our families, our places of business;

People: OUR COMMUNITY, OUR COLLEGES AND UNIVERSITIES,

Leader: Our state and nation;

People: BUT, FIRST, RECOGNIZING THAT PEACE BEGINS WITH ME—IN MY RELATIONSHIP TO GOD—AND WITH OTHERS. AMEN!

Hymns: "All People That on Earth Do Dwell" Hymnal, No. 21
"When Morning Gilds the Skies" Hymnal, No. 91

—Frank M. Witman

31.

Prayer for Community

O God, here we are. You called us, and we've come. You want us to live in your love. So we have come to worship: to listen to what you have to say to us, to give thanks for what you've done for us, and to share with you the joy you've given us. Help us to make good use of this time together. And when we go out, help us to share your love with everyone. Thank you. Amen.

—Wesley D. Taylor

32.

Why We Are Here

Leader: We have come to his place to find out who God is.

Congregation: **Now wait a minute, we have come here for many reasons, and partly out of curiosity.**

Leader: Are you not a people of God?

Congregation: **That we may be, but what does it mean to be a people of God?**

Leader: A people of God gather to discover anew who God really is, to unlock new doors for living, to come alive in the Spirit, and yes, even to dance with joy along with the Lord of Life.

—Wesley D. Taylor

33.

Prayer

Leader: Good morning God! Thank you for letting us live to see this day!

People: WE HAD A NIGHT'S REST, AND WE'RE THANKFUL FOR IT. RIGHT NOW WE'RE STILL A LITTLE SLUGGISH, BUT IT'S GREAT TO BE ALIVE!

Leader: Help us to know that we're secure in your love, so we can stop worrying about ourselves and care for others. Thank you. Amen.

—Wesley D. Taylor

34.

Call to Awareness (Everybody)

O God, we worship in your presence.

You have spoken, and given form and beauty to the world.

You have spoken, and forgiven us.

You have spoken, and freed us from the fear of death.

You have spoken, and given purpose to our life.

O Lord, speak to us now.

Awaken us to the wonder and beauty of life.

Speak, and let us respond, in praise and daily service; in Christ's name. Amen.

—Wesley D. Taylor

35.

Leader: God is here, let's celebrate!

People: WITH SONG AND WITH DANCE, WITH STRINGED INSTRUMENTS AND DRUMS, LET US EXPRESS OUR JOY IN GOD'S PRESENCE.

Leader: Let us celebrate with the old songs of praise.

People: AND CREATE NEW SONGS THAT WILL EXPRESS OUR FAITH.

Leader: Let us boldly proclaim his name and shout his praises.

—Dennis Camp

36.

Leader: Now hear this, all who seek God.

People: THE KINGDOM OF GOD IS HERE!

Leader: God is here! Let us rejoice at his presence in our midst.

People: LET US BREAK FORTH IN SHOUTS OF PRAISE AND SONGS OF JOY!

Leader: Listen, O God, to our songs of thanksgiving and respond to the hearts that reach out for you. Amen.

—Dennis Camp

37.

Leader: We have gathered here again.

People: TO SEEK THE ENDURING REALITY IN LIFE.

Leader: We have been called in.

People: TO GO OUT AGAIN AS COMMISSIONED MINISTERS IN CHRIST'S NAME.

Leader: Let us renew our commitment through worship.

People: AND MAKE AN OFFERING OF OURSELVES THROUGH GOD'S STRENGTH.

—Dennis Camp

38.

Leader: You chose to come here today. Yet there are other places you could have gone, other things you could have done.

People: AS FOLLOWERS OF CHRIST, WE ARE A WORSHIPING COMMUNITY, WHO ARE CALLED IN AND WHO GO OUT AGAIN AS CHRISTIAN WITNESSES.

Leader: Do you really think this will accomplish anything?

People: WE FIND IT NECESSARY TO COME, TO BRING OUR LIVES TO THE ALTAR FOR PRAYER AND OFFERING, AND TO MEET WITH OUR FELLOWMAN FOR ENCOURAGEMENT, COUNSEL, AND TRAINING.

Leader: Then come. Let us consider the life and way of Jesus Christ whose invitation simply is "Follow me."

—Dennis Camp

39.

Leader: Welcome Friends! I see that life has brought you here again.

People: WE COME TO CELEBRATE LIFE'S GOODNESS.

Leader: But, what's so special about this place?

People: IT CONTAINS THE SYMBOLS OF MAN'S LIFE BEFORE GOD.

Leader: Are you saying that this place is holy?

People: WHEREVER MAN HEARS GOD'S WORD OF LIFE, <u>THERE</u> IS A HOLY PLACE.

Leader: Then let us get busy speaking and hearing that word.

—Dennis Camp

40.

Leader: Good morning! What brings you to this place?

People: WE WERE TOLD THAT WE COULD MEET GOD HERE.

Leader: But, isn't that a painful experience?

People: ONLY IF WE LOVE OUR PRIDE MORE THAN GOD.

Leader: What do you expect to happen?

People: GOD WILL RENEW OUR LIVES WITH THE MEANING AND PURPOSE OF HIS LOVE IF WE WILL ALLOW IT AND WANT IT.

Leader: Then the question is: Do you really want it to happen now?

People: WE INTEND TO INVEST OURSELVES FULLY IN HELPING GOD MAKE IT HAPPEN HERE AND NOW.

—Dennis Camp

41.

Leader: O God, you are not looking for genius.

People: YOU DO NOT REQUIRE GREAT TALENTS.

Leader: You are not charmed by our panic-ridden activity.

People: YOU SIMPLY ASK FOR OUR FAITH AND OUR OBEDIENCE.

Leader: It is when we turn from self-seeking to embrace your will that we discover peace and security.

—Dennis Camp

42.

Leader: Attention please! Give your attention and join in the celebration of worship.

People: WE FOCUS OUR FAITH UPON GOD AND NEW LIFE IN CHRIST.

Leader: Bare your soul before God and know the joy of his acceptance.

People: GOD WILL HEAR OUR CRIES WITH COMPASSION AND WILL SHARE OUR INNERMOST DESIRES WITH LOVE.

Leader: Weep silently tears of joy at your own redemption.

People: OUR HEARTS SING A NEW SONG OF GRACE, BEAUTY, AND TRUTH.

Leader: Then worship—as a people who know God and share his will for all people.

--Dennis Camp

43.

Leader: Come from your separate ways and renew your covenant with God.

People: WE HEAR THE CALL TO NEW LIFE AND HOPE.

Leader: Make yourself at home and hear God's word gladly.

People: WE ARE READY TO HEAR THE JUDGMENT THAT CONFRONTS US WHEN WE ARE HONEST.

Leader: Be joyful! For unto you this day is born a new self, with new meaning and new possibilities.

People: WE HUNGER FOR THE FULLNESS OF LIFE AND KNOW THAT IT IS MADE AVAILABLE TO US IN CHRIST.

Leader: Then drink from the fountain of life.

—Dennis Camp

44.

Fifth Sunday in Kingdomtide

(World Communion Sunday)

Leader: Make a joyful noise to the Lord, all the lands! Serve him with gladness! Come into his presence with singing!

People: (Singing) JOY TO THE WORLD! THE LORD IS COME: LET EARTH RECEIVE HER KING; LET EVERY HEART PREPARE HIM ROOM, AND HEAVEN AND NATURE SING, AND HEAVEN AND NATURE SING, AND HEAVEN, AND HEAVEN AND NATURE SING.

Leader: The earth is the Lord's and the fullness thereof, the world and those who dwell therein.

People: WE KNOW THAT THE LORD IS GOD! IT IS HE THAT MADE US ALL, AND WE ARE HIS. AMEN!

—Frank M. Witman

Prayers

45.

Prayer Dialogue

(based on John 6:37b, Matt. 7:7, John 10:10b, Luke 18:27; 1:37, John 20:29b, Mark 9:24, Psalm 27:7-9, Matt. 5:6)

People: **Lord, we're talking to you, but we don't really know you, so that makes our conversation kind of awkward. But we're sure you get the message.**

Leader: I never turn away anyone who comes to me.

People: **The reason we are here in your house this morning is to worship you and to find out more about you. But usually we leave with a vague sense of disappointment—if we feel anything at all. Can this time be different?**

Leader: Yes, Ask, and you will receive, seek, and you will find; knock and it will be opened to you. I love each of you, and I have come that you might have life, and have it in all its fullness. Ask, seek, knock.

People: **But, Lord, we don't really understand. Most of us are already doing the best we can, but we fall short. Why can't we break through to you and understand what we ache to know?**

Leader: What is impossible with men is possible with me. I know your needs. With me nothing will be impossible. Ask, seek, knock.

People: **Lord, we are hungry to know you, hungry to feel close to you! Why is it so hard to believe, and to pray to you, and to see those prayers answered? The men who were your disciples and the early Christians seemed to have a lot of power and vitality. We sometimes wish we could actually *see* you like they did—then it wouldn't be so hard.**

Leader: But remember: Blessed are those who have not seen and yet believe. Ask, seek, knock.

People: **Lord, we do believe! But help our unbelief! In the words of the psalmist, we say: "Hear, O Lord, when we cry aloud, be gracious to us and answer us! Thou hast said, 'Seek ye my face.' Our hearts say to thee, 'Thy face, Lord, do we seek.' Hide not thy face from us!"**

Leader: And I say to you: Blessed are those who hunger and thirst for righteousness, for they shall be satisfied.

—Kathryn Rogers Deering

Confessions

46.

Leader: We have chosen to be Christians, a people of God, following the lordship of Christ.

People: **We fall from this way often. We often do not love our ~~brother~~ neighbour as ourselves. nor do we consistently love God above all else. We often love ourselves first, and we even do not do this well because we are blinded by our own selfish ends.**

Leader: Forgive us, Lord. We know that when we see ourselves as the measure of all, that we are at that moment not your disciples.

People: God, we gather now in your presence.

Hamline United Methodist Church
St. Paul, Minnesota

47.

Prayer of Confession

Lord,
I fake it a lot;
I do so much want to be perfect, that I fake it practically
       all of the time.
Usually nobody can tell, because they fake it too. . .
Sometimes, You know, I even fake it to myself, and
      worse, to you.
Now that's a dumb thing to do, isn't it?
Because you know more about me than I could ever hope to know
    about myself through self-examination, or handwriting
    analysis, or anything like that.
So, Lord, do your very best (and that's *the* best!) to keep
    chipping away at me, et cetera. . .
Until my inside self is as good a three-dimensional replica,
    life-size, of your model as possible.
Honest. Amen.

—Kathryn Rogers Deering

48.

Adventure and Security

(A Prayer of Confession)

O God, you've built into our personalities
    a yearning for both adventure and security.

But we have sought the safety of things
    rather than the security of your love.
Instead of getting involved
    in the venture of your kingdom
      we've reserved our limited time and money
      for ourselves.
We have tried to satisfy our adventurous spirits
      by pursuing the almighty dollar.
      by striving for success and status,
      by sex without love,
      by second-hand thrills
        thru spectator sports and color TV.

Lord, we are tired and bored
    by doing what we want to do
    instead of what we ought to do.
Father, forgive us;
    Let us taste your amazing grace.

God, I want to grow.
I know in my heart
    that I should accept Christ's challenge
    of *total* allegiance.
So jar me loose
    from the tight security of little Lord Self—
    out into the abundant adventure
    of your way of the Cross.

Lord, give me the courage to believe.
Here and now I resolve
    to seek first your kingdom,
    your righteousness,
    and the truth that makes me free. Amen.

—Phil E. Pierce

49.

Father, do I try to do your will and end up trying your patience? Do I make promises I know I cannot keep? Do I bend your words to fit my concept of the truth; rather than conceptualizing truth as fashioned by your words? And does the conflict between what I say and what I do startle you but not me? Lord, help me to prepare a place for you before tempting you to think twice before preparing a place for me. Amen

—Thomas Blowers

Prayers of Thanksgiving

50.

Father, I am a sometime ostrich living out my days, head stuck in the sand, insensitive to the problems that surround me. I am a sometime eagle perched on lofty mountain top, judging those whose lives I scarcely see and hardly understand. Lord, just for once let me stand in the middle of the action where decision comes hard and slow. And let me be a man among men before resting, content with sitting around preening my feathers. Amen.

—Thomas Blowers

51.

Thank you for making yourself and your love so real to us.
There are many concrete ways that we see you and know you.

But the most real way is when we know you in other people. Thank you for the people we know who are authentic and whose love is the real thing.

Most of all we think of Christ. How could you become more real to us? You *became* a man. You loved as we love, felt the burdens of poverty and sorrow, and even faced a real death like we face. How far you have gone to make yourself real to us! How thankful we are.

—Don Vroon

52.

It is hard, O Lord, to be really thankful. The blessings of life are often overshadowed by the burdens of life. We hold on to life, but we don't really love life like we should.

Yet when we stop to think about it, which isn't very often, we *are* thankful.

    Most of us are in good health most of the time,
    Most of us live in peace most of the time.
    Most of us eat well most of the time.
    Most of us sleep well most of the time.
    Most of us work well most of the time.
    We enjoy swimming and sports,
           shows and concerts,
           good neighbors,
           wonderful friends.
    And we live in a beautiful world, in spite of its sorrow and hypocrisy.
    So we say thank you—
           from the bottom of our hearts
           happy and joyful
                Thank you, God.

—Don Vroon

53.

We praise you, we bless you, we worship you, we glorify you. We give thanks to you for your great glory. We see it all around us—from the colors on the trees to the power of the mighty ocean.

And we see it in man, the work of your hand. How beautiful you have made us! What mystery lurks in every human heart. What sublime joy you have made us capable of. What beautiful love you have put inside us, when we are receptive to it.

Yet we can be ugly. But even when we face our own ugliness, we have much to be thankful for. You haven't let us blow up each other. You have constantly brought good out of our worst mistakes. You have patiently used our evil to teach us very difficult lessons. And you have taken our most evil deed, the brutal killing of your only Son, Jesus Christ, and made it the richest source of blessing and peace available to men.

    When we are ugly, you are beautiful.
    When we sin, you are merciful.
    When we hate, you love;
    And when we are rebellious, you are loyal.
    For all this, all we can say is "Thank you. Thank you."
                Amen.

—Don Vroon

General

54.

O Lord, Creator, we love your world and the people in it. The world has so much to offer us, and we are grateful for every bit of it.

Yet we are aware that all is not well with your world. So often we see in the eyes of our neighbors a vacant stare and a glazed-over emptiness. For so many people life seems to be an empty rat-race.

But not so for us, O Lord, You have given to each of us our portion of the joy that is in Christ. May we share that joy, and may your fullness fill the hearts of those around us, just as you have promised to fill *our* hearts. May the world and the people in it come alive as the life you offer in Christ spreads thru us to others.

We pray this for them because we love. And we love because you have first loved us, in Christ our Lord. Amen.

—Don Vroon

55.

In your strength, O Lord, we have come to the beginning of another week. You know, our Father, what a busy place your world has become. Sometimes it is hard to keep our heads. Sometimes vacation never seems to come, and when it does it goes too fast, and we are still exhausted. Hear our complaint, O Lord.

O Life-giving stream, refresh us with living water in a dry and thirsty land. Renew us with a generous portion of your strength, your courage, your confidence. Give us a little spice in life—enable us heartily to enjoy the world that you have given us. Lighten our darkness, open our eyes, and restore the joy and the enjoyment of your creative genius and saving goodness. We are a needy people, and we are confident that you can supply our every need from the riches of Christ Jesus.

All our praise, all our petitions, and all our prayers are made in his matchless name, and for his glory in us and in all men.

Amen.

—Don Vroon

Prayers of Intercession

56.

Almighty God, who taught us to pray for our daily bread, enable us to win it and use it according to your holy will. Give men skill and enterprise in husbanding the resources of the earth. Arouse our consciences, so that we may be enabled to work together to enlarge the harvests according to men's needs. Give us a deeper sense of our working together, and may each give thanks for the other's labors. This we ask in Jesus Christ.

Amen.

Hamline United Methodist Church
St. Paul, Minnesota

57.

We praise you, O God, because of your own free gift of love. You have reached out to us, and with the patience of a father, wait for us to break the chains of selfishness, and respond to your love with love. For you we seek to fill our minds with everything that is true, noble, good, and pure. Thus we know that you are the God of peace, and truly with us.

Amen.

Hamline United Methodist Church
St. Paul, Minnesota

58.

O God, who bound us all together in this bundle of life, accept our thanksgiving for each other, and for those graces in which we serve and love each other. In this day of fear and evil, keep us courageous, and trustful of each other. Grant us a righteous discontent, that we may never be perfectly at rest while injustice is done to your people. May we rejoice in loving each other, and may we seek your kingdom as the pearl of great price; we ask it in Jesus' name.

Amen.

Hamline United Methodist Church
St. Paul, Minnesota

59.

O God, we find our lives filled with things good and evil, and in your name we are called to rejoice and live greatly in the good and to confront the evil. Uncertainties surround education, politics, the life-style of the people, and the future of the church. Yet we know your Spirit moves in every time and among all people, and we give thanks for the moving power of faith in the cultures of today. The overwhelming fullness of life in Jesus Christ is possible, it is always moving us, it calls us in him. In him we would respond.

Amen.

Hamline United Methodist Church
St. Paul, Minnesota

60.

O God, let us remind ourselves of the others for whom we must give our lives. We pray for those who do not have the power to protect their own lives. We pray for everyone who must learn a concern for humanity. We pray for those who must live and die hungry. We pray for those who must learn a just use of power. We pray for those who cannot escape ignorance, and cannot earn a living. We pray for a structure in society that will enable every person to belong somewhere. We think of the Risen Lord, and his kingdom of life; may it come, beginning with our giving of ourselves to humanity. In Jesus' name we pray.

Amen.

Hamline United Methodist Church
St. Paul, Minnesota

61.

O God, our Father, we pray that we may do your will on earth, as it is done in heaven. May we see our brothers in everyone who knows the mind of Jesus. Inspire continually the universal church with the spirit of truth, unity, and concord, so that these things may be brought into the lives of men. May our weapons be justice and goodwill, our courage unfailing, and our devotion endless. We accept the limitations of our humanity, but we pray that there may also be among us the mind of Christ. In his name we pray.

Amen.

Hamline United Methodist Church
St. Paul, Minnesota

62.

O God, our Father, we remember the will of Jesus, and we pray that we may be enabled to fulfill it. Help us to gather together in one all things in him. Help us to love him, and our neighbors as ourselves. May we not be anxious for the morrow, nor judgmental upon our brothers, nor insincere in our prayers. Keep us aware of our calling to be the salt of the earth, and may the fact that we are part of the Body of Christ keep our hearts warm with love, and our hands busy in his service. In his name we pray.

Amen.

Hamline United Methodist Church
St. Paul, Minnesota

63.

People: Almighty Father, hear us as we pray for those who suffer: For all who are handicapped in the race of life through no fault of their own; for those whose livelihood is insecure, the overworked, the hungry, and the destitute; for little children, whose surroundings hide from them love and beauty; for those who are in doubt and anguish of soul, for those who are oversensitive and afraid; for those whose suffering is unrelieved by the knowledge of your love; for those who suffer through their own wrongdoing. Set free, O Lord, the souls of your servants from all restlessness and anxiety, and keep us in all perplexities and distresses, that we may be upheld by your strength and stayed on the rock of your faithfulness.

Amen.

Hamline United Methodist Church
St. Paul, Minesota

64.

Leader: O Master, we bring to you the task of this day—above all the task of being the men and women we should be. Grant us a zeal to live and work where, and as, we should. We know that for each of us there is a future in store, if only we will give you freedom to work out that future for us. Grant that in so giving we may find our true freedom; and in so living may we find your kingdom. Amen.

Amen.

Hamline United Methodist Church
St. Paul, Minnesota

65.

A Prayer for Peace

God of grace and power, we turn to you as the genius at the heart of the universe that makes life possible, that makes progress possible, that makes beautiful character possible, that made Jesus Christ the embodiment of what you will us to be.

We affirm our purpose as Christians to take Jesus as Lord of Life, to love what he loved, to admire what he admired, to be as he was.

Help us to rise above the influences that press upon us from the half-Christian world and follow after Jesus, to be true disciples, changing the world into what you want it to be.

Help us to think today about what we can do to fulfill the dream of peace on earth, of men living together in mutual trust and mutual helpfulness.

Make us instruments of your peace—not of a hopeless dream but a peace in fact. Let the time come soon when the earth shall be full of your knowledge and glory, as water covers the sea.

—James L. Ray

66.

A Springtime Prayer

As nature is praising you today, O God, we too lift our hearts and voices in praise and thanksgiving to our Maker.

Let this time of worship be exalting to our spirits as we look up to the exalted God who loves us.

As we see your hand in the long sweep of history, help us to serve the purposes you are trying to work out in our lifetime.

Fixing our eyes on Jesus, we try to understand your plan. Help us to understand, and to serve.

Surely it is your will that we should love you and love eternal truths more than prestige or pleasure in this world. Bring us to a renewed devotion to the Eternal Spirit, we pray.

Help us to see beyond the few years ahead, to the time when we shall graduate from this earth, and teach us to live so that we can hear the words, "well done."

—James L. Ray

67.

Help us to have clean motives, O God. Help us to think like Christ thought, to want what he wanted and love as he loved.

We need to reevaluate the habits of thinking and feeling that we have developed, our Father. We pause to look at what we have become, at the attitudes and motives with which we live. Point out to us the ways we fail to come up to Christ's standards. Make us sharply aware of our spiritual needs. Give us the compassion and concern that marked Christ's deed. Make us over in his image. Refine all our dross. Take from us our hate.

Father, hasten the day when mankind will no longer divide itself against itself. Hasten the day when Russians and Americans will help one another instead of wasting resources in childish competition. Hasten the day when those who have much will be deeply concerned for those who have so much less. *Thy kingdom come.* Thy will be done, on earth as it is in heaven.

—James L. Ray

68.

A Prayer for Fulfillment of Promise

Spirit of Justice and Truth, we pause in the busyness of life to think before you our thoughts about where we are going and what we are doing with the opportunities given us each day—opportunities to become what it is possible to be under your plan, to fulfill the promise and potential to rise to the noblest and finest of our kind.

Through all of our busyness, make us appreciative of the life-affirming way that is right, and turn us from the life-denying customs and attitudes, which are wrong.

Help us to see that nothing we do is insignificant, our Maker and our Judge; that in every act of life, great and small, we either think and do right, and affirm life; or our thinking and doing is out of harmony with the best in life, and is contrary to your plan.

In this moment of prayer, we confess that no relationship with other people is trivial or unimportant, that in every relationship of life we are given the opportunity to practice the perfect way Christ exemplified, or to yield to the temptation to demean persons by using them or ignoring them.

Save us from these spiritual pitfalls, and guide us into the higher way of life, in which Christ is indeed our Lord, we pray.

Amen.

—James L. Ray

69.

O Spirit of Life, it is you who guides the stars in their mysterious existence out there beyond our reach, you who laid the foundations and set the rules for the world in which we live, and it is you who oversees the growth and the fulfillment of every living thing. We know you set the destiny of a human life and will help each of us reach it when we seek fellowship with you. You are always with us.

Here and now we seek to open our minds and hearts to you. And we would that we might so experience the reality of your life in this time of worship that we will ever hereafter walk closer to you in all our experiences, both joys and sorrows.

We pray for those we know who are searching for answers to the big questions in their lives, for those who have decisions to make and seek desperately to know which way to turn. We pray that they may find fellowship with the Spirit of Life, your Spirit, to see them through safely and wisely.

We pray for those who mourn—who mourn because they are in pain, mental or physical. For those who suffer because they have been wounded by the selfishness or cruelty of some of the rest of us. And, O God, wherever any one of us has caused anyone to suffer, draw us back to make amends, to apologize, to clean the wound, to set that one free from the hurt we have done, and to set ourselves free from the guilt we have earned. Make us so sensitive to the hurts of others that we will know when others mourn and will make our dealings right and take for ourselves the work of the healer.

Make us reconcilers. And in a world divided so many ways, may we try extra hard to bring together those who are separated, who need to understand each other. Lord, we offer ourselves as those who hunger and thirst after righteousness—satisfy our hunger, we pray.

—James L. Ray

70.

Prayer of Praise

You're first-class, Jesus! You really are!! And because we know that You are Number One, and because we belong to you, we have *nothing* to fear, ever. That's good news! Your love . . . Your *love* . . . What can we even say about it that is big enough, that expresses our praise and gratitude? Here we are, just children, trying to comprehend what you did for us on the Cross. We aren't even willing to go out in the rain and get a little cold and wet helping somebody, and *you* let yourself be *tortured* and *killed* for us. Man! That's something!! After that, we've just *got to* praise You! Alleluia!

—Kathryn Rogers Deering

71.

Prayer of Petition

Laughing on the outside,
Crying on the inside;
What am I doing wrong, Lord?
Following the other blind
sheep,
When I should be following you;
When will I ever learn?
Following my old selfish ways
And forgetting about you;
When will I ever change?
Laughing on the outside,
Crying on the inside;
Help me in spite of myself, Lord!

Amen.

—Kathryn Rogers Deering

72.

Prayer for Man

(In unison following a sermon on the topic, What Is Man?)

O God, from the dust of the ground you made us. We are perishable and yet eternal. Our abilities are a part of your endowment, and yet we glory in our accomplishments. We look at the sky: We see things you have made which are so much more massive than anything we have made. We look in the microscope: We see things you have made which are more delicate than anything we have made. Forgive our tendency to glorify ourselves and help us to take our place in your creation glorifying you. Amen.

—Leon A. McCleary

73.

Prayer for Ecology and Care of the Earth (Confession)

O Creator God, we confess our careless handling of your creation. In our pursuit of our own pleasure and well-being, we have at times scarred and littered your earth, our home. Forgive us, Lord, our ways of destruction. Save us from our well-meaning, but misdirected pursuits which threaten our very survival. Teach us how to handle the abundance of your earth. Teach us how to care for the resources of your earth. Teach us how to enjoy the beauty of your earth. Amen and Amen.

—Carl B. Rife

74.

Unison Prayer

Slash us open, Father; rip us apart and throw out everything that has gone bad. Then put us back together; patch us up and make us the way we were meant to be when you first thought of us. We are trusting you when we step out with a request like this, because we know you love us. Once we are patched up better-than-new, we hope we can love you more in return. In Jesus' name.

—Kathryn Rogers Deering

75.

God, fill me with a sense of community.
Make my handshake more than skin meeting skin
my smile other than a tribute to my dentist's skill.

Transform restaurant mugs
        and paper cups
            and silver tea services
                to chalices

that I might commune with all I meet.
May my alliance with the fellow in the street
be such that I would break my body for him.
God, keep me aware
that at my worst and at my best
I am my brother's brother
        no more   no less
and it is only in communion with each other
that men fully confess and truly praise.

God, don't let winter into New York City
before the Bowery wino finds a place to sleep
and the Salvation Army can replace his coat,
or landlords turn the heat on Harlem tenements,
stretch daylight into evening to save the Beekman ambulance boys
        from junkie's knives

guard Madame Park Avenue and Fifi's evening stroll
       by Central Park
and Sister Alexandra walking home through Chinatown,
police the cops who hold down 42nd Street
have mercy on midnight pretenders
and hustlers begging quarters for a drink
this night in all that wilderness of strangers
may someone feel a little less alone.

God, touch old ladies
     who reach out at night
to metal bedrails and the empty air of sterile rooms
senility saves the souls of those with none to touch
       their cheeks
send your warm Christ who softly speaks
answers to their anxiety
and gently in the midst of their confusion
implants the needed sensual illusion
of one almost forgotten kiss goodnight.

                            —Susan Staff

76.

Lord of welfare and picket line
of corporate business large and small
of factory waste and sewage plant
of transit strike and pall
Be thou our guide on littered streets
jostled by nameless masses
lest we forget our brother's face
and shun him when he passes.
Lord of rapist and general
of president and whore
of hustler, pimp, and socialite
of junkie rich or poor
Thou art the Savior of us all
the plastic and the true
Lest we forget lest we forget
what love unleashed can do.
For all the saints in concrete cells
          strangling on prison air
for all the saviors sentenced to the chair
for every prophet crying freedom through the bars and loud
for quiet martyrs unashamed
for racist rebels proud
WE THANK THEE LORD
for this life-choked metropolis
for all the human maze
pulsating with anonymity
for ignorance and selfishness and glowing unconcern
for lack of time to listen and lack of will to see
WE THANK THEE LORD
in this dark setting
     love's miracle glows the brightest.

                            —Susan Staff

77.

A Prayer-Litany

for Christians in a Time of Change

Minister: We have gathered, O God, in a fellowship for worship, for learning and for the celebration of your love. Help us to be honest before you.

Right: To be honest means at least to admit openly that we wish the world would slow down, that life would not change quite so fast, that we could catch our breath before the next crisis breaks upon us.

Left: To be honest also means to affirm that we are not satisfied with life as it is. We do hope for peace in Vietnam, for food for the hungry, for justice for the Blacks in the ghettos, for opportunities for the Mexican-Americans, and for a sense of joy and accomplishment in our own lives.

Minister: As a congregation we lay before you, O God, our hearts that are torn between a love for quietness and a fascination with freedom, between a desire for order and a hope for change. We want to conserve all that is good, yet we dream of all the greater goods that might yet be.

Together: **Whatever our difference in attitude or motive, however differently we may see and think concerning the way life ought to be; keep us, O Lord, united in a spirit of trust that makes us aware of our common heritage in Christ.**

Right: When the prophet of a new social order speaks, help us to dream with him his dreams and not to get angry because he asks us to change our way of life.

Left: When the spokesman for things as they have been speaks, seemingly blind to the injustice that is always part of the status quo, enable us to understand the anxiety that comes with change and the fear that accompanies that which is new.

Together: **For we are all members of one family, children of the same heavenly Father. We know that the things which bind us together are greater than the attitudes that separate us.**

Minister: You have heard our words, O Father, as we have attempted to be honest, now hear us as we pledge ourselves anew as disciples of Christ.

Right: We remember how he upset the authorities in Jerusalem, how he caused many to react against him because he asked from them more than a religion of ritual but for righteousness of life.

Left: We remember how he disappointed those who would have made him a king because he had already dedicated himself to a kingdom greater than the kingdoms of this world.

Together: **Help us to affirm our citizenship in his continuing kingdom, that we may joyfully live the life you have given us, a life of joy and gladness, of responsibility and opportunity, a life made new in Christ.**
Amen.

—Myron M. Hall

78.

A Litany for Thanksgiving

(to teach us gratefulness)

Leader: Father, we have so much for which to be thankful.

People: **So much. We take things for granted, we confess, to our shame. Lord, don't let us become selfish in the midst of our blessings.**

Leader: Most of our children are well, and even when they are ill we get immediate medical attention. We have taken all this for granted.

People: **And forgotten those men and women whose children were never born or were born retarded. Forgive our forgetfulness. Let us count health as something more than what we deserve and demand.**

Leader: We came from warm homes and shall return to them. We take them for granted and

People: **Have forgotten the thousands on the streets of Calcutta and Chungking who have no houses and no place to go except the sidewalk or the alley. Father, help us appreciate our warmth tonight.**

Leader: The only noise to disturb us tonight will be that of the occasional hot-rodder or the neighbors' snowmobile. We will be apt to complain gently forgetting

People: **Those who tonight will tremble at the noise of bombs falling along their street, and the screeching whistle or rockets two seconds before they blow people from this world to the next one. Father, have mercy on their souls. Have mercy on us who are more apt to make war than make peace.**

Leader: Tomorrow our homes will echo with the gentle grumbling of people who have eaten too much and who suffer not always silently. We tend to forget

People: **Those whose homes will echo with the gentle grumbling of empty stomachs of starving children. Lord, take better care of them in heaven than we took care of them on earth.**

Leader: Lord of all who live,

People: **Teach us gratefulness for the common, small, accepted, casually enjoyed things: the doctor's phone number, the prescriptions, normal pregnancies, warmth, snow falling in silence, refrigerators with food in them, a chair on which to sit. Thank you, God, for life.   Amen.**

(South United Methodist Church
Grand Rapids, Michigan
the Rev. Kenneth McCaw)

79.

Litany of Thanksgiving

Leader: For our homes, O Lord, we thank you. For all the things in them which we take for granted—bathtubs and hot running water; electricity that runs refrigerators, washing machines, and stoves; for all the good food which is on our tables three times a day or more; for our families without whom our lives would be empty,

58

All:	**We thank you, God.**
Junior Choir:	For our pets—cats and dogs and ponies, gold fish and turtles, guinea pigs, and gerbils,
All:	**We thank you, God.**
Youth Choir:	For our schools—books and teachers, sports and activities, and especially friends,
All:	**We give thanks, O Lord.**
Leader:	For our church, God, we thank you. For the Bible and ministers who help us to learn about Jesus,
Youth Choir:	For music—organs and pianos and violins and guitars and those who play them for your glory,
Junior Choir:	For choirs and choir directors,
All:	**We give thanks, O Lord.**
Leader:	For our nation—its great beauties in parks, mountains, and lakes; its freedom of religion, of the press, of speech, of assembly.
All:	**Help us to preserve them, O Lord.**
Leader:	For the Thanksgiving holiday when we give thanks for your many gifts and remember our forefathers who made our nation great; and for this Advent season when we prepare for the coming of the greatest gift of all, your Son, Jesus Christ,
All:	**We give thanks and praise your name and rejoice. Alleluia! Amen.**

—Marybelle Landrum

80.

A Litany for Confirmation

Minister:	God loves us.
People:	**Indeed, he does.**
Minister:	We are called the children of God!
People:	**What have we done to deserve this?**
Minister:	Nothing! He loves all persons unconditionally. When you were baptized, you and the church celebrated the love of God for you and you became a member of the family of God. You were a "baby" in the Christian faith, whether you were an infant or an adult.
People:	**How do we grow? What or who enables us to grow up to maturing?**
Minister:	God does. The Spirit of God works in us and through the Christian community, his church, to bring us into ever deepening commitment to the leading of the Spirit.
People:	**Do you mean that God's loving power comes before our response of faith?**
Minister:	Yes, and that same loving power enables us to grow in Christ so that in due time we confirm by our personal commitment his claim upon us and assume our responsibility in joyful obedience to him.

People: Have these young persons come to say that they feel they are ready to make this commitment to Christ and his mission in the world?

Minister: What is your answer, you who are confirmands?

Confirmands:

We give thanks for what was done for us by God and his church that we could not do for ourselves. We are now ready consciously to affirm the meaning of our baptism, and seriously and gratefully receive the power and guidance of the Holy Spirit as we follow Christ.

People: Will you join with us in our work?

Confirmands:

Yes. With help and strength from the Holy Spirit we will accept, with you, God's commission to be the church in the world.

—Daniel T. Benedict, Jr.

81.

A Litany Based on Matthew 23:1-12

"Greatness is. . ."

Leader: Greatness is *not:*

People: LETTING THE HAPPINESS OF LIFE PASS US BY, NOR FORGETTING THE JOY OF SERVING THE LORD.

Leader: Greatness is *not:*

People: PREACHING WITHOUT PRACTICING, LAYING HEAVY BURDENS ON PEOPLE.

Leader: Greatness is *not;*

People: DOING THINGS TO BE SEEN BY THE CROWD, ALWAYS PICKING THE SEATS OF HONOR AT THE BANQUETS.

Leader: Greatness *is:*

People: BEING A SERVANT OF THE GREAT GOD, WHO MADE HEAVEN AND EARTH, AND BEING RESPONSIBLE FOR THE WORLD HE HAS ENTRUSTED TO US.

Leader: Greatness *is:*

People: FOLLOWING THE WAY OF JESUS CHRIST AND THROUGH THE SPIRIT MAKING OURSELVES AVAILABLE TO THOSE IN NEED.

Leader: Greatness *is:*

People: BELONGING TO THE CHURCH AND MAKING OUR MINISTRY REAL IN THE PRIVATE AND PUBLIC SECTORS OF LIFE.

Unison: GREATNESS IS BRINGING THE GREATNESS OF GOD TO BEAR ON THE GREATNESS OF THE WORLD'S NEEDS.

O GOD, HELP US TO BE YOUR SERVANTS, AND OUR BROTHER'S. THROUGH JESUS CHRIST, OUR LORD. AMEN.

Passing of the Peace;
(Turn to your neighbor, clasp hands, say his/her name and say:)
The greatness of God is yours today. Let it be!

—David James Randolph

82.

Litany of Thanks (for use in the family worship)

Leader: Let us say thank you to God:

People: Thank you God for things

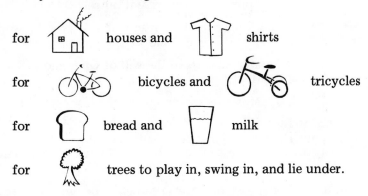

for   houses and   shirts

for   bicycles and   tricycles

for   bread and   milk

for   trees to play in, swing in, and lie under.

Leader: We thank you, Lord, for all your material gifts.

People: Let us thank God for people:
    Thank you, God, for all people

for our   fathers and   mothers

for our   brothers and   sisters

for neighbors   and   policemen

for Me   I'm glad I'm alive!

Leader: We thank you, Lord, for all your people.

People: Let us thank God that he is with us:
    Thank you, God, that you are always with us

when we   laugh; when we   cry

when we feel   alone; when we   love

when we   read and learn.

Leader: Thank you, Lord, for all things you have made and that we all belong to you.

People: Let us sing and clap our hands in thanksgiving.

—Daniel T. Benedict, Jr.

83.

The Installation of Officers

(based on Romans 12)   The People of God

Officers: O God, receive our prayers as we present ourselves to you.

Pastors: Adapt yourself no longer to the pattern of this present world, but let your minds be remade and your whole nature transformed.

People: **Then you will be able to discern the will of God, and to know what is good, acceptable, and perfect.**

Officers: Spirit of God, transform us by the renewing of our minds.

Pastors: In virtue of the gift that God in his grace has given me I say to everyone among you: Do not be conceited or think too highly of yourself; but think your way to a sober estimate based on the measure of faith that God has given to each of you.

Unison: **Teach us, O Lord, to walk in true humility of mind and soul, that we may more fully experience the measure of faith which God has granted to each of us.**

The Charge to the Officers   (leave title line)   Mr Rose
                                                                The Pastor

omit Friends in Christ, this congregation in its wisdom and in response to the influence of the spirit of Christ, has elected you to important positions of leadership. Your duties include many tasks which are necessary for the advancement of the kingdom of God, and the administration of this local community of God's people.

As you begin these responsibilities I trust that you will begin with prayer for guidance, and with a commitment to Christ which will provide the motivation to fulfill the opportunities in such a manner that the work of Christ will be enlarged by your presence.

The Vows

Officers: I will accept the office to which I have been elected, make a genuine attempt to understand its responsibilities.

People: **We will support those we have asked to provide leadership for this congregation, and to the best of our ability see that they have both the tools and help that we may fulfill our task as a congregation.**

The Installation

People: **We have chosen these people for the various offices among us as a people of God, and ask that they be installed in their respective offices.**

Pastor: In the name of Jesus Christ the head of the church Because of the authority given me by the members of this congregation and as a minister of The United Methodist Church; I welcome you to the positions to which this community of God's people have called you; on their behalf I install you each in your office.

Unison: **So be it.   Amen.**

—Frank W. Wooldridge

84.

A Litany for Night Things

(Divide congregation in two parts: "left" and "right" for antiphonal reading.)

ALL:	**We thank you, Lord, for night things**
Left:	For frogs and spiders and pondy woods
Right:	For owl and howl and prowling beast
Left:	For moon and cloud and darkling plain
Right:	For weeds and wet and murky waters
Left:	For web and vine and dangling branches
Right:	For hole and cave and black recesses
Left:	For night cry and pain and loneliness
Right:	For blues and tears and wailing voice
Left:	For healing through the fever and restless tossing
Right:	For sleep that sponges cares away
Left:	For dreams that keep our yesteryears alive
Right:	And unify our natures once again
Left:	Letting devils loose inside
Right:	And causing Christ to die again
Left:	We thank you, Lord, for Christ
Right:	Who dies in every dark, unholy place
Left:	On every dank and blackened eve
Right:	To fend off evil and sanctify our souls
Left:	Who rides the night winds
Right:	Who inhabits the howling gales
Left:	Who comes at the storm's height
Right:	And cries "Peace!"
Left:	Until the winds die
Right:	And the waves recede
Left:	And the fever drops
Right:	And calm returns
Left:	For night things
Right:	Toads, dark, and tossing on the bed
Left:	We thank you, Lord
Right:	For night things
ALL:	**Amen**

—John Killinger

Prayers of Dedication

85.

Leader: We are yours, O God,

People: **We surrender our lives to your use.**

Leader: Show us what you would have us do,

People: **And we shall do it.**

Leader: Amen

People: **And Amen.**

—John Curtis

86.

Leader: Thou hast called us, O Lord,

People: **And we shall answer.**

Leader: Use us to fulfill thy ministry,

People: **To share thy works through our church.**

Leader: Amen.

People: **And Amen.**

—John Curtis

87.

Leader: As Jesus ultimately gave his life.

People: **So we also give our lives.**

Leader: The world calls us to witness, to serve. . .

People: **Use us, O God, to fulfill this ministry.**

Leader: Amen,

People: **And Amen.**

—John Curtis

88.

Father, forgive us for cowardly faith and delinquent discipleship. We shudder to think of the costliness of true discipleship. We prefer to be one of your followers at discount prices. With such a mind in us, how can you use us at all, Lord? Father, we look to you to redeem our pitiful attempts to serve you. Take all that we are and all that we have. It's yours.
Amen.

—Charles E. Weigel, Jr.

89.

We offer ourselves, Lord, to be your people—your militant minority group, despised by all the "important" people, as Christ was. We offer our lives to be made new and to remake the society around us, so that our King may rule in every life. In his royal name.   Amen.

—Don Vroon

90.

We don't like to give to you, O God. When we give to someone else it makes us *feel* good, and we get credit for it. But when we give to you, we are reminded by Jesus that even when we have done *everything*, we have only done our duty, and we are *unworthy servants*. We know we are unworthy to give you anything, but our offering today means that we do want to be your *servants*. Thru Jesus Christ our Lord.   Amen.

—Don Vroon

91.

Jesus, lover of my soul;
Make me a lover of the souls of men.
Jesus, lover of my body,
Make me care about the bodies of others.
Jesus, giver of total love to all of me,
Help me to give total love to all my
          brothers.   Amen.

—Don Vroon

92.

We know we need you more than you need us. We know we need your gifts more than you need ours. And we know you have given us to each other. We offer ourselves again, as agents of your love, to bind men together in Christ.   Amen.

—Don Vroon

93.

Deliver us, O God, from all feelings of noble generosity as we give our small gifts for your vast work. All things are yours. We are yours. May we humble ourselves with that recognition rather than pride ourselves on parting with some of our precious money. Thru Jesus Christ our master and owner.   Amen.

—Don Vroon

Scriptural Readings

94.

A Responsive Look at War in Scriptures

Leader: We come to examine what Holy Scriptures have to say about war.

People: "AND YOU WILL HEAR OF WARS AND RUMORS OF WARS; SEE THAT YOU ARE NOT ALARMED; FOR THIS MUST TAKE PLACE, BUT THE END IS NOT YET" (Matt. 24:6).

Leader: Is this meant to be a justification and blessing of the human situation? Surely God has something better than this in mind for us.

People: "AND THEY SHALL BEAT THEIR SWORDS INTO PLOWSHARES,
     AND THEIR SPEARS INTO PRUNING HOOKS;
NATION SHALL NOT LIFT UP SWORD AGAINST NATION,
     NEITHER SHALL THEY LEARN WAR ANY MORE;
BUT THEY SHALL SIT EVERY MAN UNDER HIS VINE AND UNDER
     HIS FIG TREE, AND NONE SHALL MAKE THEM AFRAID" (Mic. 4:3-4).

Leader: Is this dream really realistic? Do we believe it? How could we ever manage to defend ourselves in such a world?

People: "WHAT CAUSES WARS, AND WHAT CAUSES FIGHTINGS AMONG YOU? IS IT NOT YOUR PASSIONS THAT ARE AT WAR IN YOUR MEMBERS? YOU DESIRE AND DO NOT HAVE; SO YOU KILL. AND YOU COVET AND CANNOT OBTAIN; SO YOU FIGHT AND WAGE WAR" (James 4:1).

Leader: So that is one cause for war! We have an inner battle to overcome, as well as the external enemy we can see so clearly and which we come to fear as a result of other sins—related to basic greed.

People: "A TIME TO LOVE AND A TIME TO HATE;
A TIME FOR WAR AND A TIME FOR PEACE" (Eccles. 3:8).

Leader: When does the time for peace come? When will we be able to spend billions for waging peace? When will we decide to spend as much effort toward peace as we have toward defense and war?

People: "HE MAKES WARS CEASE TO THE END OF THE EARTH;
HE BREAKS THE BOW AND SHATTERS THE SPEAR,
HE BURNS THE CHARIOTS WITH FIRE!" (Ps. 40:9).

Leader: The psalmist dreamed our dream before us. The prophets proclaimed a day of peace. Yet, as human beings, we have not fulfilled that for which we were created.

People: "WISDOM IS BETTER THAN WEAPONS OF WAR, BUT ONE SINNER DESTROYS MUCH GOOD" (Ecc. 9:18).

Leader: May God deliver us from evil,
May God help us to seek wisdom.

(The above litany was written to be a part of a worship service in which the sermon contained an analysis of the moral implications of our reaction to the massacre at My Lai, the conviction of Lt. William Calley, and related matters. Scripture passages are from the Revised Standard Version.)

—John J. Shaffer

95.

Responsive Prayer Scripture Reading

Leader: "He entered Jericho and was passing through. And there was a man named Zacchaeus; he was a chief tax collector, and rich. And he sought to see who Jesus was, but could not, on account of the crowd, because he was small of stature. So he ran on ahead and climbed up into a sycamore tree to see him, for he was to pass that way" (Luke 19:1-4 RSV).

People: **Lord, we are little, like Zacchaeus, trying to see you in spite of the crowd. But there are so many others trying to see you that we are being jostled and squeezed. We are even losing our sense of direction. We are trying so hard to catch a glimpse of you that we are climbing trees to get above the crowd, to get away from the confusion . . .**

Leader: "And when Jesus came to the place, he looked up and said to him, "Zacchaeus, make haste and come down, for I must stay at your house today.' So he made haste and came down, and received him joyfully. And when they saw it they all murmured, 'He has gone in to be the guest of a man who is a sinner' " (Luke 19:5-7 RSV).

People: **We are sinners, too, Lord, like Zacchaeus. We want to hear you calling us to come down to you; we want you to stay at our house today. We are eager to welcome you as our guest.**

Leader: "And Zacchaeus stood and said to the Lord, 'Behold, Lord, the half of my goods I give to the poor; and if I have defrauded any one of anything, I restore it fourfold.' And Jesus said to him, 'Today salvation has come to this house, since he also is a son of Abraham. For the Son of man came to seek and to save the lost' " (Luke 19:8-10).

People: **We admit that we are lost without you, Lord, and we want to be changed inside, like Zacchaeus. He was not content to simply say, "From this point forward, I will live an upright life." He was suddenly willing to repair all past wrongs too. Thank you for patiently waiting for us to come down to you and for giving us the faith we need to trust you.**

Leader and People: Amen.

—Kathryn Rogers Deering

96.

Responsive Scripture Lesson

Leader: "You are the salt of the earth; but if salt has lost its taste, how shall its saltness be restored? It is no longer good for anything except to be thrown out and trodden underfoot by men" (Matt. 5:13 RSV).

People: **We are the salt of the earth. Have we lost our taste? Or have we perhaps not even discovered yet that we have a taste? Let us determine to be the salt of the earth.**

Leader: "My soul thirsts for God,
for the living God" (Ps. 42:2 RSV).

People: Salt should make people *thirsty*. If we are the salt of this world, do those around us long for the living water which keeps us refreshed? Let us determine to serve as his salt and then to serve as channels for his living water.

Leader: "Whoever drinks of the water that I shall give him will never thirst; the water that I shall give him will become in him a spring of water welling up to eternal life" (John 4:14 RSV).

People: We ache to be filled with the Lord's living water. We pray that he will fill us with it and that he will renew our desire to irrigate the world.

"One thing have [we] asked of the Lord,
that will [we] seek after;
   that [we] may dwell in the house of the Lord
   all the days of [our lives],
to behold the beauty of the Lord,
   and to inquire in his temple" (Ps. 27:4).

—Kathryn Rogers Deering

97.

Responsive Scripture Lesson

Leader: The Lord tells us in his word who he is. He also tells us who we are.

People: "Even though I walk through the valley of the shadow of death,
I fear no evil;
   for thou art with me;
   thy rod and thy staff,
   they comfort me" (Ps. 23:4 RSV).

Leader: We are not afraid because we know that death and evil are only shadows—there is *light* on the other side of any shadow. And we have the presence of the Holy Spirit to see us through to the light of the Father.

People: "For once you were darkness, but now you are light in the Lord; walk as children of light (for the fruit of light is found in all that is good and right and true)" (Eph. 5:8-9 RSV).

Leader: Rejoice in the Lord! We used to be virtually lifeless and worthless. Now we have been reborn into his life and love. As long as we are his obedient children, we are fearless and growing and deathless!

People: "Therefore it is said, 'Awake, O sleeper, and arise from the dead, and Christ shall give you light' " (Eph. 5:14 RSV).

—Kathryn Rogers Deering

98.

Responsive Prayer/Scripture Reading
   (Luke 5:4-10 RSV)

Leader: "And when he had ceased speaking, he said to Simon, 'Put out into the deep and let down your nets for a catch.' And Simon answered, 'Master, we toiled all night and took nothing! But at your word I will let down the nets.' And when they had done this, they enclosed a great shoal of fish; and as their nets were breaking, they beckoned to their partners in the other boat to come and help. And they came and filled both boats, so that they began to sink"

People: **Lord, speak to us like you did to Simon and James and John! It seems that too often we have been toiling in vain, working hard for you but not really getting anywhere. If what happened to those fishermen applies to us, then we should be incredibly successful, but only if we hear your voice and act in obedience. We want that to happen!**

Leader: "But when Simon Peter saw it, he fell down at Jesus' knees, saying, 'Depart from me, for I am a sinful man, O Lord.' For he was astonished, and all that were with him, at the catch of fish which they had taken; . . . And Jesus said to Simon, 'Do not be afraid; henceforth you will be catching men.' "

People: **Lord, sometimes we feel like good fishers of men, but often we pull back empty nets. When we see how ineffective and little we are next to your power, we are ashamed and even afraid. We want you to set us straight—we want you to use us in bringing men to you. But we know that it won't work if we start feeling important, so we ask you to keep us dependent on you. We pray in Jesus' name for the sake of your kingdom.   Amen.**

—Kathryn Rogers Deering

Proclamation

To proclaim the Word of God is to carry the burden of the Lord, as Ted R. Witt, Sr., makes clear. The "burden of the Lord" however, is often made more burdensome or obscure by insensitive and uncreative prophets.

There is a need to discover fresh ways of proclamation. Those who were afraid that "new forms of worship" would diminish the role of the sermon have had their fears proven unfounded. Instead, creative worship has stimulated a creative preaching. It is neither desirable nor possible to go on with the same old style of one-way preaching in the context of the new highly participatory liturgies.

The materials included here show some effective ways of breaking through the boredom barrier. The much discussed "dialogue sermon" is demonstrated here. There are also examples of the monologue, but it becomes evident that monologue here refers to a literary and oratorical form, rather than a one-way style of communication. All preachers might learn from Kathryn Rogers Deering's sensitive work that many people can be speaking while only one person is talking when preaching is genuine.

The Prophet

Prophet of the all-caring God!
Are you preaching relaxed?
"Easy," casual-like?

When the Eternal God speaks to you!
Do you proclaim his words in soft
And subdued tones?

When the world is afire with war!
Can you only speak in a whisper
A detached platitude?

When the world is bent on self-destruction
Are prophets also sin-stricken,
Speechless and tongue-tied?

Prophet of God! Are you without a word
Of justice when half the world is
    stuffed with food,
And, the other half holds a growling stomach
And lives in half a house or
Even in the street?

Tell me prophet of the living God,
Can you be mealymouthed when
    the soul of God is in travail
About the transgressions of his people?

O holy prophet!
Thou art God's trumpet,
Have you no breath to call us back to God?

—Ted R. Witt, Sr.

Dialogues

100.

The Boss Won't Let You Down (a dialogue)

Guy # 1: ... I just give up! What's the use anyhow? This job is just like all the rest
and I hate every minute—and it sounded so good at first! ...

Guy #2: Hey, you!
      Listen!
Payday is just around the corner?
hang in there,
don't quit'
Sure, it's tough.
So much work and no pay
yet.
But the Boss won't let you down—
you can trust Him!

Guy #1: But
I'll *starve* in the meantime!
I'm penniless.
All I have is one crust of bread,
no more than that!

Guy #2: Well,
I say—
eat that crust;
be thankful
that you at least have *something*!
Soon you will have more bread
than you can imagine.
Just be patient;
keep working.
The Boss won't let you down.
I know;
He didn't let me down.
And I felt just like you do now
When I joined the company.
Remember—
He wouldn't have wanted you
in the first place
if He didn't intend to keep you,
use you,
and pay you!

—Kathryn Rogers Deering

101.

Incredibility Gap (a dialogue)

Regular Guy: The Bible? Yeah, I know I ought to read it more than I do, but you know
how things are in this day and age.

Voice: Yes, I know.

Regular Guy:	Sometimes I really intend to sit down and make myself read at least a chapter, but I'm always too worn out; you know how tired a day of hard work can make a person.
Voice:	Yes, I know.
Regular Guy:	And Sunday would be a good day to do it, but after all it *is* a day of rest, and after working all week, I need every minute to catch up on things. Besides, if I go to church, they always read aloud a verse or two. That's something anyway. . . .
Voice:	Yes, that's something.
Regular Guy:	I'm not so sure anyway that it's all that valuable. It might not be the absolute Word of God after all—I'm kind of waiting for more scientific proof. They say it was just written by different men, and it's so full of contradictions. . .
Voice:	Really?? Where?
Regular Guy:	Well, it's not that I'm anti-Bible—not at all! Why, I recommend that anyone who has the time should sit down and read it—it's an inspiring piece of literature. It's got lots of exciting stories, good historical flavor, and even advice on life. . . .
Voice:	Yes, and I *am* that life.
Regular Guy:	What? *What* did you say?? Listen, buster, that's a pretty audacious thing to say, especially for someone who's always hanging around in the background making little counter-comments to everything I say! Just what do you mean by that—"I *am* the life"?
Voice:	Why don't you read all about me and find out?
Regular Guy:	In *here*?? Well—uh—maybe I just *will*—purely out of curiosity, of course, and to prove that what you say can't be so—I'm a pretty intelligent guy, you've gotta admit—you've gotten yourself into this one. . .
Voice:	And so have you, my friend. Start reading.

—Kathryn Rogers Deering

102.

Outreach (a dialogue)

"Anyone who comes to God must believe that he exists and that he rewards those who search for him" (Heb. 11:6b NEB).

Guy #1:	You tell me to "seek the Lord while he may be found." The more I think about that, the less sure I am that you know what you're talking about. I'm just not convinced that he *can* be found. It seems like there's too much piled up between him and me—if he is even on the other side of the pile!! Just look at this newspaper—murder, wars, rioting, death, injury, misunderstanding, hate—*that's* what's *real*. How can God claim to care if all this is going on? Especially about *me*?
Guy #2:	Hey, the newspaper doesn't have the last word! The Word has the last word! And the Word is Jesus, the Alpha and the Omega, beginning and end and everything in between. And I tell you again—he loves you. It breaks his heart to see the chaos we live in. If you reach out to him, he will meet you more than halfway, and then you're *free!!*

Guy #1: I can't reach out— I can't even understand what you mean. I heard you, but I don't understand you. I do believe God exists—I think—mostly because he is real to you, but I don't understand any more than that.

Guy #2: Well then, that just proves to me all the more that you need to reach out. Once you feel his touch, your understanding will be free too. You *can* reach out! Don't you have arms and hands? Don't you have tiptoes? Don't you have a voice?? *Reach out*, before it's too late! You can reach *out*, because God has already reached *in*!!

—Kathryn Rogers Deering

103.

Yours Truly (a dialogue)

Seeker: Sir, what is truth?

Know-it-all: Truth? Truth is *facts.*

Seeker: Sir, what are facts?

Know-it-all: Facts? Facts are *actuality.*

Seeker: Sir, what is actuality?

Know-it-all: Actuality? Actuality is *reality.*

Seeker: Sir, what is reality?

Know-it-all: Reality? Reality is *truth.*

Seeker: Truth? Sir, what is truth?

Know-it-all: Truth? Truth is *truth!*

Seeker: But sir, *who* is truth?

Know-it-all: Who? Who?? Don't be silly. . . .

—Kathryn Rogers Deering

104.

One by One (a dialogue)

Guy #1: ... Whaddaya mean, you're "saved"? Ya crazy or somethin'?! You're the *last* person I would'a thought would be susceptible to this Jesus bug—Now ya won't have fun any more; now ya gotta waste Sundays in church; now ya gotta pray 'n stuff; now ya won't even laugh at my jokes—Ya must be outa your head—My _God,_ man!

Guy #2: (gently, with a smile) _My_ God, man. . . .

—Kathryn Rogers Deering

Monologues

105.

Fore and After (A monologue)

Well, sir,
Here we are,
floating
in the so-called "river of life."
(It moves pretty fast, doesn't it?)
It's easy,
you know,
to get over your head,
and anyone can
just dabble in the shallows—
it's their choice.
But—
If you want to get
anyplace,
you'd better accept the services
of a navigator,
someone who knows his business,
so you won't get snagged
and dragged
too much.

I know just the man—
Here's his card—
Why don't you give him a call?
Yes, of course he'll come;
See? "24-hour service,
seven days a week."
He really knows his business.
(I could give you references if you wish.)

Well, sure—
There are others you could call on—
his competitors.
You *could* hire one of them,
but I wouldn't risk it.
This river is rough.
It needs an expert navigator
and this man is tops!
You'd never regret having him.

What? Why isn't his *name* on the card?
That's easy to answer
Simply because
he's got so *many* names.
Everyone has his own name for him.
Call him what you like,
(I call him "Commander in chief")
but *do* call him—He'll come, I guarantee it!

What was that?
You say you aren't sure
If you even want to *go*?
Listen to me!

You've *got* to go—
that's one thing
already decided
beforehand.

So come on!
What are you waiting for?
Quit wasting time—
Make up your mind!
This is *important*—
So important—
Your *boat* is waiting—
Don't miss it!

—Kathryn Rogers Deering

106.

In Gratitude (a monologue)

I'm back, Lord!
Back from over there
on the far side of that wall.
I'm sorry, Lord—
I wish I hadn't built
that wall at all.
I acted foolishly—
The stones I piled up
were poorly-shaped
and too heavy
for me to move away
when I found myself
trapped on the far side.
I had been thinking
that just this once
I might do something
without you,
and do it right,
but I was wrong, so wrong.
I was *afraid* there.
When I called you
I wasn't sure you heard—
That wall was so tall
and *so* long both ways!!
(because of course
I had help
from other people
to build it,
to pile up all the stones.)

I called you
until I nearly gave up
in despair.
I couldn't go
    over it,
        around it,
    or under it.

I *had* to go through it.
But I simply couldn't,
alone.
You threw me that crowbar;
I tried to pry up the stones,
but I was too weak.
So you started from your side.
And of course,
being so much stronger than I,
You brought that wall to the ground
in no time at all.
I stepped
over the scattered stones
(stumbled only once)
and into your open arms.
Fool that I am—What would I do without you??

—Kathryn Rogers Deering

107.

Observation

The Word
Engulfs us like rain,
Endless downpour.
    And yet
     most of us
       Simply
       Don our raincoats
       And try to ignore it.
  We avoid the puddles
  With delicacy
     And pride ourselves
     On keeping dry.
The Downpour
Is cool and clear—
It will wash over us,
Quench our thirst,
Refresh us,
    If
    We let ourselves go—
    Forget about our raincoats
    And
      Walk in the Rain!
      Run in the Rain!
      Delight in the Rain!
Lift our faces,
     Like happy children
     And let the drops
     Bathe our cheeks
     Like tears of joy!

—Kathryn Rogers Deering

108.

Doubts (a reading)

Anyone who has ever really gotten serious about this Christianity business, who has ever stepped out on a few limbs of faith, knows what a problem *doubts* can be. Doubts can saw the limb of faith right off, causing the Christian to come crashing to the ground. They can be compared with many things:

Doubts are the greasy fingerprints on your camera lens.
Doubts are the dirt in your wristwatch which prevents it from keeping good time.
Doubts are the gravy stains on your new white tablecloth.
Doubts are the mold on that piece of bread which has been left too long in your cupboard.
Doubts are the bulletholes in the windshield of your getaway car.
Doubts are the weeds in your garden—you have to keep pulling them out.
Doubts are the keys of your piano with the ivory knocked off.
Doubts are the bent dimes which clog up your Coke machine.

But troublesome as they may be, doubts ultimately make us *stronger* by challenging us to new heights. And our Lord never lets his children be challenged too far. Doubts can never win when he is on your side in the inner battle.
Praise the Lord!

—Kathryn Rogers Deering

109.

Only Children

"Truly, I say to you, whoever does not receive the Kingdom of God like a child shall not enter it" (Luke 18:17 RSV).

We are only children,
even if we have
our own children,
grandchildren,
or great-grandchildren.

We are children
even if we have
gray hair
and arthritis
and wrinkles.

We are only children
every last one of us,
regardless of our status,
self-importance,
or maturity.

We are children,
not childish,
but child*like*
in trust, obedience,
and humility.

We are only children
and, oddly enough,
we all have the same
Father.

Yes, we are his children.
How dare we
have the audacity
to act otherwise?

—Kathryn Rogers Deering

110.

Overshadow (a reading)

He is young,
but he walks
shuffleshuffle
with his eyes on the ground.
Shuffleshuffle
from place to place
every day.
. . . . Sleep
Eat
shuffleshuffle
Study
Struggle
shuffleshuffle
Eat
Sleep. . . .
Over and over and over and over.
Making every little thing
into something big.
Why?

Doesn't he know
that his never-never-land way of life
leads nowhere?
Doesn't he know
that it could be
charged with *joy*,
love
energy
purpose?
Doesn't he know
Where to go?

No?

Why?

—Kathryn Rogers Deering

111.

Pocket Edition

      Your
            Pick-it-up-
                Put-it-in-your-pocket-
            Save-it-for-a-rainy-day-
      Religion
      Will get you nothing.
      It will take you no farther
      Than just that—your back pocket.
      (Even though you think it's best
      Because it's handy and portable.)

      Did you realize
      That the Real Thing—
      Living-religion-out-of-hiding,
      Is just as portable?
      In fact, it's so light
      It carries *you*!
      Right!
      Wouldn't that be a welcome change?

      Your
            Pick-it-up-
                Put-it-in-your-pocket-
            Save-it-for-a-rainy-day-
      Religion
      Is hardly religion at all.
      After All,
      Hell is portable too.

—Kathryn Rogers Deering

112.

Clue

Around and around we run, trying to come out on top.

Around and around we chase after that nebulous thing called happiness.

Our efforts, fluctuating, blind, and barren, seem to yield little of what we hope for. Eventually we are forced to cry out in utter emptiness, "My God! There must be a *reason* for what I see, for *me*; what is it?"

And as we ask, the answer comes, sometimes quickly, but often slowly: Real happiness, happiness without end, cannot be found unless we *give up!* Give up our*selves*, without reservation, to someone we barely know, named Jesus.

And he takes it from there.

Let us praise him!

—Kathryn Rogers Deering

113.

the myth is "He is in our midst"
        Pass it on!

Beware
        the denim-shirted brother with unruly hair
Beware the Wall Street Capitalist and the back alley bum.
the myth is "He has come"
and who will be the first to pass him by?
Emmaus stretches
        an asphalt infinity six lanes wide!
on this untimeliest of Eastertides,
He's on the loose, incognito.
there's no description but the scars will still be there
Old wounds do not erase.
so, searcher, check each hand you hold for nails
        —each face for love.
the myth is "He is in our midst"
        Pass it on.

                                                —Susan Staff

Affirmations of Faith

114.

This We Believe

We believe in a loving God as Father who has created us in his own image to love him and one another.

We believe in Jesus Christ as God's Son and our Lord who has given us the way, the truth, and the life.

We believe in the surrounding presence of God's Holy Spirit in our daily lives to know his will and the challenge to follow it.

We believe that when we falter and fail we have cleansing forgiveness for our sins which separate us from those we love.

We believe in the Holy Scriptures which tell us of man's desire to know God and to find him in the prophets, the disciples, and the apostles.

We believe in prayer which takes our concerns in communication directly to God about ourselves, our family, our community, and the communities of the world.

We believe in the sacredness of the family which enables each home to become a living laboratory of a miniature kingdom of God.

We believe in the world-wide Church of Christ which binds the grieving, the lost, the insulted, the injured, the outcasts into a caring fellowship of love.

We believe in the assurance of eternal life which makes this day a part of our own eternity, until we are wholly thine—

THIS WE BELIEVE!

—James Edward Doty
Baker University
Baldwin City, Kansas

115.

(Start in a whisper, right answering left. Get louder at each phrase until we are shouting in the end.)

Left	Right
God is alive.	His spirit is afoot.
Life is alive.	Salvation is here.
Hope is alive.	A new age is dawning.
Love is alive.	Death cannot harm us.
We are alive.	New life is given.
God is alive.	New birth is afoot.
Church is alive.	God stirs within it.
Joy is alive.	Redemption is here.
Church is alive.	Fire within it burns.
God is alive.	We love without masks.
Hope is alive.	Love is alive.
Life is alive.	We are alive.
Church is alive.	God is alive.

—James Evans McReynolds

116.

I believe that God, our Father, is the creator of life.
I believe each person must decide what he believes about God,
    considering the advice of others, but making the final
    decision himself.
I believe that God is the provider of the beauty of nature, our
    good health, the friendships that enrich our lives, and
    the satisfaction of accomplishment.
I believe that God is love and that love is the essence of our
    lives.
I believe that *all* persons are equal in the eyes of God.
I believe in one church universal in which all denominations are
    joined together.

—James L. Ray

117.

The Lord who loves us all has called us together to worship him with joyous praise. We proclaim with radiant faces what he has done for us by sending his only Son Jesus, who loves us enough to suffer and die so that we might be free. Sharing in his overwhelming love and calling on his power, in obedience, we grow closer to him every day, "finding ourselves" in the process. We are excited to think that he is always with us—in life, in death, in life beyond death! So we humbly and gratefully glorify his holy name. Our trust is in him.
    Amen.

—Kathryn Rogers Deering

118.

Father, we affirm that you are worthy of our total allegiance. You have created us as well as the world around us, everything we know and everything we don't know. You have sent your Holy Spirit to reveal your love and purpose to us. You are actively working through your people to accomplish that purpose. Even though we don't deserve it, you love us enough to have sent your Son to die for us so that we might be united with you in joy and gratitude. We say again, with new meaning, that you are our Lord and Master. We have no greater joy than to serve you.

    Amen.

—Kathryn Rogers Deering

119.

We are eager to reaffirm what we believe and live—that Jesus is our Lord and Savior. We believe that he came to live with us on earth and then was tortured and killed for our sake, because he loves us so much. We believe that he rose from the dead on the third day and that he is now on the right hand of the Father, as well as right here with us every moment. We believe that he sent his Holy Spirit to fill us with his power and to equip us to serve him. We believe that we are his Body, the Church, and that it is our responsibility to move with him into the world. We joyously state our belief that God in Christ is the only one who can effectively bridge the generation gap, the acceptance gap, and—most of all—the death gap. Jesus is Lord!

—Kathryn Rogers Deering

120.

All: I believe in God, Maker of all things, all colors, all shapes, and all of us. I believe in his son who was put here to bring peace, helpfulness, and understanding. I believe in the forgiving of sins, and in being forgiven. I believe in the resurrection of the body, and in the life after death. I believe that God is here, and always will be in the future.

Amen.

—Pam Terkelson, Confirmation Class
Trinity United Methodist Church
Los Osos, California

121.

Leader: In a time which purports to be a time of reason, but harbors within it a large measure of unwillingness to reason—

People: **We seek the source of reason in Christ and his church.**

Leader: In a time when we are aware of our lack of wholeness—

People: **We seek the missing elements in Christ and in his church.**

Leader: In a time of cynicism, mistrust, and credibility gaps—

People: **We seek to place our trust in Christ and through his power to become his children and his church in more than name.**

Leader: In a time when churches are often considered irrelevant because of past behavior—

People: **We seek to be part of a church which is aware of and responds to the present.**

Leader: In a time of increasing social conscience—

People: **We seek to continually be aware that our social consciousness stems from the love of Christ within us.**

—William Law

122.

A Creed for Youth

I believe that God, the Creator and Lord of this universe,
    knows and cares for every living person.
I believe that he makes himself real to us today
    through the Scripture,
    through our Savior, Jesus Christ,
    and through the lives of holy persons.
I believe that God's Spirit is available every moment,
    to convict me of my sinful, selfish ways and
    to enable me to rise above myself into a Christ-like life.
I believe that God has a mission for me,
    to minister in his name and
    to share his love and blessings with his needy children
      of my own community and of every race and nation.

I believe that as I give to him my life,
    my love,
    my offerings,
    and my talents,
He will bring rich meaning into my life
and will use me to help others to a better life in Christ.

—David G. Pease
    former District Director of Youth Work and Assistant Administrator
    Sunset Methodist Home
    Quincy, Illinois

123.

A Creed for Hopeful Sceptics

I wonder who Jesus was, whether he was right
        about how to live in love with others
        and at peace with oneself.
I wonder whether love shall ever overcome hatred,
        whether one can hate without becoming
        worse than one's enemies.
I wonder whether this life is all there is, or
        whether it is the beginning of something
        more.
But I am content to live in terms of these concerns,
        without final proven answers.
I believe that if there is a God who is good, he
        doesn't do half the things for which
        people blame him.
I believe that this world is the wrong place to
        look for justice, yet one should be loving
        in dealing with the vulnerable and the
        helpless.
I believe in opening oneself to the good and the bad
        of life, in order to be fully human,
        in order to find fellowship with others
        who are searching for a way.
But I am content to live on the basis of what I know,
        and trust the rest.
I hope that some holy Spirit may change my life,
        by filling it with power, purpose, meaning,
        confidence, and joy.
I hope that suffering and death are ultimate mysteries
        of life, for who would want to live in a world
        where they made sense?
I hope that life, joy, mercy, and peace shall triumph
        not just in my life, but in all this world.
But I am content to live on the basis of what I hope,
        which shall not fail me though life may pass.
These are some of the things I wonder, I believe, I hope,
in the name of Whoever and Whatever has touched and healed
the lives of so many others. Amen.

—James D. Righter (1971)

98

124.

A Personal Affirmation

(Matt. 22:37)	I love God the Father, with all my heart, and with all my soul, and with all my mind.
(Rom. 8:28)	He works for good, in all things, with those who love him.
	He is both Creator and creative, a source of steadfast love and joy.
(Rev. 5:13)	To him be praise and honor, glory and might, for ever and ever.
(Matt. 22:37)	I love Jesus the Christ, with all my heart, and with all my soul, and with all my mind.
(Rom. 8:38-39)	He keeps, forever, the souls of all those who take up their cross and follow him.
	He is both Savior and saving, a source of continual forgiveness and peace.
(Rev. 5:13)	To him be praise and honor, glory and might, for ever and ever.
(Matt. 22:37)	I love the Holy Spirit, with all my heart, and with all my soul, and with all my mind.
(Rom. 8:16-23)	He makes us God's sons and sets our whole being free.
	The Spirit joins himself to our spirits to declare the greatness of God.
(Rev. 5:13)	To him be praise and honor, glory and might, for ever and ever.
	I love the One God, who has touched my life as Father, Son, and Holy Spirit. Amen.

—James D. Righter (1971)

125.

A Creed for Advent

Our life flows from the one God and Father of us all:
    who created light to fill the dark void of space;
    who gave us the light of life, to dispel our darkness;
    who is the source of light that no darkness can ever
       overcome.
Our life flows from Jesus the Christ, his only Son, our Lord:
    who came into the world, yet the world knew him not;
    who was the one true light that enlightens every man;
    who gives, to all who believe, power to become God's
       children.
Our life flows from the Holy Spirit poured out upon us:
    who came with rush of wind, and tongues of fire;
    who witnessed to the mighty works of God;
    who fills our lives with wonder and purpose.
To our God—Father, Son, and Holy Spirit—be power and
    wealth, wisdom and honor, glory and blessing,
      now and forever.   Amen.

—James D. Righter (1971)

126.

A Contemporary Affirmation

We worship the Father God, who sent Jesus Christ,
    to whom the Holy Spirit bears witness.
We worship because we have been called out of our
    separate lives to be his church, as a way of
    saving the whole world.
We worship in the faith that love, joy, and peace
    shall endure for eternity, as this creative
    God works his purposes.
We worship, out of grateful hearts, giving thanks,
    and praising this God—Father, Son, and Spirit
    —who has claimed us.
We worship, acknowledging our sin and search for
    meaning, secure in the knowledge that nothing
    can separate us from our God.
We worship, longing for the life now and the future
    ahead that is ours for the asking.
We worship, looking always for the truth about life,
    and for the right way to live each day.
We worship, listening for the divine Word that comes
    to us through the Scriptures, the sacraments,
    the ministries of our fellowship.
We worship, seeking to be a part of God's saving work,
    as we are given the vision and power.
We worship in order that we may be touched and healed
    by God.
We worship, so that our common life may be wondrously
    changed.
We worship, as a preparation for the next change we
    shall have to make the difference in someone's
    life or in some crucial situation.
In the name of all that is Holy, Father, Son, and Spirit.
Amen.

—James D. Righter (1971)

127.

This I Believe

I believe in God, the Father of all the universe and creator of all existences
And in Our Lord Jesus Christ, his son, who lives to teach and show us his ways
    and died so we may be forgiven of our sins.
And in the Holy Spirit, who brings comfort, joy, and security in our lives by
    his everlasting presence
And in the church as a place for worship, forgiveness, belief, and union of all
    those who live for him and praise him
And in Man as one who was sent out by him to do his best in this given world
    to teach of God and help others. Amen.

—Cindy Fridley

128.

I believe in God—a smiling,
    hurting, loving God; who has
    given me everything and who
    knows all my sins and loves
    me still.
I believe in Jesus Christ,
    who came to earth with
    human joys, sorrows,
    hungers, and thirsts and
    with the perfect love of
    God in his heart and the
    perfect way of life to
    share with *all* people.
I belive in the Holy Spirit
    as the spark of the divine
    in each of us that is fanned
    into flame to strengthen and
    support us—our connecting
    link to God.
I believe that because of these
    beliefs I should *joyfully*
    share my hands in service,
    my mind and voice in prayer,
    and my life in love to all
    of God's brotherhood whether
    near or far. And I believe
    that should all men serve
    in this way, we would see the
    kingdom of God here and now.

—Janet M. Joyce
First United Methodist Church
Frank W. Wooldridge, pastor
506 S. Washington Avenue
Centralia, Washington 98531

129.

We believe in
    God the creator, who forms the present, past, and future;
    Who gives to us the universe, our lives, and each new day.
We believe in
    Jesus Christ, God's Son, his greatest gift to us;
    Who teaches us and heals our minds and bodies;
    Who sets us free to be ourselves.
    Sharing his victory in life and death we are able to live and die
        without fear.
We believe in
    The Holy Spirit, God's gift of his presence with us now.
    In his Spirit, he calls us into the church, to gather for worship,
        study, and friendship, knowing him and one another.
    In his Spirit, he sends us out as the scattered church to live the
        life of love and forgiveness, teaching others that he is God.

(Created by the Confirmation Class)
First United Methodist
Pittsburgh, Pennsylvania
William Boyd Grove, pastor

130.

(When the youth of Mason Church were asked to write an affirmation, one young woman expressed what many people honestly believe, but seldom openly admit. The following "affirmation" parodies the Apostles Creed, but it stings because it is so close to where many actually are. It might be read in conjunction with the Apostles Creed at a service of worship. This could be especially meaningful for use with a sermon or series of sermons on the Creed.)

The Offering of Our Broken Selves

I believe in Conformity, the father Almighty, maker of Sameness and Convention;

And in Security its only Son: who was conceived by the people, born of the Virgin Masses, suffered under dissent, was exalted, praised, and condoned; in the twentieth century it arose to living; It ascended into Society, and sitteth at the right hand of Government, the Big Brother Almighty, from then It shall come to quiet the protestor and the individual.

I believe in the Well-Regulated; the Holy Habitual, the sameness of saints; the forgiveness of originality; the repetition of history; and the conservative everlasting.

—Daisy Ann Baar
Mason Church
Tacoma, Washington

131.

An Ecology Creed

We believe that the earth is the Lord's; That God has entrusted the earth to us for our care, use, and enjoyment; That we live in a web of interdependence so that our acts have wide-reaching and far-ranging significance; That when we abuse the earth there follows dangerous consequences that threaten the quality of our lives, and our very existence; That when we properly care for the earth, the earth will support, nourish, and beautify our lives.

—Carl B. Rife

132.

Open Letter to the Youth of the District

From your District Superintendent

I hear voices,
      Voices of youth,
            A variety of voices
                  In a diversity of sounds and expressions.

I hear your voices of affirmation.
      You are saying,
            "We feel so young, so strong,
                  So sure of God."

I hear your voices of commitment.
>   You are aware and sensitive
>   To the values of love, human dignity,
>   And individual rights.

I hear your voices of concern,
>   About the problems of our cities,
>   Our environment, our affluence, our poverty,
>   Our crimes, and our diseases of hate.

I hear your voices of dedication.
>   You desire to create a society
>   Where life will be valued and sacred,
>   And meaningful and good.

I hear your voices of prophecy.
>   You are repeatedly predicting
>   A renewal of Christian commitment
>   Among yourselves and others.

I hear your voices of hope.
>   You are identifying with
>   And affirming your faith in God,
>   As it can be "lived out" in Jesus Christ.

And this I know,
>   If I listen, I'll hear more,
>   Much, much more.

I salute you,
>   I believe you.
>   I love you.

I hear you. . . hear you . . . hear you. . . . .

—Grantas E. Hoopert

Editor's Note: Can a letter from a District Superintendent be liturgical? This letter from Grantas Hoopert answers that question in the affirmative. It is liturgical in character and could be adapted for worship. It is included here because it is in reality an affirmation of faith.

133.

Washington Square United Methodist Church Covenant
(proposed)

We strive to become revolutionary Christians, a community of people united in love and dedicated to creating a new world and society based on trust, cooperation, and sharing. We believe the essential message of the church to be that people take priority over things or profits, that Christ's teachings take on meaning only in concrete actions that meet people's material and spiritual needs and that the church as a community must work on all levels to meet those needs.

We believe that we must be a part of all struggles for human liberation—good news to the poor, release to the captives, sight to the blind, liberty to the oppressed.

We hope to help one another grow and find abundant life.

We seek to help The United Methodist Church and the larger church of which we are a part, to find new ways to serve the present age.

We will express and promote the unity of all people.

We believe that all groups working in the church building are part of the church community, and that differences between them should be resolved in a spirit of love.

We welcome as members all people who share our goals and beliefs and who are willing to take responsibility for making them a reality in the life of the church.

To further these aims, each of us commits himself/herself:

To explore in thought and action the teachings and life of Christ, and to share these experiences with sisters and brothers for mutual encouragement and correction:

to make weekly gifts of time and/or money for the church as a whole;

to help build our community by dealing with all of us with kindness, honesty, and responsibility;

to take responsibility for people, property, program of the church when need arises.

This covenant to be entered into by all who desire to do so, including those already "members," at an agreed-upon time with appropriate ceremony. Renewable at the beginning of each year.

This covenant itself will be reviewed annually, and amended as found desirable.

(Greenwich Village, New York)

(Editor's Note: This offering from Washington Square United Methodist Church is an example of a church which desires to move from credo to covenant by way of specific commitments. The covenant came out of extensive and intensive discussions by members of just what it is to which they are committed. That process is commendable, as is the concept of this kind of covenant itself.)

134.

Stewardship Commitment
(to be used following a sermon on stewardship)

Minister: Do you acknowledge Jesus Christ as Lord of your life?

People: **We do and ask him to make us alive now and eternally.**

Minister: Does Jesus Christ have control of your life?

People: **His control is increasing as we continue to give more of ourselves to him.**

Minister: Will you covenant together with Christ to let him live in you, and through all that you have?

People: **We will, hoping that each day may bring a new awareness of his use of us.**

Minister: What will you do to attain this hope?

People: **We will support his work with our prayers, our involvement, our material possessions.**

—Leon McCleary

135.

Our Commitment

Leader: United Methodists are called upon to make basic commitments which tell us our purpose and define the nature of our objectives.

People: WE PLEDGE OURSELVES TO CHRISTIAN FAITH, TO LIVE THAT FAITH DAILY.

Leader: In our thoughts, in our speech, in our conduct.

People: WE PLEDGE OURSELVES TO THE CHURCH. THE CHURCH IS GOD'S CREATION.

Leader: Through his Son, Jesus Christ, for all humankind.

People: WE PLEDGE OURSELVES TO THE UNITED METHODIST CHURCH. OUR DENOMINATION IS NOT AN END IN ITSELF, NOR DOES IT COMPETE WITH OTHERS FOR ITS OWN GLORY.

Leader: We see our church as one expression of the love of Jesus Christ, and as a way to praise the glory of God.

People: WE PLEDGE OURSELVES TO A PERSONAL MISSION, TO BRING THE TRUTH AND COMFORT OF THE GOSPEL TO EVERY INDIVIDUAL HUMAN BEING.

Leader: To a social action that sees man and his community as the special work of God.

People: WE PLEDGE OURSELVES TO CHRISTIAN HUMILITY. OUR UNDERSTANDING COMES FROM GOD THROUGH THE HOLY SPIRIT.

Leader: This is our strength and our guidance.

People: WE PLEDGE OURSELVES TO CHRISTIAN LOVE. WE BELIEVE, AS MEMBERS OF THE UNITED METHODIST CHURCH AND AS INDIVIDUAL CHRISTIANS, THAT WE MUST LISTEN TO THE NEEDS OF OUR NEIGHBORS, AT HOME AND ALL OVER THE WORLD, AND MUST RESPOND TO THOSE NEEDS AS GOD GIVES US THE WISDOM TO UNDERSTAND.

Unison: WE PLEDGE THE CHURCH:
TO PROCLAIM THE GOSPEL OF JESUS CHRIST TO ALL HUMANKIND.
TO CHALLENGE OUR OWN MEMBERS TO A DEEPER INVOLVEMENT WITH GOD.
TO COMMIT ITSELF TO SEEKING JUSTICE FOR ALL HUMANKIND UNDER GOD.
TO LABOR FOR PEACE THAT REFLECTS GOD'S HARMONY WITH THE WORLD.
TO LISTEN AND TO LEARN FROM ALL INDIVIDUALS AND GROUPS THAT SEEK A VOICE IN THEIR OWN DESTINY.
TO DEVELOP A WORKABLE PLAN FOR FULFILLING THESE PLEDGES.

—From *The Interpreter* (September 1972, p. 29)
Adapted for responsive reading by David James Randolph

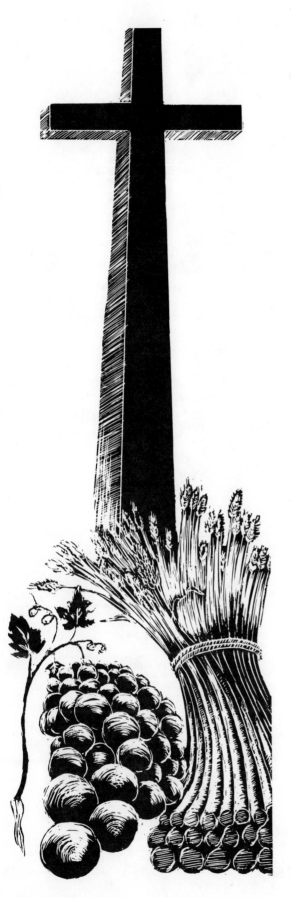

The Lord's Supper

A Layman's Ritual of Communion

(A dialogue)

"Walk Together, talk together,
O ye peoples of the earth;
Then and only then shall ye have peace."
(Sanskrit)

"I will buy with you, sell with you, talk with you, walk with you, and so following; but I will not eat with you, drink with you, nor pray with you. What news on the Rialto?"

(*The Merchant of Venice,* Act I, Scene 3)

Dialogue

(Musical background "Requiem for the Masses." Initial music fades and is replaced by Jimi Hendrix, "Purple Haze" as this statement is begun.)

First speaker:

Let us walk together, talk together, eat together, drink together, play together, think together, work together, be together.

Second speaker:
(turning away)

Why, man? Who would want to be with *you?* Who do you think you are, some kind of prize? Why should I put up with you? You gotta be kidding! You don't want to be with me. (*Returns to first speaker, faces him from six to eight inches apart, nose to nose. Everyone in the group turns to face his or her neighbor.*) Yesterday, you snubbed me downtown when I spoke to you. When I stopped at the traffic light you ran it just to get ahead of me. I waited half an hour at the movie line to get a ticket, and you knew me then— I was only fourth in line when you asked me to get your tickets too. You asked for a ride downtown, started an argument, got out, slammed the door, and didn't even say thank you. You sneered at my loyalties to family, friends, and community. You were jealous of my having an evening at home with no demands. You hate my white skin. You object to my hair, my clothes, my music, my four letter words—my immaturity. You want to make me over so I'll be like you. You retreat behind a bureaucratic front and your own special language when I want to try new ideas or need help. You avoid me so much I don't know why I should bother.

(Music ends.)

(Judy Collins, "Hey, That's No Way to Say Goodbye")

(People are standing or walking about, more in the setting of a cocktail party than of persons seated in church pews.)

(Music fades.)

First Speaker:
(slowly, a little unsettled by the response)

Yes, you have made the effort all right. And I have been guilty of all you claim—probably more. I wish it were not so, but it is a fact. Sometimes I get so busy—absorbed with one thing—it may not even be very important—but it leads me to forget the little matters, that we usually take for granted. They get out of hand.

I am truly sorry for the shabby treatment that I have given you this week. It sounds trite to say so, but it is true. Words fail to convey the way I feel. What is more, I thank you for reminding me of the self-centeredness that has run through my life this week. It extends even further than you know. Deep down, in the still and vague hours, when mists of the mind make boundaries fuzzy, I feel lonely, and I reach out to you.

Isolation is a fact of those hours, but I know it only because they are matched by others that I share in your company.

The feeling of your support—your touch, your embrace, your words, your presence—renews my spirit, opens my heart, changes my mindset. Only the outreach of you—your presence—gives me courage to overcome this isolationist destruction in me.

(Cream, "Strange Brew")

Second speaker:

But wait! You're overdoing it, man. I'm no saint. I am able to feel just as isolated as you. After all, everything that I described happened *to me*. I was at the center of all those events. I must have contributed to them. My feelings of superiority are pretty superficial. I'm upset by the whole thing and I want something more, too. But—can I make the effort? Do I dare? If I fail, then what? I don't want you to let me down, and I don't want to let you down—but I'm afraid I will—and you will—again and again. What shall we do?

(Softly, the music shifts to Peter, Paul, and Mary, "The Great Mandalla")

First Speaker:
(Grasping the hands of the other in both of his hands, looking directly into the eyes of the other)

I, too, will let you down again, if we are to be honest. But when I do, don't let it cut us off, one from the other. Let me know, so we can keep in touch. That is the important thing, and I will let you know how I feel.

110

Second Speaker:
(reluctantly, hesitantly)

Yes, but what holds all this together? Isn't it pretty chancy and loose to make all these promises? Especially when we admit we can't keep them to each other?

First Speaker:
(maintains firm grasp of the hands, but is not forcing)

There is only one promise—that we love one another and show mercy. That is the answer that men have come to in all times and all places. You and I know, because we have felt it—a deep sense of community that draws us together on a level that we cannot deny. Our doctrines talk about it, and they confuse us. They divide us. We fight over them or ignore each other because of them, but they refer ultimately to a deeper level on which we feel a need, and we feel a restraint. Our very beings cry out the truth. WE ARE. ABSOLUTELY. We are nothing in isolation. We are fulfilled in our being in community.

Isolation only half describes our being. We would not have survived infancy without loving care of mother, nor childhood without father and friends, nor youth without our friends and peers, nor adulthood without our community. My community begins here and now, with *you*. What limits it has, I cannot say. But it is silly for me to try to state the limits. What I do know is that underlying it all there is a ground of being that we all share, that is expressed in the concern we feel in our finer moments, yes, all of us. Whether we personify that concern in Jesus of Nazareth. Gibran, Gandhi, Moses, Muhammad, Buddha, Mohammed Ali, Peale, Boyd, King, or any other figure; we dare not let anything blind us to the immediacy of our meeting—here and now. Let's go, therefore, you and I, to . . .
(walking toward the table on which the meal is spread)

Together:

Walk together, eat together, drink together, then we can talk together, work together, celebrate together, play together, be together.
(With enthusiasm)

Let's Go
(Hand in hand, partners approach the table, serve each other, symbolically feed each other, and move away from the table in spontaneous conversation.)

(Softly the music shifts to The Doors, "Hello, I Love You.")

Comment of the Ritual

This ritual was written one Sunday afternoon in February, 1969, as a response to the conventional service that I had attended during the morning. It was not written with any particular thought of its being actually conducted, and to my knowledge it has not been. Instead, it served to help me consider the broadest implications that I felt from the traditional service. In particular, it took into account these events and contacts that I had experienced during the preceding week, with family, friends, associates, and even with some very hostile people. I took the proposition of the invitation, as given in The United Methodist ritual, seriously, assuming that each of the persons I had dealt with during the week might accept it.

If each of those persons accepted it, then what position could I take? Each would not accept the terms of the ritual, but he might accept the proposition of reconciliation and dedication to a renewed concern. This dedication might not even been thought of by him in Christian terms. Indeed, there were at least three people with whom I had dealt who would be deeply disturbed by an attempt to force them into an acceptance of traditional terminology and whom I could respond to only by drawing on a history of personal involvement with that terminology.

As a consequence of the commitment to people and to the underlying shared ground of our common concern as having a higher priority than the traditional terms, I followed a nontechnical language. This, in turn, led to what I now feel may be the start of a post-Christian statement. If the statement does not really go beyond the traditional Christian position, it is a reflection of my own position. If it does reach beyond the church, I should be happy to see it as an aid to expanding our expression of mission. In any case, it is an attempt to internalize and express without church jargon one layman's understanding of communion.

In retrospect, three possible settings have occurred to me as useful for actual conduct of the service:

1. A meal to be shared by ten to fifteen guests in my home. Tape-recorded dialogue and music would provide the continuity. Partners, not necessarily husband and wife, and possibly not of opposite sex, would act out the parts. By leaving periods of silence in the tapes, individuals could add their own statements. The conclusion of this service is open-ended, but an actual meal is served.

2. Within a church, in a social room rather than a pew-lined sanctuary. Dialogue is carried on live by two people, preferably laymen or laywomen, with all pairs acting out the movement. Music is taped. The shared meal is the traditional communion, but the service is open-ended to call forth spontaneous response. Partners serve elements to each other.

3. In the conventional church sanctuary, with congregation paired off in the pews. Dialogue and music are taped, but the service is acted out by an interpretive movement group. Time is allowed for everyone to commune at altar or table, with each person serving elements to his or her partner.

Any of these settings, or perhaps others, set off the routine service from this occasion. By contrast and by felt change in the rate and the pattern of service, we should draw into more sharp focus the communal relationship where the Holy Spirit dwells.

These variations on the conventional service have interested a few persons in the congregation of Wesley Memorial United Methodist Church in Charlottesville, Virginia. Probably the most appropriate comment came from one lady who said that my penned rough draft should be circulated and retained, not as a finished statement, but as an invitation to others to attempt their own statements. This is what I would like very much to emphasize. It seems that the whole point of worship experience is that something happens inside those of us who participate. An occasion shared becomes internalized, altering the way in which we respond to the ordinary affairs of the world. It is in that spirit that I consented when members of our Worship Work Area requested that it be made available for others to see and respond to.

—O. Allan Gianniny, Jr.
Charlottesville, Virginia

137.

Sacrament of the Lord's Supper

Prelude

Minister: When we bless the cup of blessing, is it not a means of sharing in the Blood of Christ? When we break the bread, is it not a means of sharing in the Body of Christ? Because there is one loaf of which we all partake, we, many as we are, are one body. (I Cor. 10:16-17)

Hymn: "The King of Heaven His Table Spreads" Hymnal, No. 325

Minister: The Lord be with you.

People: **And with you!**

Minister: Let us pray.

All: (Prayer for Purity of Heart)
Almighty God, even though our hearts are not always open, You know even those things we want most and those things we try hardest to hide. Let your love be so real to me that my mind will be clear, that I will be able to love in return, and make your name great as it is; with Christ's help. Amen.

Our God, who is within us, your name is great! We hope our earth can be free from sin. We would like everyone all over the world to have the food they need. Forgive us in the way we should forgive others. God, please help us not to do wrong things. Yours is the earth and all the people on it. Let the prayer be true!

All: Gloria (standing)
Praise and thanksgiving to God, and on earth his peace for men on whom his favor rests! God, creator of all that is, and our Father: We praise and worship you, we honor and thank you for your greatness and your love for us. God, who has come to us through Jesus Christ; who through him lifts the sorrows of the world: Have mercy on us and know our thoughts. You are the Son of God; have mercy on us. Only you are like God; only you with the Spirit of God can lead us to perfectly praise him. Amen.

Minister: (The Invitation)
If you are sincerely sorry for your shortcomings and intend to live according to God's purpose for you, join with us and accept these symbols of God's love, knowing you can be forgiven and strengthened if you are honest with God.

All: (General Confession)
Almighty God, whose son is Jesus Christ, maker of all things, judge of all men:
We know we have done great wrong and the knowledge of this makes us suffer. We know we have done this daily, in spite of our good intentions, in our thoughts, our words, and in what we do.
We want to change and are sincerely sorry for these mistakes. To remember them makes us feel guilty. Try to understand, for we know you are like a loving father. Because your son Jesus died for us, forgive us for what we have done; From now on we want to be like new people, to serve and please you because you are God. Amen.

Minister: Open your minds.

People: **We open our minds to God.**

Minister: Then, let us thank, him.

People: **Yes, it is the right thing to do.**

Minister: God, our Father, our great gratitude for what you have done for us compels us to offer our thanks to you at all times and in all places.

Therefore, in the highest way that we know, joining together with the ongoing spirit of those that you love, we applaud and praise your great name, saying:

People: **Holy, holy, holy is the Lord of all; the earth is full of his glory!**

Minister: (Prayer of Consecration)

Almighty God, our heavenly father, who loved all men enough to give your son, whose life perfectly revealed your love; we recall the night he was betrayed when his disciples were having supper together. Jesus took some of the bread and wine and when he had given thanks, he shared it; we join now in this symbolic act of remembering you.

As we consume these symbols of the bread and wine Christ had at the Last Supper, we pray that we may continually remember what you have done for us and express it in our lives.

All: (Prayer of Humble Access)

O God, we come to this moment not because we are good, but because we want to be better. We realize that only through your mercy can we begin to do your will. Come to us and give us your strength and guidance to live a new life.

Sharing of the Bread and the Cup:

Minister: The elements will be brought and passed in the pews; we will serve one another. As you pass the elements to your neighbor, say to him, "This is the Body (or Blood) of Christ," or other appropriate greeting. Hold the bread (and next the cup) until all have received a portion; then we will commune together.

Minister: Our Father, we who love you and wish to serve you pray that you will accept our act of praise and thanksgiving; and pray now with humility for forgiveness of our sins. And here we offer our whole selves as a fitting offering to you, humbly asking that all of us who took part in this supper may overflow with your love and blessing. Even though we do not deserve your pardon, we still ask for it; please accept this evidence of our intent to serve you through serving our fellow men.

We pray through Jesus whom we acknowledge as our Lord, with all honor and glory given to you, our Father all powerful.

Amen.

Hymn: "Here, O My Lord, I See Thee Face to Face" Hymnal, No. 326, Vss. 4, 5

All: The Peace (Grasping the hand of one near you)
"Peace be with you." (Or some other loving greeting)

Postlude:

(This service was developed from the work of eight groups at Calvary United Methodist Church, Nashville, Tennessee.)

138.

A Liturgy for Holy Communion

Statement of Purpose

Minister: Christ our Paschal Lamb is offered up for us, once for all, when he bore our sins on his body upon the Cross; for he is the very Lamb of God that taketh away the sins of the world: Wherefore, let us keep a joyful and holy feast with the Lord. (from I Cor. 5:7-8; I Pet. 2:24; John 1:29)

Minister: May God be present with you.

People: **And likewise with you.**

Minister: Let us pray.

All: **O Lord, you know us better than we know ourselves. We cannot hide our unworthiness from you. But we worship you because we know you accept us despite our unworthiness. We celebrate your acceptance of us this morning by keeping this joyful and holy feast with you. Help us to witness worthily to your love through what we do this morning. Amen.**

The Praise of God

(the people stand)

All: **O God, we praise you, and bless you, and worship you. We glorify you, we give thanks to you because you are God. Your mercy is unending. We know this because we have seen such mercy in Jesus Christ. Amen.**

Hymn of Praise

The Confession of Sin

(the people sit)

Minister: We are going to celebrate what the Lord has done for us by communing together and with him at his table. All of us who declare ourselves to be his are invited to the feast. Therefore, let us be sure that we who eat the bread and drink the wine belong to the Lord and to one another.

All: **O Lord, we so often forget that we belong to you. We are often trying to prove something, or be somebody when we really don't have to. You have already done something for us in Jesus Christ, and you have already made us somebody, because we belong to you. We ought to realize this, Lord, but we don't. We ought to be free to belong to each other, but we aren't. We do not serve each other, because we forget that we belong to you. Be present for us in the bread and wine, so that we may be cleansed from our forgetfulness, and know that we belong to you. Amen.**

Minister: Hear what comforting words the Scriptures say to all that truly turn to the Lord: Come to me, all who labor and are heavy-laden, and I will give you rest.

The Prayer of Intercession

The Service of the Word

Epistle Lesson

Hymn of Preparation

Gospel Lesson

Choral Response

Sermon

The Offertory and Presentation

Offertory: (An anthem may be sung during the gathering of the gifts; the people stand, and the Doxology is sung as the gifts and the elements are brought forward by lay persons to be placed on the Lord's table. The gifts and elements are presented in the following manner.)

First
Lay Person: We present these gifts of the people to the Lord.

Second
Lay Person: We present this bread and wine to the Lord. They are the work of our hands. Therefore, we deliver ourselves and our lives, even as we deliver these elements to the Lord for his use.

Minister: The Lord accepts our gifts, and will use them to make himself known to us anew.
(The lay persons return to their pews and the people are seated.)

The Prayer of Consecration

Minister: Almighty God, help us to discover you in the sacramental Flesh and Blood of our Lord Jesus Christ. Grant, we pray, that the bread and wine may become for us a feast with Christ in his kingdom. Consecrate these elements in such a way that the first Lord's Supper will happen once more for us in this celebration.

In the same night that Christ was betrayed, he took bread (here the minister may take the bread in his hands); and when he had given thanks, he broke it, and gave it to his disciples saying, "Take, eat; this is my body which is given for you; do this in remembrance of me." Likewise after he took the cup (here the minister may take the cup in his hands); and when he had given thanks, he gave it to them, saying, "Drink ye all of this; for this is my blood of the New Covenant, which is shed for you and for many, for the forgiveness of sins; do this, as often as you shall drink of it, in remembrance of me." Amen.

The Prayer of Humble Access

All: **We come to your table, O merciful Lord, because of what you have done for us—not because we deserve to dine with you. We come to you because you have graciously invited us, even though we are not worthy to gather up the crumbs from under your table. We come at your invitation because your food can make us walk in newness of life. Make the possibility of this new life actual in our lives, we pray through the Body and Blood of our Lord Jesus Christ. Amen.**

(Here the people stand.)

All: **O Lamb of God, that takes away the sin of the world, have mercy upon us, and grant us your peace. Amen.**

The Ritual of Fellowship

The Blessing (to be said to a brother or sister while joining right hands):
    May the Lord be with you.

The Response: **And with you, too.**

(When everyone has blessed his brother or sister, the people shall be seated.)

The People Commune and Give Thanks

(The people will come forward to receive the elements at the direction of the ushers. When all have communed, the minister shall cover what is left of the elements).

Minister: Let us give thanks to the Lord.

All: **We thank you God, for accepting us at your table. We thank you for accepting our offer of ourselves for you and for one another. Savior, you have fed us and nourished us in your strength. Continue to nurture and sustain us in your love, each for the other. Amen.**

Hymn of Thanksgiving

The Benediction

—Scott Wood
(Mount Comfort United Methodist Church
Greenfield, Indiana)

139.

A Liturgy of the Lord's Supper

The Prelude

Call to Worship

Processional Hymn   "Immortal, Invisible, God Only Wise"   Hymnal, No. 27

Prayer of Approach   (Congregation in unison)
    O Lord, who art ageless as the hills, and beyond, we are the young ones;
    O Lord, who art the energy of all the suns in all the galaxies, we are the weary ones;
    O Lord, who art perfect in understanding, so that nothing eludes thy knowing it, we are the confused ones;
    There is no reason that thou shouldst receive us except that we gravitate unto thee, and that we come in the name of Jesus, who has shown us why we do. Put away our confusion, our tiredness, our deceit, and take us now in one united movement. Love us down to who we are, and help us to know that that is accepted. For we depend upon thee—desperately.   Amen.

Word of Courage (Minister)

God, who in seasons past has known the saints and been the intimate source of their wisdom, strength, and hope, is likewise willing to abide with you. You have but to renounce all pretension and selfish expectation to enter now into his peace and feel at home with him. He is the Lord and we are his people, the sheep of his pasture. Relax and rejoice. We are in his presence.

The Old Testament: Exodus 3:9-15

Gloria Patri

The New Testament: Colossians 1:11-27

Prayer (Minister)

Thou hast called us to dream the impossible dream, O Lord—of nations at peace, the hungry fed, the sick and the tormented made well, the streets clean, the buildings adequate, the dark places safe, every man secure in the love and good will of all other men. Forgive us if we have not desired peace, O Lord, if we have not fed the poor or visited the sick, if we have littered our streets and countryside with the paper cartons and tin cans of our plenty, if we have condoned or contributed in any way to the existence of slums, if we have been complacent about crime and violence until it is at our very doors, or if we have withheld love from other men and so threatened the security of all men. Through Jesus Christ our Lord.

We acknowledge our sin, O Lord. If it is not ever before us, it is at least inescapable within us, and we are depressed to consider what it has done to us. Redeem us, O Lord, from the withering of our visions. Restore a right spirit within us, and make us to dream dreams again, until we are all possessed of thy spirit, through Jesus Christ our Lord.

We are called to preach, O Lord, and yet live in despair of a message. What are we to say, O Lord? And how shall we make men listen? Help us to stand in silence and awe at the foot of the Cross until we get our bearings once more, and are not overwhelmed in our task. Through Jesus Christ our Lord.

There are many books to read, our Father, many voices to hear. How shall we know what is true and what is worthwhile? Help us to be spiritually critical, our Father, as we are also critically spiritual. Through Jesus Christ our Lord.

There is confusion in many of us, Lord, about what it means to be ministers and servants in an age like ours. Who are we, Lord? What is the special nature of our calling? How can we serve thee? Breathe life into our dormant imaginations, O Lord, and stir us to adventure in our time. Through Jesus Christ our Lord.

We are anxious about many things, our Father, that have never been worthy of anxiety—place, power, honor in men's eyes. Give us instead thy presence, that we may know our own sense of presence, and be still. Through Jesus Christ our Lord.

Men need men in their midst, our Father—men like the man from Nazareth. Help us to be real men and real women, leading real lives, to real ends. Let there be nothing false or empty about our actions or about our speech. Let us be real, God. Through Christ our Lord.

Some of us have our doubts about the church, Lord; as usual, these are the best and worst of days. Help the church to be real, God. Through Jesus Christ our Lord.

Now let us all, who have eaten thy bread and drunk of thy cup, live from this oath-taking unto the next in sober introspection, in hope of grace, in the joy of life, and in the reality of love and what it demands of us, that we may be faithful stewards of the mysteries once vouchsafed unto the saints but more and more the properties of all the earth, through Jesus Christ our Lord. Amen.

Hymn   "All People That on Earth Do Dwell"   Hymnal, No. 21

Sermon

Hymn   "Lord, I Want to Be a Christian"   Hymnal, No. 286

(During the singing of this hymn, members of the congregation may come forward to make their offering)

The Act of Communion

Words of Institution for the Bread

And the Lord Jesus, on the same night in which he was
betrayed, took bread *brot*, brother, bother, mother, father,
brother
took bread, and when he had broken it
when he had borne and torn it
ripped it and hurt it
crushed it and mangled it
separated it into pieces
gave it to his disciples, betrayers all, each in his own way,
and said, "Take, eat, this is my body, which is broken for
you."

Prayer for the Bread

Distribution of the Bread *(to be eaten without waiting)*

Words of Institution for the Wine

And in like manner also he took the cup, after they had
eaten, and said, "This cup—this brimming, shimmering,
death-down liquefaction of the vine, tart and vinegary
to the taste, but dear as food to the eating of it—this
cup is the new covenant in my blood."
New covenant. New lease on life. New gift of God, whose
old gifts are always new, though needing sometimes some
new gift to discover that. New sign of love—at a skull, and
place of death. Love to the death. "All of you drink of
it. And when you do, remember me.
Bring me back to be present with you."

Prayer for the Wine

Distribution of the Wine *(to be drunk without waiting)*

Covering of the Table

Prayers for Ministry

The Bringing of the Dean's Staff

The Dean's Proclamation

Recessional Hymn   "God of Grace and God of Glory"   Hymnal, No. 470

Benediction

And now God love you, as he always has,
and use you up completely, day by day. In
the name of the Father, Son, and Holy Spirit.
                                        Amen.

—John Killinger

Holy Communion

Dear Friend,

Let me report to you what happened here at Powers Ferry last Sunday, I believe it was a happening, an event of meaning.

In the bulletin I had no order of service. I simply announced that the service would be "A Service of Holy Spontaneity." We printed the words of "Kum Ba Ya," "Michael, Row Your Boat," and "We are Climbing Jacob's Ladder." Our congregation had learned these recently for a performance of "The Winds of God." I informed our director of music and organist as to what I knew we could use, but asked them to "hang loose" because some spontaneous hymn choices might be made during the service.

The order of service was as follows:

Organ Prelude
Call to Worship   Psalm 150
Hymn No. 17

Commentary on celebration and praise
Hymn Anthem   (Hymnal, No. 77)
          Chancel and Youth Choirs
Hymn Singing: "Kum Ba Ya"
     Hymn 91 (with personal testimony)
     Hymn 228 (request with testimony)
     Hymn 184 (request with testimony)

Commentary on Confession
Call to Confession   I John 1:8
Prayers of Confession (Silent, personal)
Promise of Pardon   I John 1:9
Anthem   Chancel Choir
Parish Notices

Commentary on witness, affirmation, proclamation
Affirmation of Faith: Hymnal, No. 741
Hymn: "Michael, Row Your Boat"
Scripture Reading: Acts 1:1-9
The Witnessing

*Commentary on dedication and consecration and
     invitation and consecration of the elements*
Offertory (every worshiper comes to the altar)
Hymn
Sacrament (at the door)

The first item in the service which needs explanation is the commentary. Each commentary was *brief*—approximately two minutes. The first commentary was on worship understood as celebration of the good news of Christ. "Our freedom in Christ sets us free to worship in spontaneity." I then enumerated at least four major themes which should be present in our worship. As you can see, I gave commentaries on each of them.

The hymn singing included two songs our congregation had learned when the youth choir recently did the cantata, "The Winds of God," which is excellent. I then introduced "Amazing Grace" as the third selection with a personal story of how this hymn was indelibly associated with a person who had been crucial in the formation of my personal faith. I then invited members of the congregation to make requests of hymns meaningful to them and to "tell the story" if they desired. Immediately two requests were offered and two testimonies given briefly and effectively. Quickly I moved on with the service, judging that more would be overdoing a very good thing.

The witnessing is the next element requiring explanation. At this point I moved out of the pulpit and stood out of the chancel area, just in front of the first pews. I told the congregation that no witness to the Word could be more effective than the way the faith was being lived out in personal experience. I then made a brief witness to a recent event which had been most significant in the development of my faith. Then I announced that I would call on some lay people to make a similar witness. I suggested that the witness be a recent event of significance if possible. I also said that if anyone I called on did not feel able to do this he could just hold up his hand, and we would understand. I then called on five persons, three adults and two teenagers. Each one came forward and witnessed authentically and simply to his faith in Christ and to his experience of God's grace. (We have had a lay witness mission here, so this was familiar. However, I purposely did not call on persons who have done this sort of thing previously.)

The next element in the service was a commentary on dedication and consecration in which I lifted up Christ's gift of himself to the world. I pointed out that the greatest symbol of sacrifice and dedication was the broken body and shed blood, the bread and wine of communion. Then I read contemporary versions of the invitation to commune and of the prayer of dedication. The people came by the side aisles leaving their offering on the communion table and went out by the center aisles singing "Jacob's Ladder." At each door out were two girls (high school and junior-high age) with bread and wine. Each person was given a bit of torn off loaf bread which he dipped (intinction) in a goblet of grape juice held by the second girl. So the last acts of worship were the dedication of self and the gifts and the reception of the elements of communion on the threshold of the sanctuary as they moved out into the world again.

These two worship acts—offering and communion—were extremely moving for many. I believe Holy Communion came alive for some more meaningfully than ever before. I would appreciate your reactions to this and to the whole service. What are you doing or going to do in your churches?

—Norton Campbell
Powers Ferry United Methodist Church
Marietta, Georgia

141.

The Lord's Supper

(as it may be celebrated by a small group in an informal setting)

The Preparation

(The people may greet one another as they arrive. Any necessary announcements may be made, and matters of common concern may be shared. The ordained minister who is to preside is called herein, the president.)

President: The Lord is with you.

People: **And with you too.**

(Then at the bidding of the president there may be silent meditation, singing, prayer, or other acts appropriate for persons preparing for the hearing of God's Word.)

The Service of the Word

(There may be Scripture reading, interspersed with suitable responses of praise and followed by witness[es] to the Word. Or, the Word of God may be proclaimed and interpreted in whatever manner and through whatever media may be deemed fitting to the occasion. Then the people may respond with intercessions and other prayers in whatever form and under whatever leadership may seem appropriate.)

The Service of the Table

(The president may begin the offertory by saying the following or equivalent words.)

President: "If you are about to offer your gift to God at the altar and there you remember that your brother has something against you, leave your gift there in front of the altar and go at once to make peace with your brother; then come back and offer your gift to God" (Matt. 5:23-24 TEV).

(He may then pass to the people, in whatever way is deemed fitting, a double handclasp or other contemporary equivalent of the ancient kiss of peace.)

President and People (severally):   **Peace.**

President: "So, then my brothers, because of God's many mercies to us, I make this appeal to you: Offer yourselves as a living sacrifice to God, dedicated to his service and pleasing to him. This is the true worship that you should offer." (Rom. 12:1 TEV).

(Then the communion elements shall be brought and placed on the holy table, together with the money or other offerings, if there are such, and the president, shall prepare the elements. During this time there may be appropriate singing, other music, or expressions through other media.)

President:	Considerations
We offer these gifts (omit, if none but bread and wine),	
We offer this bread,	
We offer this cup,	
We offer ourselves,	
To be united with the one full, perfect, and sufficient offering	(1)
of Jesus Christ, who, the night before he offered himself	(2)
for us, took bread, gave thanks to God, broke it, and	
said, "This is my body, which is given for you. Do	
this in remembrance of me."	(3)
In the same way, he took the cup after the supper and said,	
"Drink it, all of you, for this is my blood, which seals	
God's promise, my blood poured out for you and for	(4)
many for the forgiveness of sins. Whenever you drink it,	
do it in remembrance of me."	
Therefore, taking this bread and this cup in remembrance of	
him, we lift up our hearts and give thanks to God.	

(The president and people shall then sing the chorus of the well-known spiritual)

A-men, a-men, a-men, amen, amen.

(The president sings or speaks his part, and the people keep repeating the chorus as indicated.)

President	People (singing)	Considerations
You are the Lord.	**A-men**	(5)
All things are yours.	a-men,	
You give us life.	a-men,	(6)
You give us the world.	a-men, a-men.	(7)
Though we have sinned,	**A-men**	(8)
You love us still.	a-men,	
You gave your Son	a-men,	
To be a man.	a-men, a-men.	

122

President	People (singing)	Considerations
He shared our life.	A-men,	
He is the way.	a-men,	
He suffered and died	a-men,	
For you and me.	a-men, a-men.	
He rose from the dead.	A-men,	
He lives with you.	a-men,	
You sent your Spirit	a-men,	(9)
To live with us,	a-men, a-men.	
Blow, Holy Wind.	A-men,	(10)
Burn, Holy Fire.	a-men,	
This bread his Body.	a-men,	(11)
This cup his Blood.	a-men, a-men.	
Come, Lord Jesus.	A-men,	
Come in your power.	a-men,	
Come in your victory.	a-men,	
May all be one.	a-men, amen.	(12)
Join us with all	A-men,	
Men and creation,	a-men,	
Past, present, and future,	a-men,	
As now we sing.	a-men, a-men.	

(From here on the president speaks to prompt the people and then joins with them in the response, which now uses other words. Or, if the people are familiar with the words they may simply be sung in unison.)

President	People (singing)	Considerations
Sing these words: Holy!	Holy!	
Holy!	Holy!	
Holy!	Holy!	
Lord God of Hosts!	Lord God of Hosts!	(13)
Glory!	Glo-ry!	
Glory!	Glo-ry!	
Glory!	Glo-ry!	
Fills heav'n and earth!	Fills heav'n and earth!	(14)
Hosanna!	Hosan-na!	(15)
Hosanna!	Hosan-na!	
Hosanna!	Hosan-na!	
O Lord most high!	O Lord most high!	(16)
Amen.	A-men.	(17)
Amen.	A-men.	
Amen.	A-men.	
Amen, amen.	A-men, a-men.	

(Silence shall be kept for a moment. Then the president and people may pray together the Lord's Prayer. Then the president shall break the loaf, or a piece of the bread, and eat a piece of it. He shall then take the cup, or one of the cups, and drink from it. Or, after breaking the bread, he may partake by intinction.)

President: Taste and see that the Lord is good.

(The bread and the cup shall be served to the people in whatever manner is deemed appropriate. As each person is served the bread, the one serving him shall say:)

The Body of Christ.

(And the one receiving may respond:)
Amen.

(And as each person is served the cup, the one serving him shall say:)
The Blood of Christ.

(And the one receiving may respond:)
Amen.

(There may then be singing, other music, or expressions through other media.)

President: Go in peace. Serve the Lord. You are free.

People: **Amen.**

(People greet one another as they leave.)

Considerations

(1) This is an attempt at a Wesleyan balance between the Catholic and Reformation concepts of eucharistic sacrifice. How successful is it?

(2) The words of institution basically follow the Today's English Version of the New Testament, except that "He was betrayed" is changed to "He offered himself for us." This puts the theological emphasis more positively, takes away even the slightest occasion for anti-Semitic interpretation, and in line with (1) above links our offerings with the self-offering of Christ.

(3) TEV omits "given," but traditional usage plus the underlying of the concept of Christ's self-offering lead me to suggest its retention. TEV translates anamnesis with "memory," but the more traditional rendering "remembrance" seems to me to have a more adequate range of meaning. I wish, however, that I knew of a still better translation of this most crucial word. Suggestions?

(4) I'm substituting "promise" for the TEV (and traditional) "covenant." While "covenant" is a richer term, "promise" at least immediately means something to the average person who has never heard of a covenant, at least in its biblical meaning.

(5) Alternative versions of the first line: "Blessed are you," "We give you thanks," "Father, we thank you." Here as elsewhere I tried to choose the president's words with the idea of their fitting the natural accents of the music, in case the president wishes to sing instead of speak the words. See, for instance, the version of "Amen, Amen" in *Risk* (No. 24). My guess is that most ministers would choose to speak these words. This begins the traditional Anamnesis.

(6) Here as elsewhere, the verb could either be in the present or the past tense, but, except for the events in the life of Christ, I lean toward the use of the present tense.

(7) In the versions I have seen of "Amen, Amen," the leader sings only three phrases to a stanza, not four—see *Risk* e.g. But I can't make the three-phrases-to-a-stanza pattern work out right so far as this text is concerned. There isn't much of a problem if the words are spoken, and if they are sung a singer can easily improvise the tune for the fourth phrase—for instance, in the *Risk* version, D, C, B-flat, A.

(8) Would "We miss the mark" be a better line here?

(9) Would the present tense ("You *send* your Spirit") be better here?

(10) This is, of course, the traditional Epiclesis.

(11) The omission of "is" has the advantages of literally translating the Aramaic, making evident the flexibility of theological interpretation, and fitting the music better than something like "*Make* this bread his body" (or, "a participation in his body," or whatever).

(12) An alternative line would be, "That all may be one," but the line as given keeps to the pattern of four syllables on the fourth line of each stanza.

(13) Something like "power" could be substituted for "hosts," but "hosts" is the familiar word, has one syllable, and, in spite of the obscurity of the word for modern men, still conveys its meaning fairly well.

(14) The COCU-Luthern-Catholic proposed version of the Sanctus uses the line, "Your glory fills all heaven and earth." This stanza approximates those words.

(15) The familiar "Glory be to thee, O Lord most high" is the *Book of Common Prayer* rendering of "Hosanna in the highest."

(16) The Prayer Book wording, "O Lord most high," fits the music much better than would "in the highest."

(17) This is of course the Great Amen, which should be triumphant and climactic, not just a single "Amen."

This use of "Amen, Amen" is an attempt to follow the principle that the musical portions tend to be the highlights of that celebration—or at least its verbal portions—and that it should be the most crucial texts, not the incidental ones, that are set to music. The great prayer of thanksgiving and consecration in the Lord's Supper does not come through as the verbal climax it ought to be, unless it is set to music.

The alternative prayer of thanksgiving and consecration, set to the tune of the Battle Hymn of the Republic, can be used in this order for the celebration of the Lord's Supper in place of "Amen, Amen." If it is objected that the "Battle Hymn of the Republic" is a military song, my answer is that the tune was originally used with the camp-meeting song, "Say, Brothers, Will You Meet Us?" The military took it away from the Church, and it's about time we took it back. "Why should the devil have all the best tunes?"

—Hoyt L. Hickman

142.

Prayer of Thanksgiving and Consecration

(an alternative for the preceding service)

(to be sung to the tune of the "Battle Hymn of the Republic" with the minister singing the stanzas and the people joining in on the chorus)

Preface

Minister: We offer these gifts, we offer this bread, we offer this cup, we offer ourselves, to be united with the one full, perfect, and sufficient offering of Jesus Christ, who, the night before he offered himself for us, took bread, gave thanks to God, broke it, and said, "This is my body, which is given for you. Do this in remembrance of me." In the same way, he took the cup after the supper and said, "Drink it, all of you, for this is my blood, which seals God's promise, my blood poured out for you and for many for the forgiveness of sins. Whenever you drink it, do it in remembrance of me."

Therefore, taking this bread and this cup in remembrance of him, we lift up our hearts and give thanks to God:

We have seen you in the grandeur of the universe.
We have tasted the abundance you have brought forth on the earth.
You have made us in your image, you have set us free to live.
Lord God of power and love.

People: **Glory, glory, hallelujah!** (3 times)
Lord God of power and love.

Minister: Though we all have sinned and fallen short, your love has
never failed.
You so loved the world you gave your only Son to be a man.
    He was born of woman, shared our lot, and lived a holy life.
    He died to save us all.

People: **Glory, glory, hallelujah!** (3 times)
He died to save us all.

Minister: He arose again and conquered the death to bring eternal life.
He ascended and with you is with us always to the end.
And through him your Holy Spirit comes with pow'r to make us one.
    He lives and reigns today.

People: **Glory, glory, hallelujah!** (3 times)
He lives and reigns today.

Minister: By your Spirit bless and sanctify both us and these your gifts.
Make this bread to us his Body and this wine to us his Blood.
As we share with one another may our sharing be of him.
    He gives himself to us.

People: **Glory, glory, hallelujah!** (3 times)
He gives himself to us.

Minister: He will come again with glory and announce the heavenly feast.
Ev'ry knee will bow and ev'ry tongue confess that he is Lord.
As this banquet is a foretaste, so that feast will be the crown.
    He'll win the victory.

People: **Glory, glory, hallelujah!** (3 times)
He'll win the victory.

Minister: So we join with all the saints of ev'ry time and ev'ry place
In the praise that all creation sings both now and evermore,
As with them we sing hosanna in the highest to our King.
    Hallelujah! Amen.

People: **Glory, glory, hallelujah!** (3 times)
Hallelujah! Amen.

(Note: This is intended to be used at the celebration of the Lord's Supper, but, with the omission of the Preface and the fourth stanza, it could be used as a general hymn of praise.)

—Hoyt L. Hickman

Editor's Note: Fundamental theological and indeed philosophical issues are involved in worship, and no meaningful change takes place without dealing with them. Innovative worship or creative worship can never be merely a mindless substitution of one element for another. Awareness of this characterizes contributors to the *Ventures* series. However, this paper by Gary W. Barbaree plumbs these issues with unusual insight and expresses some of the key theological and philosophical issues surrounding the Lord's Supper with uncommon perception and helpfulness for ongoing discussion.

The Lord's Supper: A Christian Phenomenon

(In the context of The United Methodist Church)

A Statement of Purpose

The purpose of this paper is twofold. First, it is serving as a means of understanding the meaning and function of the phenomenological study of religion. It is my hope that in the writing of this paper I have gained some insight not only on the nature of religion, but also in one discipline for the study of this nature—Phenomenology.[1] But this paper is more than just an instrument to be used as a learning device. It is an investigation into the nature of one of two sacraments of The United Methodist Church, in an effort for me to more fully understand this church as I prepare for my ministry as a United Methodist clergyman.

This paper is being prepared for presentation to Dr. Winston L. King, Prefessor of History of Religions, Vanderbilt University; Dr. David James Randolph; and the Council on Ministries of Centenary United Methodist Church, Modesto, California. I wish to express my appreciation to these people for their assistance and inspiration.

The premise of this examination of the Lord's Supper as a phenomenon within the context of The United Methodist Church is that by studying the sacrament as a Christian phenomenon and the way it attempts to structure a particular religious experience, a better understanding of the experience itself can be achieved. The Lord's Supper will be studied as the symbolic expression of certain aspects of the Christian faith. Through this study it is hoped that one may ascertain some trends in the contemporary church and their place in the continuing development of Christianity. The Lord's Supper will be used, in effect, as an indicator of current religious moods in our society.

The investigation will begin with the nature of Holy Communion in the earliest church in an attempt to grasp what function the service served for its original participants. The development of the sacrament will be examined through the point at which it became an institution of the established church. This look at the early development of the ritual will be primarily concerned with the manner in which this development influences present forms of Communion. The contemporary celebration must be understood both as the product of its history and its present social and religious environment. Since this paper is an effort to learn something about the current environment which is shaping the ceremony, it will be important to try to identify those aspects of the service which are reflections of that environment.

For the study of the actual ceremony as it is being administered currently in The United Methodist Church, two contrasting liturgies will be used. The first is an adaption from liturgies of the early church, the second is more contemporary. Both are made available for use in United Methodist churches by the Commission on Worship. After an examination of the phenomenon as it is in today's church, an attempt will be made to draw some conclusions about modern religious attitudes.

This paper should provide an understanding of several things which are of importance to any student of religion, particularly if he is involved in work with a Christian church. First, by using the methods of phenomenology, it acquaints one with a significant manner in which to describe and understand various types of religious experience or consciousness. Second, it will provide an understanding of the Christian church as a historical institution. And third, this paper should make it possible to achieve some sort of awareness of the forces which affect today's religious community.

According to Protestant tradition there are but two sacraments ordained by Christ as signs of the grace of God. They are seen not only as tokens of a Christian's faith, but also as a means by which God strengthens and confirms this faith, enabling a man to meet the demands of his faith. These two sacraments are Baptism and Holy Communion (or in the Methodist tradition the "Supper of the Lord")[2] Because of the frequency with which it is administered and its association with the crucifixion and resurrection of Christ, the Lord's Supper is a central part of the worship of the United Methodist congregation. Throughout history there have been many changes in the Communion service and its meaning, which quite possibly reflect differences in the way in which man sees his God and his relationship to him. As a central ritual, Communion would be shaped by the tone and direction of man's response to God which is his "thrust toward . . . the Ultimate." This thrust is religion.[3] The Lord's Supper functions as an expression of the Christian's religion.

An examination of the Scriptures finds the Last Supper of Jesus recorded in the three Synoptic Gospels and alluded to in the letters of Paul. The Gospel of John uses much of the language found in the Communion liturgy of today, but records no Last Supper as such. There are differences of opinion as to what actually took place during the Passover celebration prior to Jesus' death. Biblical scholars disagree greatly on the mood of Jesus' last meal with his disciples. The actual event is of relatively little importance here; of greater significance is how the infant church responded to the death and resurrection of Jesus through the institution of Holy Communion. Of major interest are the types of celebration which arose with the apostolic tradition.

By the time the Gospels became a written document (probably after A.D. 65[4]), at least two forms of the service were in practice, the Marcan and Pauline forms. But even before the ceremony had reached the somewhat stable structures of Mark and Paul's texts, it had undergone a number of significant steps in the developing interpretation. The drastic changes which possibly occurred in the form of the sacrifice prior to A.D. 65 reflect coinciding changes in the Christian faith. Willi Marxsen sees the greatest turning point in the early church as that of its move from the "Jesus-tradition" to the "Easter Faith."[5] This change was indeed demonstrated in a new interpretation of the Last Supper.

There are two major interpretations of what the Last Supper could have meant in light of the Jesus-tradition. This tradition was the religion of those who knew Jesus before the Resurrection. An examination of the two forms of Last Supper most probably will give an indication of the nature of the Jesus-tradition. The first, and most well-known interpretation of the type of celebration which the Last Supper might have been is that of a Passover celebration. Joachim Jeremias, in *The Eucharistic Words of Jesus*, takes great pains to show that the meal which Jesus and his disciples shared on that last night together was a standard Jewish Passover meal.

Jeremias studies the texts in the New Testament in light of the religious and cultural background of Jesus, and from that draws several conclusions about what he possibly meant by his "eucharistic words."[6] His methodology starts him with the historical and cultural context, and, through examination of reports of the event which survived the apostolic era (prior to A.D. 65), arrives at an evaluation of the phenomenon. Because of the time span between the original supper and its recording in written form some thirty-five years later, it is difficult to make any definite conclusions about the Jesus-tradition which would have interpreted the Passover feast of Christ. But these conclusions, however indefinite, are valuable because they are consistent with the religious environment of the first century.

The significance of the Last Supper as a Passover meal in the traditional form is well worth mentioning, not only for an understanding of the early Christian, but also for an understanding of how this may have influenced the present form of the ceremony. Jeremias believes that Jesus took the opportunity to use the Passover meal to illustrate the new covenant which he brought to man. It is also an effort to prepare the disciples for his resurrection, and to provide them with a method of reproclaiming their faith in him.[7]

A second type of Last Supper celebration is seen by Hans Lietzmann in which he calls the "Jerusalem type," because it found manifestation in the church at Jerusalen as recorded in the book of Acts. According to Lietzmann, the celebration of the Lord's Supper in the infancy of the Christian Church was based not on Jesus' Last Supper as a Passover Feast, but as another of his fellowship meals with his disciples. As a result of this interpretation of the original meal, the service by the early Christians would be different from the Passover meal of contemporary Jews. Because of the lack of detail in the biblical accounts of the service, it is impossible to say with any certainty whether the early Communion celebrations followed that of the Passover or not, but some similarities and differences are evident.[8]

In Jeremias' interpretation of the Holy Communion of the Jesus-tradition, the form of the service, that is, the order in which the sacraments are administered and the historical interpretation given by the presider, follow the procedure of the Jewish Passover feast. The celebration of the new covenant of Jesus contained much of the symbolism of the old covenant of Moses. The following is the order of service for the Passover at the time of Jesus:

A. The Preliminary Course:
    Word of blessing (the blessing of the feast day . . . and of the cup)
        spoken by the paterfamilias over the first cup. The preliminary
        dish, consisting among other things of green herbs, bitter herbs,
        and a sauce made of fruit puree. The meal proper is served but
        not yet eaten; the second cup is mixed and put in its place but
        not yet drunk.

B. Passover-Liturgy:
    Passa-Haggadha (a prayer) by the paterfamilias.
    First part of the Passover *Hallel* (from Ps. 113[9]).
    The second cup is drunk.

C. The main meal:
    The Grace spoken by the paterfamilias over the unleavened bread.
    The meal consisting of the paschal lamb, unleavened bread, bitter
        herbs with fruit puree and wine.
    A prayer over the third cup.

D. The close:
    The second part of the passover *Hallel* (Ps. 114-18[10]).
    The praise over the fourth cup.

As the Jesus-tradition separated itself from orthodox Judaism, the structure of the Passover liturgy was modified so as to be a celebration of the New Covenant of Jesus. Today's service is not generally associated with a meal, but from Paul's writing in I Corinthians 11:25, the earliest churches did at least recognize the supper; " 'This is my body which is for you, do this as a memorial of me."[11] In the same way, he took the cup, after supper, and said: 'This cup is the new covenant sealed by my blood. Whenever you drink it, do this as a memorial of me."[12] Many of the elements of the Jewish Passover were changed in their symbolism or were dropped from the service altogether. The herbs, representing the suffering of the Israelites in Egypt are not found in the Christian liturgy. And the elements of bread and wine are symbolic of Christ's body and blood. The paschal lamb is replaced symbolically by the sacrifice of Jesus on the Cross.

Hans Lietzmann holds to a different construction of the Lord's Supper for keepers of the Jesus-tradition. He sees it as a vestige of the fellowship meals which Jesus shared with his friends and disciples during his ministry. If this were the case, the liturgy would be much less formal than the Christian "Passover" of Jeremias. Lietzmann does, in fact, make a distinction between a formalized service and an informal celebration; both are typical of the earliest church at some time in the development of the sacrament. In Lietzmann's *Mass and the Lord's Supper*, he views the difference primarily in geographical terms; the less formal friendship feasts being celebrated at the church in Jerusalem, and the more formal service belonging to the other early churches.[13] However, this difference may be one of a developmental nature, since the Jerusalem church was a part of the Jesus-tradition, and the Gentile Churches were not. Perhaps now some conclusions about the religion of these Jesus sects can be made. For a study guide, the liturgy of the Jerusalem church will be used.

In *The Lord's Supper as a Christological Problem* Willi Marxsen describes the resurrection of Christ as a further proclamation of the substance of the Jesus-tradition (the "that", or *Dass*, of the message his ministry held for those who witnessed this ministry). This is an important concept for the understanding of the original institution of the Communion celebration. Marxsen formulates the *Dass* of the Jesus-tradition as "By his words and deeds Jesus puts men before God." It is Jesus who provides the direction for man's religious thrust toward God; it is through his life of action that man is shown how to respond to the Ultimate, as described in the personality terms of his Hebraic religious heritage. During his life, Jesus was not the "object of faith", rather he was the promoter of action and response. What was important about Jesus while he was alive was not "his quality, his being, or (even) his relation to God, but his function, but with this emphatic qualification: it is *his* function." [14] The means of action in the Jesus-tradition are varied in form; the functions of Jesus' action cover a wide span. But common to all of them is the eschatological nature, that is, the manner in which they function to actualize the eschaton. It was through Jesus, and more specifically through close fellowship with him, that the eschaton became a present reality. By reacting to Jesus, men were brought to the ultimate decision, not in some time after death, but now in their normal daily lives. "Jesus calls men (yes, even publicans and sinners) to his table, into his fellowship." [15] Even before Easter, the fellowship meals of Jesus and his followers were central to the themes of his teaching. The Last Supper is tremendously significant as it was an anticipation of the fellowship of the last days in the kingdom of God. The Last Supper should be seen in light of its dual purposes, which are integrated by their eschatological character. As a fellowship feast, the Last Supper had the function of allowing the disciples to share the closeness of God resulting from the actions of Jesus. But with the emphasis upon his betrayal and death in the Passover context, particularly with the paschal symbolism, the Last Supper would have been of major significance to the Jesus-tradition. This was his final promise of the eschaton, his final fellowship meal. The functions of his life of action here demanded immediate response, a sense of urgency distinguished this meal from all others. It was with this final act with his apostles that Jesus affirmed the thrust of his life. The Last Supper marked the end of a period in which the nature of Jesus' being was relatively unimportant. It wasn't necessary to know who he was, only to react to his call to a new life, in the fellowship of God through him.

After Easter there was a further proclamation of the Jesus-tradition. The life of Jesus still functioned as before, only without his presence. Because of his absence, any ceremony which recreated the fellowship and eschatological promise, would be of tremendous importance. Consequently, it was the final fellowship meal, with its easily recognized implications of the eschaton, which was adopted by early Christians. The phenomenon served to keep alive the Jesus-tradition. The ceremony itself at this time probably attempted to emphasize the elements of the Last Supper which were closest in meaning and function to Jesus' fellowship and eschatological themes.

Because of Jesus' being no longer present after Easter, there was a danger that the new life which the tradition proclaimed would be doctrinalized. The message of his life would no longer be "*Jesus* makes God actual," "*Jesus* anticipates the future," "On *Jesus* depends the final decision." The message might easily be understood as "*There is the possibility* to experience now already the actualization of God, already now to anticipate the future." [16] Jesus would then be separated from his kerygma (teachings), it becomes not an ideology but a doctrine. Jesus would still be recognized as the person who began the tradition, but his actual life of action would have no meaning for the present.

It was then as a protection of the function of the life of Jesus that the tradition developed a Christology. The sacrament of Holy Communion changed significantly as the tradition sought ways to cope with the Easter problem. It was now necessary to establish who Jesus was, the quality of his being and his relation to God. This period of adjustment to Jesus' absence is marked by what is known as the Easter faith. It was from this faith that the true church structures developed, in order to retain a sense of the relation between Jesus and his kerygma. The letters of Paul and the first written gospels were products of the Easter faith. [17] The early church was characterized by its definite attempts to interpret the life of Jesus, not merely in light of its function, but in the context of his relation to God and man, his being Son and Savior. An examination of some of the changes in the liturgy of the Lord's Supper give evidence of new trends the religion which grew up around Jesus.

The two prominent liturgies of this period were the Marcan and Pauline formulas. These accounts of the Last Supper are as follows:

> During supper he took bread, and having said the blessing, he broke it and gave it to them, with the words: "Take this, this is my body." Then he took a cup, and having offered thanks to God he gave it to them; and they all drank from it. And he said, "This is my blood, the blood of the covenant shed for many" (Mark 14:22-24 NEB).

> For the tradition which I handed on to you came to me from the Lord himself: that the Lord Jesus, on the night of his arrest, took bread and, after giving thanks to God, broke it and said: "This is my body, which is for you; do this as a memorial of me." In the same way he took the cup after supper and said: "This cup is the new covenant sealed by my blood. Whenever you drink it, do this as a memorial of me" (I Cor. 11:23-25 NEB).

In the reports of interpretations of the sacrament by Jesus there are considerable differences implied by the wording of Paul's formula and that of Mark. Paul's formula says: "This cup is the new covenant sealed by the blood." Here the emphasis is clearly on the covenant, not on the blood. Willi Marxsen outlines the interpretation in Corinthians in this way:

cup—covenant
this covenant is then interpreted further by "blood"[18]

Mark, on the other hand, gives a different emphasis. His gospel reads: "This is my blood, the blood of the covenant." The major symbol here is the blood. Marxsen's outline of Mark's formula is:

contents of the cup—blood
this blood is then interpreted further as blood of the covenant.[19]

Paul shows a relationship of cup-covenant-(blood). While Mark's liturgy follows a contents-of-the-cup-blood-(covenant) word of the sacrament.

The first word of interpretation of the sacrament, concerning the bread, shows no difference between the two formulas. It is interesting to compare the word of the bread with the word of the cup. Paul reads: "This is my body, which is for you"; Mark says: "Take this; this is my body." Both are equations between bread and body. The following outline shows the incongruency of Paul:

bread—body
cup—covenant[20]

Whereas Mark is congruent:

bread—body
contents of the cup—blood[21]

The incongruency of the Pauline formula was apparently corrected by the later liturgy of Mark. Paul, quite possibly, indicates the types of changes being made in the interpretation of the life of Jesus by Easter-faith congregations. The discrepancy within Paul's text, even though it is basically stylistic, seems to show both the interpretation which was that of the Jesus-tradition and also the one which arose out of the Easter faith. Paul's word of the blood is reminiscent of the significance of the Last Supper lying in the new covenant of Jesus which was a view held by the Jesus sects. But the word of the bread makes an equation between the sacramental bread and the physical body of Christ. This is a definite attempt to identify Jesus the person with the elements of Holy Communion. Such an identity would not have been necessary if the emphasis of the ceremony were on fellowship or on establishing new meanings for the Passover of the old covenant of Moses. Here in this one passage are indications of the different thrusts, however subtle, which influenced the development of the liturgy of the Lord's Supper. The Jesus-tradition sought an expression of the action of Jesus and the meaning of his life while he lived. The Easter faith sought a ceremony which would make this a part of the lives of people who had no way of knowing the man without an association between him and the teachings which the apostles brought them. The people who knew the living Jesus (as opposed to the Risen Christ of Paul) would never have separated the man from his teachings; it is for this reason that Communion in the Jesus-tradition probably did not make an equation between the holy elements and the man Jesus.

The first century after the birth of Christ saw significant developments in the church as it sought methods of incorporating changes in religious attitudes and concepts brought about by the life, death, and resurrection of Jesus. The changes in religious environment were reflected in the ritual structures which the church instituted in order to remain at peace with its world. The Lord's Supper developed concurrently with the Christology of the church. A look at liturgical forms being used in today's church should give some idea of the religious attitudes of its culture and some of the religious problems with which the church is faced.

Both of the liturgies used here in a study of the Lord's Supper are currently being administered in United Methodist churches. The first is an adaption from the Canons of Hippolytus (Hippolytus lived between the late second century and the early third century), and from hymns and prayers of the church at Alexandria, Antioch, and Ethiopia, during the second and third centuries. The second liturgy is for a service in contemporary language.

A Liturgy from Hippolytus
and the Early Churches

The order of service:[22]

Presider: Peace be with you.

People: **And with your spirit.**

Deacon: (Reading from the Old Testament)

People: (A Psalm)

Deacon: (Reading from an apostolic writing)

People: (Reading from a gospel)

Presider: (Sermon)

Deacon: (Dismissal of the catechumens) Let the catechumens depart. Let no catechumen remain. Let the catechumens depart.

All: Prayer of the Faithful (all standing)—(adapted from the church at Alexandria)

Deacon: Pray for the peace of the one holy catholic and apostolic orthodox Church of God.

(Silent Prayer by all the faithful)

Presider: We pray and ask your goodness, Lover of mankind: remember, Lord, the peace of your one holy catholic and apostolic Church which is from one end of the world to the other: bless all the people and all the lands: the peace that is from heaven grant in all our hearts, but also graciously give us the peace of this life.

Deacon: Pray for our Bishop, _____ , of this city of _____ , and for all orthodox bishops, elders, and deacons.

(Silent Prayer by all the faithful)

Presider: We pray and ask your goodness, Lover of all mankind: remember, Lord, our leaders. Preserve them to us in safety many years in peaceful times, fulfilling these holy offices which you have committed to them according to your holy and blessed will, rightly dividing the word of truth, feeding your people in holiness and righteousness; and with them all the fullness of your one only holy catholic and apostolic Church.

Deacon: Pray for this holy assembly and our meetings.

(Silent prayer by all the faithful)

Presider:　We pray and ask your goodness, Lover of mankind: remember, Lord, our congregations. Grant that we may hold them without hindrance, that they may be held without impediment, according to your holy and blessed will: through the grace of your only Son, Jesus Christ, our Lord. Amen.

Peace be with you.

People:　**And with your spirit.**

All give the kiss of peace as a sign of reconciliation to their neighbors

Offertory:　*The deacons present bread, wine, and other gifts (if any) to the presider at the table. The congregation stands and sings "Let All Mortal Flesh Keep Silence" (from the church at Antioch, Hymnal, No. 324).*

1.　Let all mortal flesh keep silence,
And with fear and trembling stand;
Ponder nothing earthly-minded,
For with blessing in his hand,
Christ our God to earth descendeth,
Our full homage to demand.

2.　King of kings, yet born of Mary,
As of old on earth he stood,
Lord of lords, in human vesture,
In the body and the blood,
He will give to all the faithful
His own self for heavenly food.

3.　Rank on rank the host of heaven
Spreads its vanguard on the way,
As the Light of light descendeth
From the realms of endless day,
That the powers of hell may vanish
As the darkness clears away.

4.　At his feet the six-winged seraph,
Cherubim, with sleepless eye,
Veil their faces to the presence,
As with ceaseless voice they cry,
Alleluia, Alleluia,
Alleluia, Lord most high!　　Amen.

The presider and all the elders place their hands on the offering of bread and wine. The presider, giving thanks, says:

The Lord be with you.

People:　**And with your spirit.**

Presider:　Lift up your hearts.

People:　**We lift them up to the Lord.**

Presider:　Let us give thanks to the Lord.

People:　**It is fitting and right.**

Presider:　We return thanks to you, God, through your beloved Son Jesus Christ whom you sent to us, in these last days, as Savior, Redeemer, and Messenger of your will. He is your word, inseparable from you. Through him you made all things. Being well pleased with him, you sent him from heaven into the womb of a virgin. Dwelling there, he was made flesh and was revealed as your Son, born of the Holy Spirit and the Virgin.

133

He, fulfilling your will and winning a holy people for you, stretched out his hands when he suffered that he might set free from suffering those who trusted in you. He was handed over to death, a death he freely accepted that he might destroy death, shatter the chains of the devil, trample hell underfoot, lead the righteous to light, set the limits of hell, and show forth the resurrection. It was then he took bread and gave thanks to you, saying: "Take eat, this is my body which is broken for you." Likewise, he also took the cup, saying: "This is my blood which is poured out for you. When you do this, do it in memory of me."

Therefore, remembering his death and resurrection, we offer to you this bread and cup, giving thanks that you have considered us worthy to stand in your presence and to serve you. And we ask that you send your Holy Spirt on the offering of the holy Church. Unite all who share in these holy mysteries that they may be filled with the Holy Spirit for the strengthening of their faith in the truth, so that we may praise and glorify you through your Son Jesus Christ. Through whom glory and honor be to you with the Holy Spirit in your holy Church both now and always.   Amen.

The presider breaks the bread.

Distribution *(After the clergy have received Communion, the faithful receive, standing about the table.)*

Presider:　　　　The bread of heaven in Christ Jesus.

Communicant:　Amen.

Elder or Deacon: *(to each person as the cup is offered)*　　In God the Father Almighty.

Communicant:　Amen.

Elder or Deacon: In the Lord Jesus Christ.　Amen.　*(or)*
　　　　　　　　In the Holy Spirit and the holy Church.　Amen.

Presider:　　　　(post-Communion prayer and benediction — late additions from the church in Ethiopia):

God Almighty, the Father of our Lord Jesus Christ, we give you thanks because you have imparted to us the reception of the holy mystery: Let us not be for guilt or condemnation, but for the renewal of soul and body and spirit, through thine only Son through whom to you be all honor and glory, world without end.　Amen.

Eternal God, Almighty, the Father of the Lord and our Savior Jesus Christ, bless your servants, protect and help and prosper them by your power. Keep and confirm in them your fear by your greatness; provide that they shall both think what is yours and believe what is yours and will what is yours; grant peace without sin and anger, through your only Son, through whom we pray. Amen.

When this is finished let everyone hasten to do good works, to please God, and to live rightly, serving the Church, doing what he has learned and advancing in piety.

The first part of this liturgy follows the form of present-day worship services in the United Methodist churches. There are the initial greetings between the pastor and the people; followed by readings and hymns from the biblical heritage of the church. These statements from the past serve to give authority to the service which is to follow and also to show a continuity between past and present religious experiences. The most striking feature of this liturgy is the great concern it expresses for the church and its leaders. This is indicative of a strong ecclesiastical government which definitely sees itself as an entity apart from the people. Note that the catechumens are not allowed to stay for the actual Communion service. The church, at the particular time in history in which this order of service was more or less standard, had achieved at least some sort of autonomy and could afford to be somewhat exclusive. Little is given in the liturgy concerning the requirements which a catechumen must meet before he is allowed to partake of the sacrament, but the overall view of the church expressed there is one of a highly organized machine, the function of which is to make the truth known to its members. Such phrases as "one holy catholic and apostolic orthodox Church of God" show an attempt to establish the church's identity among the members of the congregation, and quite possibly, within the community. Either the church was already a powerful force in its cultural environment, or it recognized that it could become such a force. All the prayers preceding the offering are for the church, its leaders and congregations. The church itself is seen as an illustration of the power of God in the world.

The picture which this liturgy draws of God, as seen most clearly in the offertory hymn, is also one of power. God is seen in conflict with the "powers of hell," over which he is finally triumphant. Perhaps this is a reflection of the way the church saw its place in society: an instrument of God's will, instituted to spread the understanding of God's spirit to the "earthly-minded" world of "mortal flesh" in which the church found itself. This is a picture of a crusading church which is obligated to spread the "Light of lights" to all realms of a world removed from heaven.

An examination of the presider's statements concerning the life of Jesus and the meaning of the Last Supper are the results of a doctrinalized Christology not found in the liturgies of the Jesus-tradition or the Easter faith. The service has incorporated the theology of the gospel tradition into its sacramental formula. There is an emphasis on the death which Jesus "freely accepted" so that he could conquer death, Satan, and hell, and "lead the righteous to light." It is reported that only after Jesus accepted his death, he took the bread. Here the bread is equated with the body of Christ, as it was in the formulas of the Easter faith. However, the significance of this equation is considerably different. Christ has acquired a sacrificial symbolism. Unlike the Easter faith, in which the equation of bread and body served to identify Jesus with his teachings and make his kerygma valid after his death, the function of the association of bread and body of Christ is to bring the sacrifice of Jesus into the life of the communicants. It is not the life of Jesus which is of prime importance, but his sacrificial death and his resurrection. Anticipation of the eschaton is all but lost. In its place is the promise of deliverance from death. It is possible that somewhere in the development of the church's Christology the eschaton became identified with the apocalypse. This was not the case in the earliest Christian traditions. The eschaton referred to the time when God called all men to be judged. It was after this judgment that those who had refused the call of fellowship with God would be obliterated. The Communion which this liturgy expresses is one in which men may "Praise and glorify (God) through (his) Son Jesus Christ."

This liturgy starts with who Jesus was. The major concern is with how Jesus is related to God. From the starting reference point of Jesus as the Son of God, Lord, and Savior of mankind, the service eventually gets around to a celebration of his life. Even then, it is not primarily a life of active fellowship with God, but of hope that someday man will be "set free from suffering." The message of Jesus was one of reward through service to God. The themes of sacrifice, passion, and suffering, which are central to this ceremony, were barely discernable in the fellowship and new-covenant expressions which were the liturgies of earlier traditions.

The service of Holy Communion in the churches of the second and third centuries evidences a strong centralized church with comparatively exclusive membership. It contains reflections of a religion set against an "earthly-minded" culture, and concerned with suffering and redemption. Participation in the Communion is participation in a memorial service in honor of the God who promises to free his "holy people" from suffering.

This liturgy is of use to the current church for several reasons. First, its historical nature helps to provide an understanding of some of the background of contemporary theological themes which have shaped the church and are evident in modern liturgies. It also expresses a dimension of God which has been played down in recent years, but is nonetheless valuable. The stress upon the responsibility of the church as God's instrument in the world helped to unify the religious community around a protecting God of power. By remembering the passion of Jesus, man can see a loving, sacrificing God; through the sacrifice of the Communion man shares, for a time, the passions of Jesus. Themes which underlie modern

Christology were once in the foreground. Some of these themes, now obscured in the Lord's Supper, are easily seen in the liturgies of the post-apostolic church of the late second century.

The church of today has undergone tremendous upheavals since the Canons of Hippolytus. It finds itself in a far different world from that of the early church and the post-apostolic church. The liturgy of today's Lord's Supper is the product of developments which have come out of both of the earlier traditions and out of its present cultural framework. The Communion Service which is being used as a means of studying contemporary thrusts and responses toward God reflects many themes inherent in today's society and the way in which it sees itself and the Ultimate. In this liturgy can be seen the values which are held by modern religious men in a secular environment. Both eschatology and ecclesiology have been greatly reworked in the context of the modern world. Fellowship and covenantal relationship have acquired a renewed vitality.

The liturgy of today is a contrast not only with both liturgical forms already studied, but in some instances points out contrasting features between the two earlier ones, by sharing certain aspects with one and not the other.

A Communion Service in Modern English

It is every pastor's duty to serve this sacrament regularly to God's people as he was ordained to do.

Where the full order cannot be used, one may begin with the Invitation.

The Lord's Table should be set before the people, covered with a clean white cloth. Either the traditional elements or modern substitutes, common to the life of the people, may be used. If contemporary elements are used, it should be agreed upon and announced publicly beforehand.

While it is customary to come forward to kneel for Communion, the pastor and people may agree to receive the sacrament standing or seated, as in other Christian traditions.

All people who hope to find or to lead a Christian life are invited to receive this sacrament. Neither race, denomination, dress, nor personality should bar anyone who comes to worship God in this way.

The service may begin with an instrumental prelude or with congregational singing. Any popular or classical instrument and music can be used, so long as mechanics do not disrupt the service. The place of worship may be decorated with contemporary expressions of faith.

The service itself may begin with a sung hymn or prelude with a short statement about Communion, or with Scripture sentences. Whatever is used should be in everyday language familiar to the people wherever possible.

The Order of Service[23]

Prelude

Call to Worship   Choir

Hymn of Praise

Scripture Sentences:

Pastor: We come together to celebrate Holy Communion. This acted-out parable of God's love was begun by Jesus with his first disciples. In this service, the token elements of (here name the elements) will be used as symbols of the presence and love of Jesus Christ our Lord.

The Holy Spirit may be saying to us, as he did to John of Patmos:

"Listen! I stand at the door and knock; if anyone hears my voice and opens the door, I will come into his house and eat with him, and he will eat with me" (Rev. 3:20 TEV).

In faith, John recorded this saying of Jesus in his Gospel:

"I am the living bread, he will live forever. And the bread which I will give him is my flesh, which I give up so that the world may live" (John 6:51 TEV).

136

Listen to this urgent appeal from our scriptures:

"Dear friends! Let us love one another, for love comes from God. Whoever loves is a child of God and knows God. . . . This is how God showed his love for us: he **sent his only Son into the world that we may have life through him. . . . Dear** friends, if this is how God loved us, then we should love one another" (I John 4:7-11 TEV).

Hear this incredible insight of Paul:

"What no man ever saw or heard,
What no man ever thought could happen,
Is the very thing God prepared for those who love him"
(I Cor. 2:9 TEV).

(Then the pastor and people shall greet one another.)

Pastor: The Lord be with you.

People: **And with your spirit.**

Pastor: You may be seated, and let us pray.

Pastor and People (bowed):

O God, our Father, before you our whole lives are exposed, and all our needs are known. Be at work in our lives. Wipe out all our old secrets and wrong desires, so that we may perfectly love you and truly worship you, in Jesus Christ our Lord. Amen.

Our Father, may all men come to respect and to love you. May you rule in every person and in all of life. Give us, day by day, the things of life we need. Forgive us our sins, for we forgive everyone who has done us wrong. Let nothing test us beyond our strength. Save us from our weakness. For yours is the authority, and the power, and the glory, forever. Amen.

(Then all shall stand to sing, solemnly at first but with increasing tempo and joyfulness.)

(Tune—"Jacob's Ladder")

O Lord Jesus, cast our sin out.
    Lord, have mercy; Christ, have mercy.
Take away our life of sin now.
    Jesus, hear our prayer.

Fill our empty lives with love.
    Give our lives some great purpose.
Send your Spirit to live in us.
    Jesus, hear our prayer.

You, alone, Lord, can transform us.
    You, alone, can we depend on.
You, alone, can give us power.
    Jesus, hear our prayer.

Glory to God, peace to all men.
    Let us praise him, let us bless him.
Let us give our lives to serve him.
    Jesus, hear our prayer.   Amen.

Invitation to Communion:

Pastor: Friends, if you sincerely turn your back on your sins; if you want to live in love and peace with everyone; if you desire to lead a new life doing God's will from now on; then prepare to come forward in faith to receive this sacrament. Now let us make our peace with God, confident of his forgiveness, by joining in this prayer of confession:

General Prayer of Confession (seated and bowed):

All: O God, whom Jesus called Father, we admit that we have done many wrong and wicked things. We admit that we have ignored many opportunities to do the loving thing. We are sorry we have thought, said, and done such foolishness. Now we turn away from our mistakes. We are sick at heart, Father, when we think of them. Forgive us for not knowing what to do. Please forgive us. In the name of Jesus, forgive us. Grant that we may so love and serve you in all our days, that others will praise you.   Amen.

Words of Assurance

Pastor: God our Father has promised to forgive all who turn to him in faith. Even now he forgives us, and sets us free to live new lives in Jesus Christ our Lord. Henceforth we may live, not in fear or dread, but secure in his power and love. Nothing can separate us from the love of Christ. Therefore, let us rejoice in the Lord, our God!

Anthem   Choir

Scripture Lesson   Pastor

Communion Meditation   Pastor

Prayer

Offertory   Choir

Presentation of Tithes and Gifts

(When the collection is received, the offering of Communion elements may be brought to the Lord's Table or uncovered there.)

People: **We offer these gifts,
We offer this bread,
We offer this cup,
In the name of Jesus Christ our Lord.**

Pastor: Let us give our lives to God!

People: **We do offer our lives to God!**

Pastor: Together, let us thank the Lord God!

People: **For it is the least that we can do!**

Pastor: Thanking God our Father is the very least we can do! For now we can live all of life without fear. We can face even death without anxiety. For we know that whether we live or die, we belong to Jesus Christ our Lord. Therefore with all who love God and their fellow men, let us join in praising Him!

(When the people are seated, the pastor shall recall the origin and purpose of this sacrament in the life of the Christian church.)

Pastor: Jesus went forth in God's name to save the world. We remember in this sacrament his life and death. We call on him to live in us and with all men. We look forward to being with him forever. This, according to Scripture, was his intention.
    He wanted all people to receive these symbols of his love. At the dinner table, on the very night he was betrayed, he told his disciples:
        "I have wanted so much to eat this Passover meal with you before I suffer.
        "Take and eat this bread; this is my body given for you.
        Drink this, all of you, for this is my blood poured out for you.
        "Do this, whenever you want, in memory of me, until I come again."
    Then Jesus and the disciples sang a song and went out into the darkness to the Mount of Olives.

We use these symbols of his body and blood, in memory of his life and death, in faith that he is risen to be with us, and in the hope we will be with him to the end of time. Let us pray that as we receive this sacrament, Jesus will become a living reality in our lives and in our life together.

The Communion Prayer (seated and bowed):

All: **We do not come to this table, O Lord, counting on our own goodness. For we know that we have missed the mark of our high calling. We trust only in your love. We would gladly eat the leftovers from your table. But we rejoice that your love is so great that you invite us as guests. Grant that we may receive this sacrament as a turning point in our lives. May we grow to be like you, as you become the center of our living. Amen.**

(The minister and others helping serve Communion shall commune first, then the choir and congregation as the minister directs, and the elements are distributed.)

Pastor: May the body and blood of our Lord Jesus Christ preserve your soul and body unto everlasting life. Eat and drink this, remembering that he died for you, and feeding on him in your heart by faith, with thanksgiving.

(After all have been served, the elements are covered.)

Pastor: The peace of the Lord be with you.

People: **And with you, also.**

Pastor: Let us thank God with all our hearts.

Prayer of Thanksgiving and Dedication (seated and bowed):

All: **O Lord our Father, please accept our offering of praise and thanksgiving. We thank you that in Jesus Christ we find forgiveness for all that is past, and a new future of meaning and purpose. Here and now, Lord, we offer ourselves to you. We are yours, body and soul. May we all find our lives filled with grace and goodness. Though none of us deserves it, lead us to a new life together. In Jesus Christ our Lord. Amen.**

Closing Hymn of Celebration and Dedication

Benediction:

Pastor: This service is ended. But our life in Jesus Christ our Lord goes on and on. We go now, in his name, into all the world. Let our light so shine, and our joy be so obvious, that all who see us will come to praise God! Amen.

Choral Amen   Choir

Postlude

This modern liturgy for celebration of the Lord's Supper is characterized by its attempt to break away from traditional procedures which had lost their impact through overuse. At the same time, it can be seen as an outgrowth of its religious heritage. The form and language of the service are modern, but many of the symbols and concepts contained within it can be found in the earliest liturgies. This form of the ceremony represents some new developments within the Christian faith and also some themes which have been maintained since the ministry of Jesus. Those ways in which modern man is different from the man of Jesus' time are reflected in this service as well as those ways in which they are the same.

One noticeable difference between this liturgy and the one from the second century is its appeal to all men of faith. Christianity in the twentieth century is making a definite effort to escape from ties to exclusionism which grew up early in the church as it pitted itself against a world of corruption. No one is barred from participation in the service who wishes to worship God in this way.

This particular service might rightly be called a "celebration of love" for celebration and love are two key words in the liturgy. The meaning of celebration here is similar to that of the celebration of the fellowship feasts of the Jesus-tradition. It is the active loving of Jesus which is celebrated. However, unlike the feasts of the Jesus-tradition, there is no eschatological meaning attached to the modern meal. Love (*agape*) achieves a sort of autonomy, standing by itself as a product only of the grace of God.

There is a definite effort to personalize the life of Jesus. After centuries of identification of Jesus with his kerygma, modern man again finds it difficult to separate the two. Consequently, there is seen in this ceremony a reproclamation of the fellowship with God which is possible through a positive reaction to Jesus' call to loving. Jesus is viewed not only as the promoter of God's love, but as the product of this love.

God is also seen as a God of power who protects those who have faith and trust in him. However, this power is not the same as that of the postapostolic church. The forces from which protection is desired are those within the man himself which keep him from loving his fellow men. The fear from which release is sought is not fear of death and suffering, but it is fear of separation from the love of Christ. This fear is removed when one understands the Resurrection as God's promise that his Holy Spirit will be forever present in the world.

It is important to note the new interpretation of the sacramental elements. They are used not as symbols of Jesus' sacrifice but "as symbols of the presence and love of Jesus Christ our Lord." This is very close to their function within the Jesus-tradition. The bread is described as "the living bread which came down from heaven" as Christ Jesus. Here, the bread symbolizes not the physical presence of Jesus, but the spiritual presence of his love. Christ is seen as the Redeemer of the world in the sentence: "The bread which I will give . . . is my flesh, which I give up so that the world may live." Christ's sacrifice on the Cross is taken as a symbol of his love for mankind. The purpose of the sacrament is for Jesus to become a living reality in the lives of each man and the life which the Christian community shares.

An aspect of this service which was not emphasized in the earlier ones is the necessity of commitment to the life which is possible through Jesus. It is not so much a matter of repentance as one of acceptance of his call to love and life. The congregation seeks the filling of their empty lives and a sense of purpose.

The emphasis of this ceremony seems to be upon each man's reaction to God's love as seen in the life of action which Jesus led. Although the language is not even similar to the eschatological references of the Jesus-tradition, there is a call here, too, to make a decision about Jesus now. Any eschaton which is viewed by the modern man would have to be one which was possible through his reaction to God at the present time.

Judging from the structure of this modern liturgy, there is a trend for modern religious men to internalize their God. The major emphasis is upon response to God. This response is left up to the man's own free will. He must choose to live the new life in Jesus. There is an effort to understand Jesus in terms of his earthly ministry and in his continuing presence in the lives of modern man as the model of *agape* love.

Trends which may be reflections of modern society are numerous. There is a loss of the deep sense of history as a means of establishing the authority of anything. Jesus is not important because of what he once meant to religious men, but because of what he means to men today. Also the celebration is pervaded by a sense of festivity. For too long man was trapped by his own solemnity and rationality. This ritual expresses a desire to let go and live.

The modern celebration of the Lord's Supper indicates a new sense of religion. It is no longer determined by what church building one goes to once a week or what words he says when he prays. Rather, religion is something which a person carries inside of him which guides the ways in which he responds to people around him. It is the system by which he orders his world, the structure of his cosmos.

Notes

1. Edmund Husserl describes what he means by the phenomenological method in *Ideas: General Introduction to Pure Phenomenology* (New York: Collier Books, 1962).
2. *Discipline of The United Methodist Church,* 1968 (Nashville: The Methodist Publishing House), 1968; pp. 40-41.
3. Winston L. King, *Introduction to Religion: A Phenomenological Approach* (New York: Harper & Row, 1968) p. 12.
4. Dr. Richard Mead, from a lecture delivered at Vanderbilt University, February 13, 1970, on the Gospel of Mark.
5. Willi Marxsen, *The Lord's Supper as a Christological Problem* (Philadelphia: Fortress Press; 1970), p. 2.

6. Joachim Jeremias: *The Eucharistic Words of Jesus;* (Oxford: Basil Blackwell, 1955), pp. 57-60.
7. *Ibid.*
8. Hans Lietzmann; *Mass and the Lord's Supper: A Study in the History of the Liturgy;* (Leiden: E.J. Brill, 1953) fasc. no. 1.
9. Jeremias, *Eucharistic Words,* p. 3.
10. *Ibid.*
11. *Ibid.,* pp. 58-59.
12. All biblical quotations are from the *New English Bible;*
13. Lietzmann, *Mass,* fasc. no. 1, pp. xiii-xvi.
14. Marxsen, p. 3.
15. *Ibid.,* p. 2.
16. *Ibid.,* p. 3.
17. Dr. Richard Mead; a lecture delivered at Vanderbilt University, February 6, 1970, on the Easter faith.
18. Marxsen, p. 7.
19. *Ibid.*
20. *Ibid.*
21. *Ibid.*
22. Based on *Ventures in Worship,* ed. David J. Randolph (Nashville: Abingdon Press, 1969), pp. 82-85. "A Basic Liturgy" prepared by Dr. James F. White.
23. *Ibid.*; pp. 85-90; "A Communion Service in Modern English", prepared by Dr. James D. Righter.

—Gary W. Barbaree
El Dorado, Arkansas

Communion Table Dismissals

144.

Some of you are students. Remember God goes to school too—every time you do. When you go try to act like God is there. That may be the only way someone else will ever know. You may go.

—Donald L. Slover

145.

Tomorrow is Monday. It starts all over again. When it starts we'll all be with you. Don't let your friends down. You may go.

—Donald L. Slover

146.

When Jesus ate with his disciples he said, "One of you will betray me." You are Jesus' disciples. You are eating with him now. Pray that it not be you who betrays him. You may go.

—Donald L. Slover

147.

Some of you are parents. It's hard to be a parent—God knows it's hard. Don't ever forget that your child's God is a lot like you. You may go.

—Donald L. Slover

148.

It is so easy to forget Jesus. We want our own way. But what we do hasn't much meaning apart from him. Whatever you do, do it in Jesus' name. You may go.

—Donald L. Slover

149.

There's a lot of work ahead this week. Some of it will be drudgery; some may be exciting. Don't let either kind keep you from doing it for Christ's sake. You may go.

—Donald L. Slover

150.

Sometimes discouragement comes. Have you ever felt the roof falling in upon you? Then you know how Jesus felt in Gethsemane. He'll be with you—even when the roof falls in. You may go.

—Donald L. Slover

151.

A lot of folks don't have it as good as you do. Some have to move with no place to go. Some have babies crying and no milk in the house. Be glad for what you have. But don't waste it. You may go.

—Donald L. Slover

152.

Sometimes we almost let our masks slip. And then we fix them back again. God wants his people to be *real.*—Can you accept the real people around you? Let someone let his mask slip a little before you. You may go.

—Donald L. Slover

153.

It's a changed and changing world—and so uncomfortable. But it's still the world God loves enough to die for—Let him *live* in it in you. You may go.

—Donald L. Slover

154.

It's hard to love—when war comes, when someone derides, when a person is mistreated, when a bad man wins, when a good man suffers, when someone hates—it's hard to love. But Jesus did.

—Donald L. Slover

155.

This has been a good day. Our service has been a celebration. Life is good. Lord, help us not to forget that all of life and everyday are worth celebrating. You may go.

—Donald L. Slover

Benedictions

156.

May the God who inspires men to endure, and gives them a Father's care, give you a mind united toward one another because of your common loyalty to Jesus Christ. And then, as one man, you will sing from the heart the praises of God the Father of our Lord Jesus Christ. So open your hearts to one another as Christ has opened his heart to you, and God will be glorified. (Rom. 15:5-6, Phillips)

—Kathryn Rogers Deering

157.

We have worshiped here together;
We have celebrated the miracle of our new life in Jesus.
Now go forth in peace—but not passive peace, *powerful* peace.
Powerful peace.
This week's hard knocks will be taken for God's glory.
This week will be full of chances to be used by him, to share him with others.
We'll all meet together here next week to celebrate our victories—*his* victories.
    Peace!

—Kathryn Rogers Deering

158.

The Lord has showed you, O man, what is good;
    and what does He require of you
    but to do justice and steadfast love
    and to walk humbly with your God?
—He is with you as you go forth. . .
        Amen.

—Kathryn Rogers Deering
(based on Mic. 6:8)

159.

In conclusion, my brothers, fill your minds with those things that are good and deserve praise: things that are true, noble, right, pure, lovely, and honorable. Put into practice what you learned and received [today]. And the God who gives us peace will be with you. Amen. (Phil. 4:8-9 TEV).

—Kathryn Rogers Deering

160.

Go forth once more, as channels of God's love.
Go into your world and spread the Good News, which says we are all loved for what we are.
Such Good News may seem too good to be true, but it is true just the same.
God is with you.

—Kathryn Rogers Deering

161.

We worship together as we live, as the children of God, in the name of the Father, the Son, and the Holy Spirit. Today is a new challenge to us, and we move out with eagerness to see what will happen. May the peace and power of God go with every one of you. Amen.

—Kathryn Rogers Deering

162.

The world awaits—the world where you live and work, which is your special mission field. It awaits your word of hope, your smile of love, your touch of Christ. A person can find him everywhere and miss him anywhere, out there. Let us leave this place resolving to guide people to him, as he leads us. Amen.

—Kathryn Rogers Deering

163.

Leader: Go and show others the good life.

People: **Live as Jesus taught us to live.**

Leader: Let love influence all that we do,

People: **That we may be found acceptable when we see God.**

Leader: Amen,

People: **And Amen.**

—John Curtis

164.

Leader: Go and share with others the GOOD NEWS.

People: **That God loves you and me,**

Leader: And Jesus Christ leads us to grace

People: **That we might sense his VICTORY.**

Leader: Amen,

People: **And Amen.**

—John Curtis

165.

Leader: Go, prepare for the cross and the crucifixion.

People: **Love the Lord with all thy heart.**

Leader: Come and serve as one who knows the Resurrection.

People: **Love thy neighbor as thyself.**

Leader: Amen,

People: **And Amen.**

—John Curtis

166.

Leader: Go and serve the Risen Savior.

People: **His hands have become our hands.**

Leader: He lives within our hearts,

People: **His heart will become our heart also.**

Leader: Jesus said, "Go and serve . . ."

People: **We will carry his GOOD NEWS to all the world.**

Leader: Amen,

People: **And Amen.**

—John Curtis

Baptism

167.

Service of Baptism

"God is love."
"We love because He first loved us."

Dearly Beloved,
We are here to celebrate life!
We are here to celebrate the
        wonder that is birth,
           the mystery that is love,
               the fulfillment that is marriage,
                  and the glory that is God.

We rejoice with thankful hearts! God has accepted us as partners in creation. He has entrusted to us a child, a gift of love, a gift of life through birth. We rejoice with grateful hearts that God has entrusted to us *this child*.

We celebrate the covenant of marriage established in trust by the God of love, whom we see in Jesus, the Christ. We affirm this covenant and charge these parents to dedicate their lives in faith, to be human instruments, agents of God, who will convey their faith in God and his purposes to this child.

We celebrate God's rich grace. "We love, because God first loved us through Christ." A child learns to love through being loved. A child knows the grace of God because he is first loved by those whom he touches. Baptism is an outward and visible sign of the personal grace of the indwelling presence of the Spirit of God.

(A passage from Kahil Gibran may be read here. *The Prophet* [New York: Alfred A. Knopf, 1951]. See pp. 17-18.)

Do you in presenting *this child* confess your faith in the God who has created and loved us all regardless of our abilities and hindrances and before whom the distinctions of race, class, and intelligence are as nothing?

I do.

(A passage may be read here, from Pat Floyd, *A Baby Is For Loving* [Nashville: Graded Press, 1964], See pp. 99-114.)

Will you endeavor to live before *this child* in such a way that life might become Good News to *him?*

I will.

Will you endeavor to keep *this child* under the ministry and guidance of the church until *he* by the power of God shall accept for *himself* the call of the Christ to be an instrument of his witnessing community?

I will.

What is the name given this child?

N———.

———, I baptize you in the name of the Father and of the Son, and of the Holy Spirit. Amen.

To the Congregation:

Dearly Beloved, *this child* is a member of Christ's Church because *he* is a child of God and thereby a child of the covenant. And you the people of this congregation in receiving this child promise with God's help to be *his* sponsor to the end that *he* may confess Christ as *his* Lord. I commend to your love and care *this child*, whom we this day recognize as a member of the family of God.

Let us pray (in unison):

O God, the giver of every good and perfect gift, we praise and thank thee for this gift of new life and the power to create life. Thou has allowed us to join with thee in the creation of a human personality with an eternal soul. Prepare us in thine own way for the rearing of the child thou hast entrusted to us that *he* may be duly brought up in the light and love of Thy Son Jesus, who is the Christ.   Amen.

—W. B. Pratt

168.

The Sacrament of Baptism of Infants

Minister: Dear friends, baptism is a sign of the grace of the Lord Jesus Christ, through which we share his righteousness and become participants in eternal life. Those receiving this sacrament are thereby marked as Christian disciples, and initiated into the fellowship of Christ's holy church. Our Lord has expressly given to little children a place among the people of God. "Let the children come to me," he said. "Do not hinder them, for to such belongs the kingdom of God." N____ and N____, you are presenting your child for holy baptism, and thus declaring your desire and intention to raise him as a Christian. Do you now, therefore, confess your own faith in the Lord Jesus Christ?

Parents: **We do.**

Minister: Will you keep alive and nurture the sense of privilege and responsibility that is now yours to live before this child as persons who demonstrate the reality of the gospel of Christ? Will you do your best to see that he is brought up in the Christian faith, that *he* is exposed frequently to the teachings and influences of Holy Scripture, and that *he* learns to revere and worship God?

Parents: **We will.**

Minister: Will you encourage *his* participation in the life of the community of God's people, the church, that *he* may receive its ministry and guidance until, under God, *he* shall accept for *himself* the gift of salvation, and be confirmed as a full and responsible member of Christ's holy church?

Parents: **We will.**

Minister: What name is given this child?

Parents: **N _____.**

Minister: N____, I baptize you in the name of the Father, and of the Son, and of the Holy Spirit. To you, the members of this church, we commend N____, whom we this day recognize as a member of the family of God in Christ. Speaking to you, I declare our mutual intention and promise to surround *him* and *his* family with prayerful affection and concern, and with the influences of our own lives, which we shall endeavor to pattern after the example of Christ, that N____ may be led to the fullness of the Christian life.

Let us pray (extemporaneously).

—John N. Strout
The United Methodist Church
Simi Valley, California

Weddings

A Service of Marriage

Marcella Sue Buehler and Bruce A. Sloan

David L. Semrad, presiding

A Statement from the Bride and Groom:

We are honored by your presence at this service of worship at which time we will enter the marriage covenant. We invite you to share in this, one of the happiest and holiest moments of our lives. It is hoped that you will join freely with us as we worship.

The Prelude

"Wedding Prayer"
"Whither Thou Goest"
"One Hand One Heart"
"O Perfect Love"

The Processional   "Trumpet Voluntary"   Purcell

The Call to Celebration and Worship

Hymn of Praise   "Praise to the Lord"   Hymnal, No. 55

The Prayer of Confession (in unison):

Almighty God, who has shown to man that life's meaning begins and ends in thy love, we admit that our search for personal meaning has been elsewhere. We have endlessly engaged in acquiring material possessions, expecting the ultimate to break through in such things as new cars, new homes, new clothes. We have deceived ourselves, as we have erected false idols. We have sought meaning in social relations, offering our lives and reputations for the sake of being where the action is. We have deceived ourselves, thinking that sociability means fulfillment. Even in our personal relationships, we seek to assert ourselves by saying and doing what people want us to say, for the sake of acceptance. We have deceived ourselves, for we have become carbon copies.

We offer these lives, O God, which speak of brokenness and boredom, hyperactivity and aloofness, self-centeredness and conformity. Make us whole with thy love. Help us to realize that all human activity is meaningful only as an expression of one's fundamental commitment to the reality of divine love. In the spirit of Christ which is love we pray. Amen.

The Word Which Makes Us Whole

Revelation 21:5
II Corinthians 5:17-18

The New Covenant Lesson

I Corinthians 13

The Witness to the Word

Sermon

The Charge to the Bride and Groom:

I require and charge you both, as you stand in the presence of God, that having considered the holy covenant you are about to make, you now declare before this community of faith your pledge of commitment, each to the other. Be well assured that if this commitment is kept ever before you in love, you will experience life's deep meaning in relationship, and your home will provide fulfillment for each of you.

The Questions:

(Bruce/Marcella) do you promise to take *(Marcella/Bruce)* as your *(wife/husband)*, to live together with *(her/him)* before the Lord of history and his creation? Will you love *(her/him)*, trust yourself to *(her/him)*, both in weakness and in strength, and receive *(her/his)* trust in you? Will you seek *(her/his)* growth toward freedom and maturity and in your life together say yes to the world?

The Giving of the Bride

The Exchange of Vows:

Joyfully and with utter seriousness, I *(Bruce/Marcella)* make with you *(Marcella/Bruce)* this covenant of marriage to share with you the task of freeing ourselves and others to receive and live the Word of Life. I promise to love and trust you, to speak the truth to you and hear it from you, to sustain and nurture you in faith and tenderness, and with you to receive every day as a gift of the Lord, until we are parted by death.

The Exchange of Rings:

In token and pledge of our constant faith and abiding love, with this ring I give myself to you, in the name of the Father, and of the Son, and of the Holy Spirit. Amen.

The Response of the Congregation:

As members of Christ's church, we rejoice with you in the covenant you have made. We pledge to support and strengthen your life together, to speak the truth to you in love, and with you to seek the way of life for others.

The Prayers and Lord's Prayer

The Benediction

The Recessional   "Trumpet Tune"   Purcell

Postlude

170.

The Celebration of the Marriage
of
Katherine Isabelle Kennedy
and
Richard Forrest Collman

The Preparation

Psalm 150 (NEB)   Minister

"Fanfare"   Dietrich Buxtehude, Organ, Brass

Processional

"Trumpet Voluntary"   Henry Purcell (1658-1696) Organ, Brass, Timpani

Invitation to Celebrate   Minister

Dear friends and loved ones of Katherine and Richard:
Throughout religious history, man has felt a need to celebrate the great moments of life. At those times he calls upon his friends to help commemorate the high moment. Man felt he could not do justice to the moment alone. But even more so he has felt the need to hold these experiences up before God. Thus in this sanctuary, before those loved ones and friends, and the presence of God, Katherine and Richard come to receive the sacrament of marriage.

"In Thee is Joy"	Organ
Chorale Prelude	J.S. Bach
Two Wedding Chorales J.S. Bach	Organ and Trumpets
"What God Hath Done, Is Rightly Done" "Now Thank We All Our God"	
"Toccata for Flutes" John Stanley	Organ
"My Spirit Be Joyful" J.S. Bach	Organ and Trumpets
Four Short Pieces Anthony Holborne	Brass Quintet

"The Marie-golde"
   "The Choise"
   "The Last Will and Testament"
   "The New-Yere's Gift"	

Chorale Prelude	
"Deck Thyself, My Soul, with Gladness" Johannes Brahms	Organ
"Rondo Franciase" Leon Boellmann	Organ
Invocation	Minister

O God, our Father, source of infinite love, bless us with a sense of your indwelling presence as we worship here. Keep us sensitive to the wonder of things which fill our days and give meaning to life. Deepen in us the level of our loving, both for those near and dear to us, and for those who, though strangers, need our concern.

Especially do we pray your blessing on these two who come here in this high moment of their lives. Be near to them as they make their promises to each other, that they shall pledge their vows with deepest sincerity, knowing full well the meaning of the words they say.

And do grant to us all, we pray, a heightened sense of the joy of life because we share this moment with them, in your loving spirit. Amen.

Hymn "For the Beauty of the Earth"	Hymnal, No. 35

The Confession

Call to Confession	Minister

Life is not all joy and happiness. We confess our shortcomings in the hope that a self-conscious awareness of who we are will enable us to overcome our faults.

Prayer of Confession	Minister and People

O God, we acknowledge the fact that too often we are alienated one from another. We choose to ignore our neighbor; we follow our own selfish inclinations. We confess our mistakes, made daily, and ask that those we offend and those we ignore may forgive us our weaknesses. Keep us from treating one another as objects, as persons who can serve our own selfish interests and needs. We are humble when we consider how ineffectual we are at really loving our neighbor. The words we speak and the ideas we preach turn to stones in our mouths when we fail to act on the principles in which we claim to believe. Amen.

Silence for Inward Renewal

Words of Assurance	Minister

The Almighty and merciful Lord grant you true repentance, forgiveness of all your sins, time for amendment and newness of life, and the grace and consolation of his Holy Spirit. Let us stand to celebrate our forgiveness!

Gloria Patri	Minister and People

God's Word and Man's Response

Call to Praise

    Minister: O Lord, open our lips.

    People: **And our mouths shall show forth your praise.**

    Minister: Praise the Lord!

    People: **The Lord's name be praised!**

Act of Praise (based on Isa. 61:10–62:5)

    People: **As the groom rejoices in his bride,**
                 so will God rejoice in you.

    Minister: God has clothed you in garments of light.
                 As the groom awaiting his bride,
                 And as the bride adorned in her jewels.

    People: **As the groom rejoices in his bride,**
                 so will God rejoice in you.

    Minister: As the earth makes seeds to spring up,
                 As the trees are blooming in the sun,
                 So will the Lord fulfill your future.

    People: **As the groom rejoices in his bride,**
                 so will God rejoice in you.

    Minister: You shall be named "No longer forsaken,"
                 Thus be your name forever "The Wedded,"
                 For the Lord is delighted with you.

    People: **As the groom rejoices in his bride,**
                 So will God rejoice in you.

Old Testament   Genesis 2:18-25 (NEB)

Musical Interpretation: "Der Herr Segne Euch" (May God Bless You)   J. S. Bach
    (Duet for tenor and baritone from the Wedding Cantata, No. 196)

    Der Herr segne euch, je mehr und mehr.
    euch, euch, und eure kinder,
    Der Herr segne euch!

    May God bless you, ever more and more.
    you, you, and all your children.
    May God bless you!

A Reading from the Song of Solomon 1:15–2:13 (NB, omitting 2:8, 9)
    "Dialogue of the Bride and Groom"

Musical Interpretation: Antiphon II "His left hand is under my Head,   Marcel Dupre
                and his right hand doth embrace me"

New Testament Lesson Colossians 3:12-17 (NEB)

Musical Interpretation: "They'll Know We are Christians by Our Love"   Peter Scholtes
        (printed on insert, introduced by organ, sung a capella)

The Contemporary Word   Rev. Richard Mathison

    "When Love is New"
    Text Colossians 3:16c "Sing thankfully in your hearts to God"

The Covenant of Marriage

Charge to the Couple   Minister

I require and charge you both, as you stand in the presence of loved ones and of God, that having considered the holy covenant you are about to make, you do now declare before this company your pledge of faith, each to the other. If the vows you make this day are kept, your life together will be full of joy and peace, and the home which you make shall abide through every unknown future.

Blessing of the Families

Minister: Who gives Katherine and Richard to each other and gives blessing to their marriage?

Parents: **We, their families, do.**

Vows (*said by bride and groom to each other, joining hands and facing each other*)

I, N____, take you, N____, to be my (wife/husband), to love and to trust from this day forward; for better, for worse; for richer, for poorer, in sickness and in health. As we continue to grow in our love for each other, I shall adore you with my body, listen and speak the truth to you, and seek to live each day as a gift of God, as long as we both shall live.

Blessing of the Rings   Minister

Wedding rings serve as the symbol of the covenant you have just spoken. They are the outward and visible sign of an inward and invisible love which binds your hearts together. As they are of the finest of earth's materials, so your love is of the richest of spiritual values. As rings are without edge or seam, having no beginning and no end, so they symbolize the perfection of a love that cannot end.

Let us pray: Bless these rings, our Father, to be the visible sign of the vows here made, that each who gives a ring and each who wears one may ever be reminded of their promises, evermore living and growing in the spirit of your love. Amen.

Bride and Groom:

N_____, I give you this ring as a sign of our covenant.

Declaration of Marriage   Minister

May your mutually exchanged covenant be for you both, again and again, a source of happiness and life-giving strength. I now proclaim that Katherine and Richard are husband and wife, in the name of the Father, through the Son, and in the Holy Spirit (pause for kiss). Let all people here and everywhere recognize and respect this holy union, now and ever.

Congregational Response:

We who witness their vows today will so order our lives that Katherine and Richard may be surrounded by our constant love, strengthened by our wise counsel, encouraged by our thoughtful concern, and supported by our steadfast love.

"The Call"   Words by George Herbert, Music by R. Vaughan Williams

The Wedding Prayer (husband and wife kneeling)   Minister

The Lord's Prayer   Minister and People

Hymn   "Now Thank We All Our God"   Hymnal, No. 49

The Sending Forth   Minister

Recessional:

"Trumpet Voluntary" Organ, brass, timpani   Henry Purcell

(Wedding party followed out by parents, families, ministers)

—Richard Collman
Appleton, Minnesota

171.

An Experimental Liturgy for Marriage

(At the announced hour, when the guests have assembled, let the wedding party take their places, the bride and groom facing the minister.)

Minister: Let us give attention to the purpose of this gathering.

People: **We have come here to rejoice,**

Minister: To unite N_____ and N_____ in marriage.

People: **This is a celebration in their honor.**

The Explanation of Marriage

Minister: This celebration is a proper act for the friends and relatives of this couple. Our participation in this ceremony signifies the good wishes we have for the bride and groom.

We recognize in this celebration the fulfillment of dual importancies. First this is a civil ceremony, a social custom signifying that the laws of the state of _____ have been properly observed in the marriage of this man and this woman. As the representative of this state, I charge you with being truthful in your exchange of vows and being faithful in the life you will share.

This is also a religious ceremony. Religious, as when a man and a woman promise together in marriage to love and honor each other; then, they stand in the presence of all they cherish. In the presence of justice, beauty, truth, and honor; may your love for one another be the very center of human experience.

The Exchanging of Vows

Groom: N_____ , I promise to be your faithful husband, to love and serve you as long as love or life shall last.

Bride: N_____ , I promise to be your faithful wife, to love and serve you as long as love or life shall last.

Minister: Marriage within our culture has traditionally been sealed by the exchanging of vows of man and woman. It is fitting that this tradition be continued in this marriage. To signify these vows in the visible world, rings are exchanged. These rings become symbols that this man and this woman are husband and wife.

The Exchanging of Rings

Groom: N_____ , I give you this ring as a sign of my promise.

Bride: N_____ , I give you this ring as a sign of my promise.

The Joining of Hands

Minister: The Scriptures: "Love is patient and kind; love is not jealous nor boastful; it is not arrogant or rude. Love does not insist on its own way; it is not irritable or resentful; it does not rejoice at wrong, but rejoices in right. Love bears all things, believes all things, hopes all things, endures all things. Love never ends" (I Cor. 13:4-8 RSV).

The Pronouncement of Marriage

Minister: N_____ and N_____ , you are now husband and wife according to the church and the law of this state. Become one another. Fulfill these vows. Love and serve one another.

The Marriage Kiss

The Response by the People:

People: **We have witnessed it. They are married.**

Minister: Mr. and Mrs._____, I affix my seal to these proceedings.

People: **We recognize you as husband and wife.**

The Dismissal:

Minister: Go into the world and fulfill your lives. Hold fast to your ideals. Give one another new experiences of joy. Challenge one another that you might grow together. May this love now sealed with marriage mature and enrich the experiences of you both. May your home be a happy one and your lives fulfilled. Go, the marriage is complete.

(Let there be a celebration and rejoicing.)

—John H. Curtis

172.

A Service for the Celebration of Marriage

Description:

This wedding service is the result of several student weddings where the couple and the minister have worked together to develop an order which 1) places the celebration of marriage in the context of a meaningful liturgy; 2) offers the congregation an important place in the total act of worship; 3) recognizes the responsibility of the parents and friends; and 4) uses language which is contemporary.

The service here presented is a basic liturgy which can be augmented with music, contemporary readings, or other acts of celebration.

Prelude

Processional

Call to Worship

Minister: We come this afternoon to share in the celebration of the marriage of N_____ and N_____.

People: **We rejoice in their love and gladly celebrate this occasion with them.**

Minister: Their love is grounded in the love of God as understood through Jesus whom we call Christ.

People: **We receive them in their faith and pray that God may bless them in their marriage covenant.**

Hymn of Praise

Contemporary Reading

The Word in Scripture (I Cor. 13 TEV)

Minister: I may be able to speak in the languages of man and even of angels,

People: **But if I have not love, my speech is no more than a noisy gong or a clanging bell.**

Minister: I may have the gift of inspired preaching; I may have all knowledge and understand all secrets; I may have all the faith needed to move mountains—

People: **But if I have not love, I am nothing.**

Minister: I may give away everything I have, and even give up my body to be burned—

People: **But if I have not love, it does me no good.**

Minister: Love is patient and kind; love is not jealous, or conceited, or proud;

People: **Love is not ill-mannered, or selfish, or irritable; love does not keep a record of wrongs;**

Minister; Love is not happy with evil, but is happy with the truth.

People: **Love never gives up: its faith, hope, and patience never fail.**

Minister: Love is eternal. There are inspired messages, but they are temporary; there are gifts of speaking, but they will cease; there is knowledge, but it will pass.

People: **For our gifts of knowledge and of inspired messages are only partial; but when what is perfect comes, then what is partial will disappear.**

Minister: When I was a child, my speech, feelings, and thinking were all those of a child; now that I am a man, I have no more use for childish ways.

People: **What we see now is like the dim image in a mirror; then we shall see face to face. What I know now is only partial; then it will be complete, as complete as God's knowledge of me.**

Minister: Meanwhile these three remain: faith, hope and love;

People: **And the greatest of these is love.**

Homily

Questions

To the Groom: N_____ , will you have N_____ to be your wife? Will you live and work with her in building a Christian home? Will you share with her your joys and sorrows, your needs and dreams? Will you offer her the freedom and support she needs to fulfill her own life?

Response: I will.

To the Bride: N_____ , will you have N_____ to be your husband? Will you live and work with him in building a Christian home? Will you share with him your joys and sorrows, your needs and dreams? Will you offer him the freedom and support he needs to fulfill his own life?

Response: I will.

To the Parents: Mr. and Mrs. N_____ and Mr. and Mrs. N_____ , will you give your blessing to N_____ and N_____ in their new relationship? Will you support them with the freedom and love which they need? Will you share your experience and wisdom with them, and seek to learn from them as well?

Response: We will.

To the Congregation:

    Will you pledge your support to N_____ and N_____ in their new relationship? Will you share with them the fellowship and joy of their new home? Will you be with them in time of need when they seek your help?

Response: **We will.**

Exchange of Vows and Rings

I, N_____ , take you, N_____ , to be my wife, to live with you according to God's purposes. I promise to love and trust you; to speak the truth to you and to hear it from you; to sustain and nurture you; and with you to receive each day as a gift from God. As a symbol of our precious and eternal love, I give you this ring. Amen.

I, N_____ , take you, N_____, to be my husband, to live with you according to God's purposes. I promise to love and trust you; to speak the truth to you and to hear it from you; to sustain and nurture you; and with you to receive each day as a gift from God. As a symbol of our precious and eternal love, I give you this ring. Amen.

Pronouncement of Marriage

Wedding Prayers

Minister:	God, who gives life to all people and meaning to every moment; we pray that N_____ and N_____may be faithful to the covenant they have made before us. May the home they establish be a place of peace and love in which all may share. May your grace and love be their constant companion as they fulfill their life together. Amen.
Bride and Groom:	Our Father, as we begin this new relationship together, give us the understanding, the patience, and the skills to fulfill your purpose in our lives. We ask your continued presence that we may learn the art of lasting love. Amen.
Congregation:	**Our Father, we rejoice with N_____ and N_____. We thank you for their families and friends who have helped to shape their lives. We thank you for the opportunities and events which challenge them to their life's work. We thank you for their ever-deepening relationship and their decision to share the future together. We pray that we may be responsible witnesses to them, enabling them to share their lives for the sake of all mankind. Amen.**

Hymn or Song of Celebration

Benediction

Postlude

—Don Collins
United Ministry in Higher Education
Wisconsin State University
Oshkosh, Wisconsin 54901

174.

Music in the Christian Marriage Ceremony

I. The Ceremony

A) It is an act of Christian worship in which God is the center.

The order for the solemnization of matrimony is a part of the ritual of The United Methodist Church. It is clearly to be regarded by United Methodists as a specifically Christian act, distinguished alike from a civil ceremony or the rite of a non-Christian religion. The minister, authorized by the church to officiate at this sacred service, instructs the congregation in the first sentence of the ritual that the gathering is "in the sight of God." The ceremony is thus marked as God-centered worship.

The minister, therefore, along with the Worship Commission, the Music Committee, and the responsible musicians in the local church, must cultivate a sense of worship with regard to the wedding ceremony, including the arrangement of music in keeping with both the joy and the solemnity of the occasion.

B) It is the Christian Church's corporate worship, not a private act.

Having instructed the congregation that the act is performed "in the sight of God," the minister continues to acknowledge that the ceremony is "in the presence of these witnesses." The ceremony is thus marked as corporate worship of the Christian community.

The community has a great deal at stake in the establishment of a new home. Through legal and professional agencies society seeks to guide, and even control, some aspects of marriage. The Christian fellowship should be especially eager to offer its counsel and support to the young people, just as it rejoices with them in their happiness. One of the many ways in which this can be accomplished is through the presence and participation of the worshiping congregation in the sacred act of marriage. Music should be chosen to help accomplish this end. Hymns should be encouraged as elements of the service in which the people participate audibly. The congregation may sing the processional, or a hymn of praise after the processional. Clergymen, choirs, or soloists should not be allowed to offer the Lord's Prayer, which according to the New Testament and the United Methodist ritual belongs to the disciples together.

We may take our clue for music within the ceremony from yet another phrase delivered by the minister in his opening statement. We should enter into this sacred act "reverently, discreetly, and in the fear of God." Merrymaking and the many social customs have a place in family celebrations and receptions. It is with regard to the church service that a holy dignity is appropriate, and likewise that the minister, music committee, and organist or director must assume direct obligations.

If, for example, a bride has a favorite wedding song which does not belong in Christian worship, it is the duty of pastor and music leader to urge that it be sung at a family dinner or at the reception, but not at the ceremony.

II. The Music

Whatever else we may say concerning the wedding ceremony we must begin with the basic statement that it is an act of worship. There is ample evidence to support this position in the words of the ritual itself and in the biblical understanding of Christian marriage. Clearly God is the center of this service as he is the focal point of all worship!

We may determine what we should do, say, play, or sing by asking the one question that is relevant—how can we *properly* and *adequately* honor God on this occasion when persons come to deepen their understanding of their relationship to him and to each other in the context of the establishment of a new Christian home? We are equipped to answer this question only to the degree that we see clearly the difference between Christian marriage on one hand, and required civil procedure and societal custom on the other. This difference should be the sole reason we come to the church rather than the courthouse or a judge's chamber. This difference is the sole reason for asking how shall we express thanksgiving to God for our understanding of Christian marriage and pledging ourselves to the faithful living-out of our understanding, rather than simply asking what would we like to do or have done at our wedding. This difference allows us to witness to the unique nature of Christian marriage rather than be placed in the inadequate role of entertaining our guests. This difference lifts up God's church with all her banners flying to challenge the best in men rather than allowing the world to turn God's church into a servant of societal custom and whim!

The music we choose will be in keeping with the joy and solemnity of the occasion, selected because it expresses the unique nature of Christian marriage rather than because of the personal desires of the participants. Minister, musician, bridal couple, having mutually asked how they may honor God and celebrate the formation of a new Christian home, may together seek adequate texts and music for such expression. The musicial portions of the service will thusly be chosen with purposeful intention rather than from custom, tradition, or nostalgia.

In the final analysis we must decide upon specific musical items, using our understanding of the nature of Christian marriage as a primary criterion in the selection. Openness to the biblical understanding of Christian marriage will be required as we examine specific pieces of music, and the task will not be a simple one. It will be helpful to isolate the component parts of music and to analyze the relationship each bears to the act of worship.

A) Texts

During their captivity in Babylonia the Jews asked the pointed question, "How shall we sing the Lord's song in a strange land?" Our task is identical with theirs, for we are called to sing the Lord's song, and we cannot go out and do our own thing! Our thing is not necessarily the Lord's song, and we are not in the entertainment business, nor for that matter, are we primarily concerned with the creation of aesthetics. However, before we can ask, How shall we sing? we must ask the prior question, What shall we sing? It was not because they did not know how to sing that the Jews could not sing the Lord's song. They could not sing precisly because they did not know what to sing.

What then, is the Lord's song? This is indeed a theological question. What shall we sing is a question of content in terms of a given text. How shall we sing is a question of form and strategy. The question of content is the one that forces every man to be a theologian, a thinker about God. The alternatives open to us are not, as is often supposed, to be or not to be a theologian, but rather to be a diligent and responsible theologian, or to be a misinformed, inadequate one.

We shall never sing the Lord's song if we do not weigh the content of our singing before the tribunal of biblical evidence concerning the nature and mission of the church, subsequent scholarly study, and historical practice.

Texts set forth specific intellectual ideas, or at least pretend to do so. In most cases it is not difficult to determine if a text is concerned with a secular or Christian view of marriage, although the mere mention of God or Christ is in itself not sufficient to insure the latter, especially in recent times. Texts that promote an obviously non-Christian position are compatible with a civil ceremony or appropriate on the occasion of the rehearsal dinner or reception, but cannot celebrate our understanding of the nature of Christian marriage, adequately express our praise and thanksgiving to God, the center of our worship, or give testimony to our understanding of this sacred act to those who have come to join with us on this occasion.

Texts, then, must be of a specifically Christian nature, supporting the biblical view of Christian marriage and avoiding the promotion of the secular interpretation of matrimony.

B) The Music Itself

If content is a theological matter and form is a matter of strategy and communication, how shall we think about the media in which some explicit verbal message is attired, or more difficult, how shall we evaluate the media when the verbal message is absent? For the student of musical style and history, and for those whose background and exposure has given them a sense of aesthetic appreciation, the task is academic. They are turned on by quality and skillful writing. They are turned off by shoddy and cheap work. But there is one other element of music, the most significant element as far as music in the church is concerned, that all recognize and to which all respond, although few would verbalize concerning it. It is the *symbolic nature* of music which affects each person at the gut-level—where he lives. No one has to be a scholar to recognize that all musical styles possess symbolic qualities. No one needs technical understanding to recognize the folk-rock style, which conjures up for each of us the current youth sub-culture of which it is symbolic. Older individuals even though they may be totally incapable of telling one note from another, immediately perceive the peculiar style of love ballad made popular by Jeanette MacDonald and Nelson Eddy. Along with the perception of the style, comes a haunting nostalgia which the symbolic music has power to arouse. This music holds up certain values, a certain life-style, and evokes from the listener a predictable reaction. Those of us who perform this music have an obvious obligation to know what we are apt to cause to be the center of concern for those who listen. Let us explore a bit further.

A sixteenth-century motet seems to be symbolic of the Renaissance view of the educated man and his society. The individual vocal lines, while complete and independent in themselves, nevertheless complement each other in an organized scheme. Each has a complete life in itself and none dominates the others. The harmonious whole is a result of the several parts living within the rules of a prescribed system, but doing so with individual character and completeness.

The folkrock music of the young speaks eloquently for their culture. The rudimentary and limited harmonies are perhaps reflections of a deep desire for a return to the basic and elemental in human living. The parallel movement of these harmonies seems to be an appeal for unity and comradeship, with no divisive individualism to disturb the almost regimented conformity of parallel movement. To participate in this music, one has only to participate.

That is to say, the desire to be a part of the scene is the only requirement for participation, which is based upon desire rather than discipline. I could suggest that this is symbolic of the reaction on the part of the young to a feeling of having been locked out by adults. No one is locked out in their culture.

The point to be made is that all music is symbolic of a life-style. It remains for us—the church—to ask if it is symbolic of the Lord's song. If we want to sing the Lord's song in this very strange land the task is clear. We must first determine what the Lord's song really is, and select the media that effectively symbolize that song to our times. I am not really certain any of us know what those media are, or will be. I am not certain any single medium can be selected to speak to our pluralistic society. However, if each of us—clergy, laity, musicians—will continue to ask why we think specific texts and music, both theologically and symbolically represent the Lord's song, we will have made a beginning.

C) Idiomatic Composition

All music is composed with specific instruments in mind. Good musical composition is idiomatically compatable with the nature of the instruments upon which it is intended to be performed. It is seldom, if ever, possible to effectively perform violin, piano, or vocal compositions on a pipe organ. Additionally, we must raise the question of our right to use the creative work of a composer in a way he did not intend it to be used. There is an inexhaustible supply of organ literature. Music performed on the organ should be limited to the compositions intended for performance on that instrument.

D) The Integrity of the Performer

Every man knows what he does best. When a church musician plays to the glory of God he has an inherent right to be allowed to do those things which he feels he is most capable of doing. This, I suppose, is the major distinction between being a church musician and a popular entertainer. The former offers his best as an act of praise to God, the latter selects his material by the demands of the market. If we allow the church to bow to the demands of the popular taste, we have forgotten what our business is, and in effect, we have put the church of Jesus Christ out of business.

Our business is not to entertain, or to create pure aesthetics, or to arouse nostalgia, but rather to challenge men to a better way of life through our witness to the good news of our common faith.

—Charles Merritt

(Note: Some of the above material was derived from *A Wedding Manual* [Nashville: Abingdon Press, 1965].)

Funerals

174.

A Remembrance Service
for
Mona Edith Kewish, Deaconess
The Interchurch Center, New York City

Organ Voluntary: Mary Monroe Payne, Organist

Call to Worship: Betsy K. Ewing, Deaconess
                    Assistant General Secretary, National Division, Board of Missions UMC

Leader: We ~~have gathered~~ are here to celebrate the entry of ~~Mona Kewish~~ George Empey into life ~~eternal.~~ beyond life

People: **To affirm with praise and thanksgiving the goodness of the Lord.**

Leader: Let us rejoice in his presence with us, in death as in life, among those who mourn as with those who now see him face to face.

People: **Our lips will ~~shout for joy~~ praise, for his love is over all that he has made. Blessed be his glorious name forever!**

Hymn of Thanksgiving "Now Thank We All Our God"   Hymnal, No. 49

Prayer ~~of Confession~~ (unison):

O God, our Father, from whom we come, and unto whom our spirits return, we confess to thee our slowness to accept death as part of thy plan for life. We confess our reluctance to commit to thee those whom we love. Give us grace, in the presence of death, to worship thee and to trust thy care with confidence. Through Jesus Christ our Lord, Amen.

~~Words of~~ Assurance: of Pardon

Jesus said, "If you believe, you will see the wonder of what God can do. I myself, am the Resurrection and the Life. The man who believes in me will live even though he dies, and anyone who is alive and believes in me will never die at all."

Take heart, then, that in faith there is life for us all! By his great mercy, we have been born anew to a living hope.

The Psalter   Hymnal, No. 563

The Lord is my light and my salvation;
  WHOM SHALL I FEAR?
The Lord is the stronghold of my life:
  OF WHOM SHALL I BE AFRAID?
When evildoers assail me, uttering slanders against me,
  MY ADVERSARIES AND FOES, THEY SHALL STUMBLE AND FALL.
Though a host encamp against me,
  YET WILL I BE CONFIDENT.
One thing have I asked of the Lord.
  THAT WILL I SEEK AFTER:
That I may dwell in the house of the Lord all the days of my life
  TO BEHOLD THE BEAUTY OF THE LORD, AND TO INQUIRE IN HIS TEMPLE.
For he will hide me in his shelter in the day of trouble.
  HE WILL SET ME HIGH UPON A ROCK.
And now my head shall be lifted up above my enemies round about me.
  I WILL SING AND MAKE MELODY TO THE LORD.

Hear, O Lord, when I cry aloud
 BE GRACIOUS TO ME AND ANSWER ME.
Thou has said, "Seek ~~ye~~ my face."
 MY HEART SAYS TO ~~THEE~~, "THY FACE, LORD, DO I SEEK."
I believe that I shall see the goodness of the Lord
 in the land of the living!
 WAIT FOR THE LORD: BE STRONG, AND LET YOUR HEART TAKE
 COURAGE: YEA, WAIT FOR THE LORD!

Hymn of Affirmation: "Ten Thousand Times Ten Thousand"

Words of Faith from Scripture: George Teague, Associate Minister,
 Christ United Methodist Church, New York City

Comfort from the Gospel: John 14:1-7. 15-21, 24-31 (NEB)
Confidence from the Epistle: Romans 8:14-25, 28, 31-32 (Phillips)

Prayer of the Faithful:

~~Father~~ of all, we have joy at this time in all who have faithfully lived and in all who have peacefully died. We thank ~~thee~~ for all fair memories and all living hopes: for the sacred ties that bind us to the unseen world: for the ~~dear and~~ faithful dead who compass us as a cloud of witnesses, and who make the distant heaven a home to our hearts. May we be followers of those who now inherit the promises; through Jesus Christ our Lord. Amen.

The Word of Comfort and Victory: Tracey K. Jones, Jr. General Secretary,
 Board of Missions, UMC

Prayer

Hymn of Victory "For All the Saints"   Hymnal, No. 537

Benediction:

Leader: We feel the pain of separation; we are conscious of our loss, but we have hope in Jesus Christ.

People: **We have given thanks to him from whom comes life and death and who surrounds us in both. We have affirmed our faith and rejoiced in Christ's victory over death, which is his promise to us.**

Leader: Well, then, shall tribulation, or distress or persecution, or famine or nakedness, or peril or sword separate us from the love of Christ?

People: **No, in all these things we are more than conquerors through him who loves us. For we are sure that neither death nor life, nor angels nor principalities, nor things present nor things to come, nor powers nor height nor depth, nor anything else in all creation will be able to separate us from the love of God in Christ Jesus our Lord!**

The Doxology

—Jeanne Audrey Powers
Room 1375
475 Riverside Drive
New York, New York

172

175.

A Service to Honor
The Memory of
The Rev. Edwin H. Witman
September 18, 1971
Santa Monica, California, First United Methodist Church

Order of Worship

Prelude (*from the hymns of praise and thanksgiving in the Hymnal*)

Procession

(*The five participating clergy, the closed, plain and unadorned casket, followed by the eight pallbearers—four sons, two granddaughters, one grandson, and one nephew. Organ music was Bach's "Jesu, Joy of Man's Desiring."*)

Call to Worship — The Rev. Joseph Parshall

Hymn   "O For a Thousand Tongues to Sing" — Hymnal, No. 1

Invocation

Old Testament Lesson — The Rev. Irwin Trotter

Psalm 100 read responsively

Affirmation of Faith *(to be shared by all):*

We know that in everything God works for good with those who love him, who are called according to his purpose. What then shall we say to this? If God is for us, who is against us? Who shall separate us from the love of Christ? Shall tribulation, or distress, or persecution, or famine, or nakedness, or peril, or sword? No, in all these things we are more than conquerors through him who loved us. For I am sure that neither death, nor life, nor angels, nor principalities, nor things present, nor things to come, nor powers nor height, nor depth. nor anything else in all creation, will be able to separate us from the love of God in Christ Jesus our Lord. (selected from Romans 8, RSV)

Gloria Patri

New Testament Lesson — The Rev. Mortimer Dean
    II Timothy 4:1-8
    I Corinthians 13

Hymn   "Amazing Grace! How Sweet the Sound" — Hymnal, No. 92

Biographical statement — The Rev. Paul Woudenberg

Eulogy — The Rev. Kenneth A. Carlson

Anthem   "Hallelujah Chorus" — Handel

Closing Prayers (*a collection of prayer in felt response to the experience of worship.*)

Hymn   "For All the Saints" — Hymnal, No. 536

Benediction

Recessional   "A Mighty Fortress is our God"

(*clergy and pallbearers with casket go out. The congregation was invited to dismiss as they would from any other service of worship. The casket was immediately placed in the hearse by the pallbearers.*)

Postlude (*Powerful, exultant music*)

—Frank M. Witman
The United Methodist Church
Simi Valley, California

173

Editor's Note: Frank Witman has been one of the most consistent contributors to the *Ventures* series. Few articles received have been as moving as this service prepared by Mr. Witman for the funeral of his father and the correspondence which accompanied it. There is certainly a "powerful, exultant music" that sounds through a service of worship like this.

Annual Conference Worship — Ordinations

This section is significant because some of the most important acts of worship take place in the annual conference. The service of the Northern Illinois Conference is an excellent example of how the historic dimensions of faith come alive today. The services of ordination are thoughtful explorations of the way in which this crucial act can most meaningfully and adequately be expressed in our day.

Annual Conference Commissions on Worship are becoming both more active and more creative. The Minnesota Conference has prepared an anthology of contemporary liturgy, Part 2, entitled "A Time to Celebrate," which is edited by Richard F. Collman. Copies are available from the Minnesota Annual Conference. The United Methodist Church, Room 400, 122 West Franklin, Minneapolis, Minnesota, 55404.

Another outstanding annual conference anthology is that of the Virginia Conference entitled "Living Acts of Worship." It was prepared by a task force under the leadership of James D. Righter, and further information on this project may be secured from the Rev. Raymond F. Wrenn, 4016 West Broad Street, Richmond, Virginia, 23230.

In the Washington area, annual conference worship has been enhanced by booklets for worship from the Baltimore Annual Conference, which show an excellent combination of the traditional and the contemporary. Further, this Conference Commission on Worship prepared a booklet entitled "Worship Concepts," edited by Stanley G. Harrell, which provides helpful commentary on basic aspects of worship.

The Peninsula Conference prepared a series of pre-conference meditations in 1970 on the theme of peace, which developed the resource of personal devotions in an uncommon and socially sensitive way.

In a time when authenticity is a special hallmark of worship regional units such as the annual conference have a distinctive role to play, both in stimulating worship and helping develop standards for it. Indications are that this responsibility is being assumed and this Project on Worship encourages the annual conference commissions and invites them to submit materials for wider sharing.

176.

The Northern Illinois Conference
At Worship

Celebrating: *Church*

Historically, Methodists have known church more in conference than in congregation. For Methodists parish means world, not locality. Clergy, and more and more, laity too, are itinerants, moving from place to place from time to time. So our more abiding abode is the "Connexion." We may live, grow, and die in this, our family of faith.

John Wesley himself initiated the singing of the following hymn in conference worship, and for more than two centuries Methodists have sung this hymn celebrating the journeying mercies of Providence which bring together, each person in place, the church in conference. So now we stand to celebrate this very great grace of God:

"And Are We Yet Alive?"   Hymnal, No. 336

(still standing)

The Lord is with you,

AND WITH YOU ALSO,

Lift up your hearts.

WE LIFT THEM UP TO THE LORD.

Let us give thanks to the Lord our God.

IT IS ALWAYS RIGHT TO GIVE HIM THANKS AND PRAISE.

For your covenant with us that makes us church, and for our commitment to you and one another which makes us ministry.

WE EVER GIVE THANKS TO YOU, LORD OUR GOD.

For all promised empowering from on high: to proclaim your Word, fulfill all prophesy, and to practice every love,

YOUR CHURCH EVER PRAISES YOU, LORD OUR GOD.

For every correction and chastisement of your church until our union with you with one another is made perfect.

TEACH US TO BE GRATEFUL, LORD OUR GOD.

For all the faithfulness in all the years, passed to us as heritage in your church; for all testings in our time; for children who follow us,

WE ASCRIBE ALL GLORY TO YOU, LORD OUR GOD.

Most of all, for the whole world which we serve that you may save, with sure and certain hope that a better world is to come,

WE PRAISE AND BLESS AND MAGNIFY AND WORSHIP AND HONOR YOU, LORD OUR GOD, THROUGH JESUS CHRIST, YOUR SON, OUR SAVIOR. AMEN AND AMEN.

Confessing: *Church*
(seated bowed)

If as conference we are content to be less than church,

FORGIVE AND REDEEM US, JESUS CHRIST.

If we do not manifest the graciousness of your grace in debate and dispute,

GENTLE AND SUBDUE US, JESUS CHRIST.

Bend the hearts of the older to the younger, and the spirits of the younger to their elders, so that all may hear one another in love, and thus hear you in truth,

WE HUMBLY PRAY, JESUS CHRIST.

Make us open to strangers among us and warm our welcome to newcomers, so that all may share the richness of a mutual ministry.

WE ASK OF YOUR GRACE, JESUS CHRIST.

Teach us to have watch-care over one another's souls, to gladly bear one another's burdens, to seek the fullest enlargement of every ministry among us,

HEAR OUR PRAYER, JESUS CHRIST.

Save us in all our strivings: from every suspicion and every rejection of one another, from all rivalry for place or power or position, from all the drives of ambition, from every sin and selfishness,

IN YOUR MERCY, IN YOUR GREAT MERCY, IN YOUR VERY GREAT MERCY, JESUS CHRIST!

Now, as newly forgiven, we stand to sing Charles Wesley's greatest hymn of hope and assurance. He wrote it to mark the anniversary of his own conversion. This hymn is said "to strike the key-note of the whole of Methodism, that multitudinous chorus whose voices, like the sound of great waters, encompassed the world."

"O for a Thousand Tongues to Sing"   Hymnal, No. 1

Called: *Church*
(still standing)

Send us from church here to be church everywhere, every way with pure lives, by honest work, in loving care.

WE ASK IN FAITH, OUR FATHER.

Steady us with courage, inflame the passion of our discipleship, but temper us with sound judgment and disciplined obedience; unfold among us every gift and grace of ministry.

WE ASK ONLY FOR JESUS' SAKE, OUR FATHER.

Now open to us all the doors of service we are to enter; give us every word of your Word to speak openly before men; make plain our pilgrimage as we walk by faith; and finally bring us as good and faithful servants, together, and at last, to the church made perfect in heaven.

FAITH MAKES US BOLD IN BELIEVING, AS WE ASK IN THE NAME OF ONE GOD, FATHER, SON, AND HOLY SPIRIT. ALLELUIA!

So we may sing now Charles Wesley's hymn for closing conference worship:

"And Let Our Bodies Part"   Tune: Boylston

This is the ascription offered at your baptism. Let us renew it together in sacramental grace:

Now unto him who is able to keep you from falling, and to present you faultless before the presence of his glory with exceeding joy, to the only wise God our savior,

Unison: be glory and majesty,
              dominion and power,
              both now
              and evermore.
              Amen.

—William F. Dunkle, Jr.

Service of Ordination

June 27, 1972
First United Methodist Church
Albany, Oregon

Preparation Music

Hymn of Celebration   "Here We Are"   *Ventures in Song*, p. 104

Call to Celebration

> Liturgist: In the name of Jesus and in the spirit of community, I call you to celebration.
>
> Community: **We come to join together in that place we call the church, to lift up our lives, words, thoughts, and actions so as to make this time together a celebration.**
>
> Liturgist: The Spirit of the Lord is upon us, he has called us to this time and to this life of love and service.
>
> Community: **We recognize the great call that Jesus speaks to us, we accept his call, and gather here into that special community, the Church, to renew our lives, make new loyalties, and revitalize our commitment to the Christian way of living and loving.**

Call to Confession

> Liturgist: We have gathered to celebrate, but there is much that is wrong in our world and much that is not right in our own lives.
>
> Community: **It is hard for us to recognize ourselves as sinners, but when we remember the life and ministry of Jesus, we know we have a long way to go in living the Gospel fully.**
>
> Liturgist: In the spirit of prayer, I call you to confession.

Prayer of Confession (Community)

We confess to you, O God, that we are not the people we would like to be. Yet we believe that you know us as we are, and love us. Teach us to accept ourselves as you do. Give us the courage to put our trust in your guiding power. We also sense that we share in the unrest in our world. Forgive indifference to human suffering, reliance on weapons of terror, and any preoccupation with material things. And forgive us Christians for being unsure of our good news, and slow to invite others to join in vital worship. Amen.

Words of New Life

> Liturgist: We have confessed our sins, now it is time to forget the past and to live new lives in the present. God forgives us, our hope is that we can start anew, following a new life of loving, forgiving, serving, and caring.
>
> Community: **In the newness of this moment, which is filled with exciting possibilities, we make this statement of faith and belief.**

Affirming the Church (Community)

We gather in the name of Jesus, and we think that is all to being the church. But the church is much, much more. It is a holy community. It is a place where men walk as brothers. There may be differences of belief, but the differences should not divide, for division breaks down the holy community. It destroys the ministry of Jesus.

The church is more than people, but its strength arises through faithful living.
The church gathers to celebrate the possibility of new life,
But then it scatters into all the world to work and serve.

If we only practice the church on Sunday morning, it becomes corrupt, destructive, and only a club.
It is in service done for others, that brings the reason for the church to be.

Offering (*for Ministerial Education Fund*)

Reading of the Scripture   II Timothy 3:10-4:5

Ordination Sermon "Wesley, This Is Your Life"
        Bishop W. Maynard Sparks

Liturgy of Ordination *(all ministers present responding)*

Liturgist:	Be a good minister of Jesus the Christ, filled by the Word of God, and directed by his Spirit. Become a faithful steward of Word and sacrament, in preaching, teaching, worship, service, and witness. Be a useful servant of the people of God; rejoice in beauty, endure affliction with patience, and in all things seek to identify the forms of God's presence.
Ministers:	By so doing, we would commend ourselves to every man's conscience in the sight of God.
Community:	**Beware of pride and sin.**
Ministers:	We have a treasure in earthen vessels, to show that the transcendent power of God belongs to him and not to us.
Community:	**But can you endure?**
Ministers:	Although afflicted, we shall not be crushed; although perplexed, we shall not be driven to despair; although struck down, we shall not be destroyed; for it is the God who said, "Let light shine out of darkness," who has shone in our hearts to give the light of the knowledge of the glory of God in the face of Christ. We have the same faith as the one who wrote, "I believed, and so I spoke." We too believe, and so we speak.
Community:	**But what does it profit if a man says he has faith but not works?**
Liturgist:	It is written; You will know them by their fruits; every sound tree bears good fruit, but the bad tree bears evil fruit. A sound tree cannot bear evil fruit, nor can a bad tree bear good fruit; thus you will know them by their fruits.
Community:	**Tend the flock of God that is your charge, not by constraint, but willingly, not for shameful gain, but eagerly, not domineering over those in your charge, but being examples to the flock.**
	Do your best to present yourself to God as one approved, a workman who has no need to be ashamed, rightly handling the word of truth.
Ministers:	We would speak clearly and simply as followers of him who came to preach good news to the poor, to proclaim release to the captives, and recovering of sight to the blind, to set at liberty those who are oppressed, to proclaim the acceptable year of the Lord.
Liturgist:	Let us pray.
All:	**O Lord God, Heavenly Father, who has called us through Christ to be partakers in this gracious covenant, we take upon ourselves with joy the yoke of obedience, and engage ourselves, for the love of thee, to seek and do thy perfect will. We are no longer our own but thine. Put us to what thou wilt; put us to doing; put us to suffering; let us be employed for thee or laid aside for thee, exalted for thee or brought low for thee, let us be full, let us be empty, let us have all things, let us have nothing; we freely yield all things to thy pleasure and will, through Jesus Christ our Lord. Amen.**

Ordination Epistle   Ephesians 3:7-9; 4:11-13

Presentation of Ordinand

The Examination *(Statement by the Bishop)*

The Examination Questions

Bishop: Do you believe in one God, Father, Son, and Holy Spirit, and do you confess Jesus Christ as your Lord and Savior?

Ordinand: I DO.

Bishop: Are you persuaded that the Scriptures of the Old and New Testaments convey the Word of God and are the unique and authoritative standards of the church's life, its worship, witness, teaching, and mission for the world?

Ordinand: I AM SO PERSUADED.

Bishop: Will you be diligent in understanding the faith to which the creeds, confessions, and doctrines of the church bear witness, and in proclaiming by word and action the truth of the Gospel as God gives you opportunity?

Ordinand: I WILL, THE LORD BEING MY HELPER.

Bishop: Do you believe in your heart that you are truly called of God in this sacred ministry, with its obligations and opportunities for the service of God and men?

Ordinand: IN SO FAR AS I KNOW MY OWN HEART, I DO SO BELIEVE.

Bishop: Will you faithfully preach and teach the Gospel proclaiming forth the judgment and healing of God? Will you give faithful service to the people committed to your care, minister the sacraments as ordered by our Lord Jesus Christ, and care for the poor, the bewildered, and the oppressed for Christ's sake?

Ordinand: I WILL, THE LORD BEING MY HELPER.

Bishop: Will you endeavor to be a steadfast and prayerful disciple, daily following the rule and teaching of our Lord, to the end that your life and the lives you touch may be fashioned by the Gospel?

Ordinand: I WILL, GOD BEING MY HELPER.

Bishop: Will you be loyal to the fellowship of this church, accepting its order and discipline, to the end that it may more and more realize the will of God in Christ for this world?

Ordinand: I WILL, BY THE HELP OF GOD.

Conferring of Orders

Veni, Creator Spiritus

Liturgist: Come, Holy Ghost, our souls inspire,

Community: **And lighten with celestial fire.**

Liturgist: Thou the anointing Spirit art,

Community: **Who dost thy sevenfold gifts impart.**

Liturgist: Thy blessed unction from above

Community: **Is comfort, life, and fire of love.**

Liturgist: Enable with perpetual light

Community: **The dullness of our blinded sight.**

Liturgist: Anoint and cheer our soiled face

Community: **With abundance of thy grace.**

Liturgist: Keep far our foes, give peace at home;

Community: **Where thou art guide, no ill can come.**

Liturgist:	Teach us to know the Father, Son,
Community:	**And Thee, of both to be but one:**
Liturgist:	That through the ages all along,
Community:	**This may be our endless song:**
Liturgist:	Praise to thy eternal merit.
Community:	**Father, Son, and Holy Spirit. Amen.**

The Laying of Hands

Bishop: By the authority of the church through the imposition of our hands, send forth your Holy Spirit upon your servant, N_____ , for the office and work of an elder in your church, O God, with authority to minister your Word and sacraments, to declare your forgiveness to repentant sinners, and to shepherd your flock; in the name of the Father, and of the Son, and of the Holy Spirit. Amen.

(Then the Bishop and those participating in the service shall deliver the Holy Scriptures into the hands of the Elder.)

Bishop: Take the Holy Scriptures as you exercise the authority you have received to preach the Word of God and to celebrate the sacraments. Amen.

Hymn of Dedication   "We Thank Thee, Lord" Hymnal, No. 203

Going Forth

Liturgist: Go, knowing that you are continually loved and charged with the task of loving others.

Community: **We go to be a special quality of people, sustained by God's love, directed by this time of worship and celebration, and recharged for a life of Christian service.**

Liturgist: In the midst of our world, where hatred, mistrust, criticism, and violence seem to be the accepted way of life, we are seeking to find that love which is unique to God.

Community: **We are seeking not only to find that special love, but to live it, hoping to bring peace and compassion to our world and to our lives. Amen.**

(Ordination Party in the Fellowship Hall)

Oregon Conference
Wesley Taylor, Chairman,
Commission on Worship,
and, in this service, ordained

178.

Service of Ordination

The Preparation

The Prelude

The ordinands are preparing for this service of ordination in meditation and prayer. We ask the congregation to join them in the same spirit.

The Processional Hymn   "Praise to the Lord"   Hymnal, No. 55

(Let the congregation stand and join in singing).

Introductory Statement   The Bishop

The Scriptures teach us that each Christian is a minister, and together we are the body of Christ, the Christian church. The church as the body of Christ calls all its members to Christ's ministry of reconciliation. Some persons, however, are called to a particular ministry within Christ's body. From the beginning these persons have been the ordained ministers of the church called to the special task of helping others join the body of Christ and grow in their faithful relationship to God and in their loving service to others. In the New Testament we find two orders, and therefore the ordained ministry of The United Methodist Church consists of deacons and elders.

Ordination is the rite by which these orders are conferred. It is an act of God in his church. We recognize that in all ordination the true ordainer is God. In response to the prayers of his church, and through the words and acts of her representatives, God commissions and empowers those to be ordained for the office and work to which they are called.

The Presentation

(The Chairman of the Board of the Ministry or some other duly appointed person presents the candidates for ordination to the Bishop.)

Presenter: Bishop, we present to you these persons to be ordained deacons and elders in The United Methodist Church.

Bishop: Let the authority for their ordination be declared.

(The chairman of the Board of Ministry shall report the vote of the annual conference. He will then introduce each candidate for ordination to the congregation by stating his name and the immediate work to which he has been called. When all names have been called the candidates will turn and face the Bishop for the examination.)

The Examination

Bishop: Each person who is presenting himself here today for ordination has considered deeply and seriously the tasks to which he has been called. He has been examined concerning his calling and his commitment. He has studied in great detail and in depth the Christian faith and the expectations The United Methodist Church has of her ordained ministers. Today we are asking each person standing before you to share with you his or her commitment to this high calling of ordained minister. The questions to be asked will center on the basic expectations which the church has for those who enter into the ordained ministry.

Bishop *(addressing the ordinands)*:
              Do you trust that you are truly called by God to this ministry in his church?

Answer: I do so trust.

Bishop: Are you persuaded that the Holy Scriptures contain all things necessary for salvation, and are the supreme and decisive standard of faith? And are you determined to study these Scriptures diligently and instruct the people committed to your charge in the truths that they contain?

Answer: I am so persuaded and determined, by God's grace.

Bishop: Will you endeavour to maintain peace and love among the people committed to your charge, to bring sinners to repentance, and to declare to them God's forgiveness?

Answer: I will, the Lord being my helper.

Bishop: Will you constantly endeavor to inspire the people committed to your charge, so that their continual concern will be with the world for which

Christ died—especially for those in the world who are poor, needy, and oppressed.

Answer: I will, the Lord being my helper.

Bishop: Will you help people to be good stewards of the many gifts of God, that every member may be equipped for the work of ministering?

Answer: I will, the Lord being my helper.

Bishop: Believing you are called to exercise this ministry with The United Methodist Church, will you accept its discipline and submit yourselves as ministers of the Gospel to those whom this church shall appoint to have authority over you?

Answer: I will, by the help of God.

Bishop: (*This question is addressed only to the deacons.*) A minister in the church of God is one inwardly moved by the Holy Spirit to serve God and his people. He is one who believes the Holy Scriptures and seeks diligently to read and expound them. The responsibility of the deacon is to conduct divine worship, to assist the elder in the administration of the Holy Communion, to baptize, to instruct the youth, and to conduct other pastoral functions that will serve the needs of God's people. Will you accept these responsibilities of a deacon?

Answer: I will, by the help of God.

Bishop: (*Addressing the people*) Beloved, these are they whom we intend, God willing, to ordain ministers. You have heard them presented and examined. They are persons of sound learning and godly life, and we find them to be duly called to serve God in this ministry. We therefore ask you to declare your assent.

(*The people stand*)

Bishop: We are not sufficient of ourselves; our sufficiency is from God. Do you trust that these persons are, by God's grace, worthy to be ordained?

Congregation: **We trust that they are worthy. To God be the glory!**

The Ministry of the Word of God

Bishop: The Lord be with you!

Congregation: **And with your spirit.**

Bishop: Let us pray.

Bishop and
Congregation: GRACIOUS GOD, OUR ETERNAL FATHER, HEAR OUR PRAYERS AS WE DRAW NEAR TO YOU.

Ordinands: Hear our prayers of thankfulness, Lord. We are truly grateful for the lives of all the people who have led us to this moment of dedication. We are thankful for the challenge that now lies ahead; for the great potential of your kingdom made real in our lives.

Bishop and
Congregation: WE TOO ARE THANKFUL. FATHER, WE GIVE TO YOU THANKS FOR THE LIVES OF THESE YOUR SERVANTS. MAY YOUR LOVE BE MADE INCARNATE IN THEIR LIVES. GIVE TO US THE POWER TO HELP THEM AND TO SUPPORT THEM IN THEIR HOLY WORK.

Ordinands: Pour into our lives your Holy Spirit, and enlighten the paths our feet must take. Lead us into the lives of others, those who are in sorrow and those who are in joy. Help us to carry your Gospel to all peoples. Give us courage to speak in word and action of your wrath and judgment. Give us gentleness to speak in word and action of your humility and compassion.

Give us the wisdom to discern the time of courage from the time of gentleness.

Bishop and
Congregation: INSTILL YOUR LOVE IN OUR HEARTS, LORD, SO THAT IN LOVE WE MAY ACCEPT THESE YOUR SERVANTS, AS THEY LEAD YOUR CHURCH HELP US ALL TO GROW IN SPIRIT AND CONCERN TO THE END THAT WE MAY BECOME THE BODY OF CHRIST.

Ordinands: These things we pray in the name of Jesus Christ who, with the Father and the Spirit, reigns, eternally and to whom belongs all power and majesty.

All: AMEN.

The Hymn "Sing Praise to God Who Reigns Above"   Hymnal, No. 4

(As the congregation sings let the ordinands return to their seats.)

The Affirmation of Faith "The Korean Creed"   Hymnal, No. 741

Minister: Where the Spirit of the Lord is, there is the one true Church, apostolic and universal, whose holy faith let us now declare:

Minister and
Congregation: We believe in the one God, maker and ruler of all things, Father of all men, the source of all goodness and beauty, all truth and love.

We believe in Jesus Christ, God manifest in the flesh, our teacher, example, and Redeemer, the Savior of the world.

We believe in the Holy Spirit, God present with us for guidance, for comfort, and for strength.

We believe in the forgiveness of sins, in the life of love and prayer, and in grace equal to every need.

We believe in the Word of God contained in the Old and New Testaments as the sufficient rule both of faith and of practice.

We believe in the Church as the fellowship for worship and for service of all who are united to the living Lord.

We believe in the kingdom of God as the divine rule in human society, and in the brotherhood of man under the fatherhood of God.

We believe in the final triumph of righteousness, and in the life everlasting. Amen.

Lessons from the Holy Spriptures

The Call	Isaiah 42:1-9 (NEB)
The Task	Matthew 20:25-28 (NEB)
	II Corinthians 5:17-20 (NEB)
The Resources:	Ephesians 6:10-20 (NEB)

The Sermon

Prayer by the Bishop:

Almighty and most merciful God, giver of all good things, look with favor upon these your servants. Cleanse and purify them of all sinfulness and iniquity so that their work may be carried on with modesty and humility. Grant them the grace necessary to fill their high calling and strength needed to observe all spiritual discipline. Give to them that quality of life that men call hope. Make them always hopeful and never embittered with their life of service. Endue them with the mixture of the wisdom of patience and the impatience of love. Guide them in their ministry so that it may reveal your unending love, through Jesus Christ our Lord. Amen.

The Hymn   "Come Holy Ghost, Our Hearts Inspire"   Hymnal, No. 467
(Let the congregation stand to sing.)

The Investiture

(The chairman of the Board of the Ministry calls the names of those to be ordained deacon. As their names are called they present themselves before the Bishop.)

Prayer by the Bishop

We glorify you, O God, that of your great goodness you sent your Son Jesus Christ to take the form of a servant and to humble himself, becoming obedient even to the death on the Cross. We praise you that you have exalted him and given him the name which is above every name. We are grateful that through him we have been taught that he who would be great should be the servant of all. We thank you that you have graciously called these servants to be deacons in your church. Make them, O Lord, to be modest, humble, and constant in their ministry, and to have ready will to observe all spiritual discipline. Make them stable and strong in your Son, Jesus Christ, so that they may be found worthy to be called into the higher ministry of your church: through your Son our Saviour, Jesus Christ, to whom be glory and honor, world without end. Amen.

(To each ordained the chairman of the Board of the Ministry delivers an open Bible and the Bishop lays a hand on his head.)

Bishop: Send down your Holy Spirit upon this servant, N_____, whom we ordain as a deacon in the church, committing to him the authority to execute this office, to read the Holy Scriptures in the Church of God, to preach the Word, and to serve His people. Amen.

(After the above is said for each ordinand, let the congregation respond.)

Congregation: **Amen.**

(After all deacons have been ordained they shall stand. The Bishop hands each a certificate of ordination.)

Bishop: We give you the right hand of fellowship and receive you to share in this ministry.

(After all have received the certificate the ordinands turn to face the congregation, and the Bishop addresses them.)

Bishop: We declare these as deacons in the church of God, in the name of the Father, and of the Son, and of the Holy Spirit.

Congregation: **Amen. Thanks be to God!**

(The deacons return to their seats. The chairman of the Board of the Ministry asks each of those to be ordained elder to stand and come and kneel at the altar as his name is called.)

Prayer by the Bishop:

We glorify you, O God, that of your infinite love and goodness you chose a people for your own possession to be a royal priesthood and a holy nation, and have given your only Son Jesus Christ to be our great High Priest and Author of eternal salvation. We thank you that by his death he has overcome death, and by his resurrection has poured his gifts abundantly upon his people, making some apostles, some prophets, some evangelists, some pastors and teachers, for the building up of his body, the church. Give to these to be ordained elders grace to offer with all your people spiritual sacrifices acceptable to you. Enrich them in all utterance and all knowledge, that they may proclaim the Gospel of your salvation. Make them watchful and loving guardians over your flock, as followers of the Good Shepherd who gave his life for the sheep. Enable them in all things to fulfill their ministry without reproach in your sight, so that abiding steadfast to the end, with all your faithful servants they may be received into your eternal joy, through Jesus Christ our Lord, who lives and reigns and is worshiped and glorified with you, O Father, and the Holy Spirit, one God, world without end. Amen.

(The chairman of the Board of Ministry calls each ordinand's name. As his name is called he is joined by two sponsoring elders and two lay sponsors, and presents himself before the Bishop for the investiture.)

N_____, the Lord pour upon you the Holy Spirit for the office and work of an elder in the church of God, now committed to you by the authority of the church through the imposition of our hands. Be a faithful dispenser of the Word of God and of his holy sacraments to the people, in the name of the Father, and of the Son, and of the Holy Spirit. Amen.

(After the above is said for each ordinand, let the congregation respond.)

Congregation: **Amen.**

(After each elder has been ordained he shall stand and the Bishop hands to each a certificate of ordination.)

Bishop: We give you the right hand of fellowship and receive you to share in this ministry.

(After all have received the certificate of ordination, let the ordinands face the congregation.)

Bishop: We declare these as elders in the church of God, in the name of the Father, and of the Son, and of the Holy Spirit.

Congregation: **Amen. Thanks be to God!**

(The Bishop invites the congregation to stand.)

Prayer by the Bishop:

Direct us O Lord, in all our doings, with your most gracious favor, and further us with your continual help, that in all our works, begun, continued, and ended in you, we may glorify your holy name, and finally, by your mercy, obtain everlasting life; through Jesus Christ our Lord. Amen.

The Doxology

The Postlude

(Kansas East Conference
United Methodist Church)

179.

A Time of Ordination Recognition

Leader: We listen to the sounds of the world, and know that they carry the calling of God.

People: **The tinkling of glass, the laughter of children;**

Leader: The din of the traffic, the cry of new jungles;

People: **The spilling of blood and the wailing of sirens.**

Leader: The tasting of birth, the hushed tones of dying;

People: **The pleas of the captive, and the praying of saints.**

Leader: We look for the sights of the world and see in them the pointing of God.

People: **The wires of computers, the eyes of the forgotten,**

Leader: The grandeur of mountains, and the smog over factories,

People: **The bustle in airports, the homes for the aged,**

Leader: The flags of the nations, the pages of history,

People: **Front pages of newsprint, and youth around schoolyards.**

Leader: We sense the touch of the world and feel in its presence the finger of God.

People: **The fist of a fighter, the hand of a child,**

Leader: The creasing of bullets, the peace of the forest,

People: **The wound of an insult, and the heat of new fires,**

Leader: The crowd on the busses, and the dust in the air,

People: **The taste of good food, and the hollow pit of depression.**

Leader: There are other sounds and sights and feelings. There are words of the Bible, and visions of pulpits, and hands of the bishop. These are also the pointing of God.

People: **The sounds of the world we know, the sights of life we understand. These fingers of God we can accept. But those of the church are special. They are for you alone, for you are better equipped, more forcefully called.**

Leader: The sounds are the same, the visions are equal. We feel the same finger in world and church. God's finger is one. There is no division. Stand with me or we must all be seated.

People: **God's calling is one, let its hearers be one. Give us the courage to accept one ministry, common in call, yet differing in function.**

Leader: As I accept one function of ministry, so let us all find the special functions in which we might express our common call.

People: **As we celebrate your ordination, and continue the search for our own. Amen.**

Editor's Note:
This responsive act of worship is for use in a parish church, recognizing the ordination of its minister.

—William A. Ritter
Livonia, Michigan

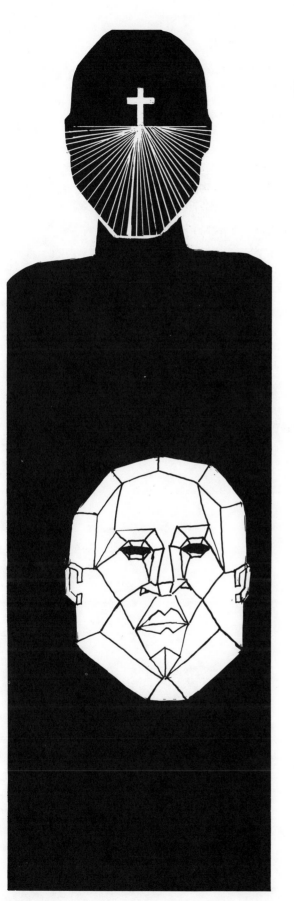

Special Services

A Festival for Workers

Prelude

Invocation:

Here we are, Lord. We have come as teachers, as students, as factory workers and business executives, housewives, secretaries, doctors, and engineers. This is who we are, Lord. We offer our vocations into your care. Take our lives and our labors and fashion them into the building blocks of your kingdom. Give us back the tools of our professions, transformed and sanctified by our renewed awareness that they are the instruments of our ministry. Here and now, O God, we accept once more your commission to be your workers in the world. Amen.

Procession of the Workers   "O Master Workman of the Race"   Hymnal, No. 171

(During the singing of the hymn, you are invited to process to the altar and to place there a symbol of your work. Return to your seats by the side aisles.)

Call to Confession:

God has given us life, but we have not lived. He has given us jobs to do, but we have turned away from work, for we have found the burden heavy and the anxiety painful. May we admit commonly our willfulness and our weakness in denying what is given. Let us confess our sins:

Prayer of Confession (by all):

LORD OF ALL THAT IS AND IS TO BE, SENSITIZE OUR SIGHT THAT WE MIGHT REALLY SEE WHAT IS AND UNDERSTAND WHAT OUGHT TO BE. WE CONFESS THAT OFTEN WE SEE ONLY WHAT WE WANT TO SEE. WE STRIKE FOR MORE VACATIONS AND MORE BENEFITS WHILE THOUSANDS ARE COLD, DISEASED, AND POVERTY STRICKEN. WE BELIEVE THAT NO ONE CAN STARVE IN AMERICA, AND SO WE SPEND OUR TIME WORRYING ABOUT THE STOCK MARKET AND WONDERING IF INFLATION WILL EASE IN TIME FOR US TO BUY ANOTHER CAR, WHILE CHILDREN DIE OF MALNUTRITION, SOMETIMES HERE IN OUR OWN CITY. WE SPEAK OF EQUAL RIGHTS, EDUCATION, AND JUSTICE FOR ALL, BUT CANNOT FEEL THE FRUSTRATION OF OVERCOMING PRE-JUDICE OF RACE OR NATIONALITY AS IT HAPPENS IN OUR COMPANY OR IN OUR CITY. WE CREATE TECHNOLOGY, BUT FAIL TO CONTROL IT. WE COMPLAIN ABOUT EDUCATION, BUT GO TO SLEEP IN CLASSES. WE SUPPORT STUDIES OF ANTIPOLLUTION, BUT SCATTER OUR TRASH DAILY. LORD, HELP US TO SEE THE INCONSISTENCY OF OUR WORK AND OUR DISTORTION OF LIFE WHEREIN WE BECOME DESTROYERS RATHER THAN CREATORS. HAVE MERCY.   AMEN.

Words of Pardon and Assurance:

Listen! Your life is good. Whatever the last moment was, this one is now. It is God's mercy that first clears away the rubble of our lives, in order to make us free and open to life. The hands that are his will battle the real war on poverty. The minds that are his will create life in the city. The hearts that are his will bring humanness to man's labors. The last Word is that the new Word is given! Arise, then, as those who know that such a word demands shouts of joy!

Gloria Patri

Anthem

Scripture Lessons   Exodus 20:8-11, St. Matthew 9:35-38, I Corinthians 3:10-15

Hymn   "When Through the Whirl of Wheels"

Sermon   "Not All Strike Breakers Are Scabs!"

Concerns of the Church

Prayers of Intercession

—George Engelhardt

181.

A Liturgy of Human Identity

(Worshipers may be seated throughout the service. Readers will read in turn, each person beginning with the text following the one his neighbor read. At the time for spontaneous prayer, you are to be free to offer short expressions of prayer as you are moved to do so.)

Leader: In the beginning God created the heavens and the earth
          (Gen. 1:1 RSV).

All: **The Lord God formed man of dust from the ground, and breathed into his nostrils the breath of life; and man became a living being.**

Leader: The Lord is God and he has given us light.
          (Ps. 118:27 RSV).

All: **Praise the Lord God!**

Leader: Let the Redeemed of the Lord say so.
          (Ps. 107:2 RSV).

All: **Blessed be the Lord God, the God of life here now and here tomorrow; and let all the people say, "Amen!"   Praise the Lord!**
          (Ps. 106:48 RSV).

Song of Praise

Reader 1:   He spent twenty-five years
            at diagramming sentences
            And adding $2 + 2 = X^2$
            And reading that there really was a spirit in '76
            For that investment he got a real
            signed and sealed note saying he is
            qualified to add $2 + 2$ and diagram.
            He has official sanction to live.

Reader 2:   He awakes to that dreadful ring
            and stumbles to the shower
            to begin his creative day at the
            security-risk-mutual-underwriters-
            safety-life and casualty-assocation;
            Where-you-can-put-forty-down-a-month-
            and-know-you-are-secure-for-the-future-
            and-when-you-die-the-children-are-
            taken-care-of. Amen.

Reader 3:   She makes the coffee and turns on
              "As the World Turns" to see if
              Grandma Baker will survive open
              heart surgery so she can see the
              grandchild who was illegitimately
              fathered to the granddaughter
              who ran away from home because
              she hated her parents for being
              her parents. And it will be
                    continued
                    Tomorrow and
                    Tomorrow and. . .

Reader 4:   For this domination of the good
              life they have a forty-year
              mortgage—a big-bright-green
              ego machine with white
              side walls (of course), a built-in
              self-cleaning, fully automatic
              burner with a brain.
              A stainless steel, two-basined,
              even-flow, hot and cold kitchen
              sink with a built-in disposal
              worth $19.95 of anybody's money.

Reader 5:   And as the world turns,
              lives are twisted inward
              and smiles become hollow,
              and hair turns wintry,
              furrows reveal erosion
              and stainless steel rusts,
              the light bulb breaks
              and the garbage disposal isn't fun anymore.

Leader: We curse the lives we're living.
              we curse reality.
              and God should be damned
              for creating such a shoddy,
              hideous joke,
              The mouths that once were full
              now choke to spit out the ashes.

              Jesus taught that prayer is the expression of the continuous relationship we
              have with God. He taught us to pray the Our Father. Let us pray.

All: **Our Father. . .**

Leader: Let us confess our sin to God.
              We seek pleasure in big, bright, green machines.

All: **Forgive us, O Lord.**

Leader: We hate.

All: **Forgive us, O Lord.**

Leader: We cannot tolerate difference.

All: **Forgive us, O Lord.**

Leader: We use each other for selfish reasons.

All: **Forgive us, O Lord.**

Leader:	We seek the easiest way.
All:	**Forgive us, O Lord.**
Leader:	We sell ourselves for status, prestige, wealth.
All:	**Forgive us, O Lord.**
Leader:	We often neglect your will.
All:	**Forgive us, O Lord.**
Leader:	We often say our will is your will.
All:	**Forgive us, O Lord.**
Leader:	For what is in our minds. . . *(silent confession)*
Leader:	For what we crowd from our minds. . . *(silent confession)*
Leader:	For the concerns we now express openly... *(spontaneous, vocal prayer)*
Leader:	Forgive us, O Lord.
All:	**Forgive us, O Lord.**
Leader:	To be alive is to know hurt.
Reader 1:	For the creation waits with eager longing for the revealing of the sons of God; for the creation was subjected to futility, not of its own will but by the will of him who subjected it in hope; because the creation itself will be set free from its bondage to decay and obtain the glorious liberty of the children of God (Rom. 8:19-21 RSV).
Leader:	To be human is to ask, "Why?"
Reader 2:	God's wrath is revealed coming down from heaven upon all the sin and evil of men, whose evil ways prevent the truth from being known. God punishes them, because what men can know about God is plain to them. God himself made it plain to them. Ever since God created the world, his invisible qualities, both his eternal power and his divine nature, have been clearly seen. Men can perceive them in the things that God has made. So they have no excuse at all! They know God, but they do not give him the honor that belongs to Him, nor do they thank him. Instead, their thoughts have become complete nonsense and their empty minds are filled with darkness. They say they are wise, but they are fools; they exchange the glory of the immortal God for images made to look like mortal man or birds or animals or reptiles (Rom. 1:18-23). TEV

Leader: These words are harsh, He is not mocked.

Reader 3:   And now, go, write it before them on a tablet,
and inscribe it in a book,
that it may be for the time to come
as a witness forever.
For they are a rebellious people, lying sons,
sons who will not hear the instruction of the Lord;
who say to the seers, "See not";
and to the prophets, "Prophesy
not to us what is right;
speak to us smooth things,
prophesy illusions,
leave the way, turn aside from the path,
let us hear no more of the Holy One of Israel"
   (Isa. 30:8-11 RSV).

Leader: We want only peace and happiness.

Reader 4:   Do not think that I have come to bring
peace to the world; no, I did not come to
bring peace, but a sword. . . .
Whoever does not take up his cross and follow
in my steps is not worthy of me. . . Whoever
tries to gain his own life will lose it;
whoever loses his life for my sake will gain it. . . .
Whoever gives even a drink of cold water
to one of the least of these my followers,
because he is my follower, will receive his reward
   (Matt. 19:34, 38-39 TEV).

Leader: To be human is to need love.

Reader 5:   I have told you this so that my joy may be in
you, and that your joy may be complete. This
is my commandment: love one another, just as
I love you. The greatest love a man can
have for his friends is to give his life
for them. And you are my friends, if you do
what I command. I do not call you servants
any longer, because a servant does not know
what his master is doing. Instead I call
you friends, because I have told you
everything I heard from my Father.
You did not choose me; I chose
you, and appointed you to go and bear
much fruit, the kind of fruit that
endures. And the Father will give
you whatever you ask of him in my
name. This, then, is what I command
you: love one another
   (John 15:11-17 TEV).

Leader: To be God's men we are free, yet bound in covenant.

Reader 6:   We have, then, brothers, complete freedom
to go into the Most Holy Place by means
of the death of Jesus. He opened for us
a new way, a living way, through the curtain—
that is, through his own body. . . ,
Let us come near to God, then, with

a sincere heart and a sure faith,
with hearts that have been made clean
from a guilty conscience, and bodies
washed with pure water
    (Heb. 10:19-20, 22 TEV).

Leader: Let us hold on firmly to the hope we profess,

All: **Because we can trust God to keep his promise.**

Leader: Let us be concerned with one another,

All: **To help one another to show love and to do good.**

Leader: Let us not give up the habit of meeting together. . . .

All: **Instead, let us encourage one another, all the more**

     (Heb. 10:23-25 TEV).

The Sermon

Leader: To be in Christ is to eat his Body and
drink his Blood. To be in Christ is to know
that incarnation means God's love in man. Christ
is incarnate in us if his love captures us in
servanthood.
Now we take the bread for his Flesh
to remember who we are and why we are here
and to emphasize who he was and why he
was here.

(The loaf of bread is passed around with a dish. Each person breaks off a small piece and places it in the dish. The dish of pieces is returned to the leader to be consecrated.)

We also take the wine for his Blood
to remember who we are and who he is. He
promised to be with us in all times. He died to
prove it. He rose to show it.

(The pitcher of wine and the communion cup are passed, each person pouring his portion. These are returned for consecration.)

Take this and eat: This is my Body.

(The leader holds up the dish if he so desires.)

Drink from it, all of you. For this is my
Blood, the blood of the covenant, shed for
many for the forgiveness of sins.

(He may likewise raise the cup.)

(The dish of bread is now passed. As the bread is passed the person giving it says to the one who takes it, "N___, the Body of Christ," each of those communicating takes a piece. When all have been served, all will communicate simultaneously.)

(Now the cup is passed, each person drinking approximately the amount he poured. As the cup is passed, "N___, the Blood of Christ," is said.)

Leader: We have shared the Body and Blood of Christ's resurrection.

Reader 1:   After breakfast Jesus said to Simon Peter: "Simon, son of John do you love me more than all else?"

Reader 2:   "Yes, Lord," he answered, "You know that I love you."

Reader 3:   "Then feed my lambs."

Reader 4:   A second time he asked: "Simon, son of John, do you love me?"

Reader 5:   "Yes, Lord, you know I love you."

Reader 6:   "Then tend my sheep."

Reader 7:   A third time He said: "Simon, son of John, do you love me?"

Reader 8:   "Lord, you know everything; you know I love you."

Reader 9:   "Feed my sheep."

Hymn of Celebration

(The ceremony concludes with the passing of the peace. "The Peace of God be with you." "And with you." The peace is exchanged until all have been recognized.)

—Larry Don Hollon

Commentary

As the Project on Worship grew, it seemed desirable to the director and to the Commission committee with which we worked to have a thorough and "objective" analysis of *Ventures in Worship* and *Ventures in Worship 2*. Professor Louis W. Bloede was selected for this task and his compact but perceptive analysis is included here because it is suggestive and helpful, not only to those who worked with the Ventures series, but for anyone who is concerned about the direction of contemporary worship. The analysis is included here as Professor Bloede wrote it, although he and the director continue to engage in discussion about some of the basic issues involved. The editor is grateful to Professor Bloede for his incisive work and for the thoroughness of his study and the fine spirit with which he has carried out his assignment. Louis W. Bloede is associate professor of Worship and Homiletics at the Evangelical Theological School in Naperville, Illinois.

An Analysis of *Ventures in Worship* and *Ventures in Worship 2*

and suggestions for the future
by Louis W. Bloede

Some explanation of how I became involved with this project may be in order. At a meeting of the Board of Trustees of Evangelical Theological Seminary in November of 1969, Bishop Lance Webb learned of my request for a sabbatical leave. As chairman of the General Commission on Worship of The United Methodist Church, he was especially interested in my desire to spend some of my time engaged in research in worship. He suggested that I contact Dr. David J. Randolph to see if my sabbatical plans might include some relationship to the Project on Worship in which Dr. Randolph was engaged. I wrote Dr. Randolph and received a very encouraging reply.

In February of 1970, I met with Dr. Randolph and the Committee on Creative Sources of Worship and learned more about the worship project, which involved the collection and publication of various contemporary worship materials. At this meeting I agreed that I would plan to devote some of my sabbatical to an analysis of these materials.

In 1970 I was one of the Fellows in Residence at the Institute for Ecumenical and Cultural Research, Collegeville, Minnesota.[1] Here I had ample opportunity to do further background reading in worship, to experience Roman Catholic, as well as Protestant worship, to engage in ecumenical dialogue about worship, and to devote time to an analysis of *Ventures in Worship* and *Ventures in Worship 2*.

This task of analysis has proved to be both exciting and frustrating. As I read through these materials a number of times and jotted down my comments and reactions, I was excited about the creativity of many of these contributions. Obviously, in a variety of places throughout this land people are concerned that the worship life of the church be renewed and made as relevant as possible to the day in which we live. However, I also experienced frustration. In this present report I want to briefly note my personal analysis and reactions to the packets.

The Usefulness of the Packets

In the Articles of Religion of the former Methodist Church, now printed in the *Discipline* of The United Methodist Church, we find two paragraphs dealing with the "Rites and Ceremonies of Churches." Included in these paragraphs are these words: "It is not necessary that rites and ceremonies should in all places be the same, or exactly alike; for they have always been different, and may be changed according to the diversity of countries, times, and men's manners, so that nothing be ordained against God's Word."[2]

While not exactly a mandate for change, the statement certainly allows for considerable freedom to change the rites and ceremonies of worship. Because of this tradition of freedom, which finds expression locally, as well as denominationally, The United Methodist Church would seem to be a fruitful source of contemporary expressions of worship. Indeed several annual conference Commissions on Worship (Minnesota, Kansas East, and Southwest Texas, to name a few) have developed their printed collections of contemporary worship materials. However, by collecting such materials on a national basis, greater selectivity can be exercised, materials can be printed rather than mimeographed, and much wider distribution is possible.

My investigation has not revealed any other denomination publishing anything quite like these packets. In fact, although there is great interest on the part of many persons in making changes in worship, there are surprisingly few examples of contemporary worship materials available in any organized fashion. The large number of packets purchased indicates the great interest in materials of this nature.

One area of additional research that might be considered is that of learning how the packets are actually being used by the pastors and congregations which purchased them. How useful have they found them? What criticism would they make? What have they been encouraged to do locally because of the packets? What suggestions do they have for the contents of future packets?

While negative comments can be made about specific contributions, in general the quality of materials included is high. This undoubtedly reflects the fact that selectivity and editing have been exercised. Certainly not all the new expressions of worship being introduced and used in local churches are as carefully thought out and constructed as the materials in these packets.

Now let me make some specific observations about the material in the two packets.

1. To use Dr. James White's phrase, "the worldliness of worship"[3] stands out in these materials. For the most part the writers of these materials see the problems of the world as being the continuing concern of the church and thus the proper focus of worship.

Dr. David Randolph's comment in the foreword of *Ventures in Worship* is very significant when he notes that "prayers of confession were among the most numerous items submitted." This seems to be where people are today—very much aware of what we might call "the human condition," the social sinfulness of the world, the need for contrition and confession.

It almost seems as if some of the people writing these new worship materials have discovered the printed corporate prayer of confession. This is the modern-day counterpart to the personal prayers of confession spoken at the altar rail by the penitent sinner in the days of revivalism. This strong emphasis upon confession is needed today, because it can lead to cleansing and renewal. Our worship must include the concern to get the view of the worshiper outside the "four cozy walls" and into the world. But we must also be concerned that the worshiper not simply wallow in remorse over his guilt. In young Isaiah's experience in the temple, his sense of guilt, and words of confession were followed by the symbolic cleansing of his unclean lips.[4]

Our worship must give reassurance of the cleansing of sin. The note of hope must be emphasized, and in some of the materials in the packets it is. (A good example of this being done is found in *Ventures* p. 28, no. 36). But this note of hope and joy is not expressed in some of the other materials as much as it could be if we are really "celebrating" as we worship.

There is a kind of over done pessimism in some expressions of worship today—the attitude that everything is wrong and nothing is right. Perhaps this is inevitable because of the frustration and disillusionment of many youth, and we know that many of the changes in worship are being planned by and for youth. But it is at this very point that the Gospel becomes very relevant. We have good news to proclaim. As the authors of *The Celebration of the Gospel* remind us, in worship we are celebrating God's victory in Christ.[5]

2. In looking critically at the materials in these packets one must raise the question of what kind of theology underlies these expressions of worship? How we worship is determined to some extent at least by our understanding of whom or what we worship. Even if this is not verbalized, some image of the deity must be in the mind of the one preparing the worship materials.

I find in these materials greater emphasis upon the immanence of God than upon the transcendence of God. God is not regarded as Mystery, or as the Wholly Other, but he is more like the man next door, and one just talks with him in ordinary fashion. There is almost an easy going familiarity with the Deity. For example, in one call to worship, the worshiper is told, "Take off your mask of formality and be yourself."[6]

This matter-of-factness in relating to God can be partly explained by our up dating of language, but I believe there are theological dimensions to this as well. Although this assertion is difficult to pinpoint, one has the feeling that there is a kind of humanism that permeates our worship even as it permeates our theology. Thus, we are given the impression that this is really man's world now and not God's world, and thus man alone is responsible for improving it. I much prefer Paul's idea that "we are workers together with God."[7]

3. The use of fresh, contemporary language must surely be noted as an outstanding characteristic of these materials. The King James English of Scripture and prayer is no longer used as the language of worship. The vocabulary of worship and the vocabulary of daily conversation do not differ as much as they once did. The result is usually (but not always) greater clarity and ease of speaking.

One must be cautious about taking a classic prayer and attempting to improve it by changing a few words. For example, one prayer ends with the phrase, "The credit all goes to you."[8] To me this suggests a God who is very concerned about who gets the credit. The original phrase must have spoken of giving God the glory and praise, but somehow "credit" has a different connotation than "glory," and in this instance a less positive one.

If we look critically at the language and structure of these contemporary worship materials, we soon discover how difficult it is to create them and improve upon the past. God does not expect perfection before he will hear us, but we surely want to offer him our best. This means creative imagination, hard work, and a willingness to refine and rewrite.

Some of the materials "read" better than they "say." One wonders if the author rehearsed them aloud before using them with a congregation. Was he really aware of what constitutes good written language for speaking purposes?

Another concern that must be kept in mind is whether the material is really an expression of corporate worship or whether it is more useful for personal devotional practice. This is a difficult distinction to make, but in some instances the pronoun "I" is used entirely, or the pronouns "I" and "we" are both used within a single prayer.[9]

Even in contemporary worship we are still plagued with the problem of the prayer that sounds more like a sermon than a prayer. The one who is praying seems to be addressing the people rather than God. Again, the distinction is a difficult one, but something of which we must be aware.

In connection with language and structure I was impressed with the strong use of contrast in some of the selections. For example, traditional words of scripture are alternated with current news headlines or descriptions of the human situation. The result is almost a kind of verbal multi-media effect, which can jar us from complacency regarding the Scripture and the news.

4. Even though the language used in these materials is contemporary, the contents of the packets suggest that worship is primarily a verbal experience. Almost everything in the packets is material that would be printed in the worship bulletin and read as part of the service. These are useful materials, but in the future more attention may need to be given to such questions as the physical setting in which worship takes place, the ceremonials of worship, vestments, symbols and art work, music, dance, etc. Some of these are alluded to in the contributions in the packets, but in most instances need to be discussed more fully.

5. The traditional benediction at the conclusion of the worship service is being replaced by a sending-forth of the people, a commissioning for service. Oftentimes this is in the form of a shared response between pastor and congregation rather than simply spoken by the pastor.

Undoubtedly this sending-forth underscores the concern of present-day worship to motivate people to action in the world. Dedication can sometimes be clarified or reinforced by verbal expression, and thus this commissioning to service in the world is to be commended. In the past this kind of response was often called for immediately after the sermon, so perhaps the emphasis has only been shifted to the conclusion of the worship service. However, I personally feel that something important is lacking if the blessing of God upon his people is not expressed. Thus I would urge that the sending-forth either include or be followed by a benediction.

6. The creation of new worship forms is apparently still almost entirely the work of the clergy. Perhaps this is to be expected, because the primary responsibility for worship rests with the clergy, but does it really have to be this way? Why can't we involve lay people more than we do, not only in the leadership of worship, but in the creation of worship materials?

I was pleased to note that lay people were actively involved in the survey of worship that took place at Wesley United Methodist Church in Charlottesville, Virginia. Likewise, as changes were made in worship at University United Methodist Church at Goleta, California, a committee that included lay people met frequently through the year. And the pastor of the Baughman Memorial United Methodist Church in New Cumberland, Pennsylvania, submitted a meaningful prayer that was prayed by John Langdon as the high point of a sesquicentennial pageant. But these references to the involvement of lay people seem to be the exception rather than the rule.

7. Judging from the materials in these packets the offering has been neglected as a vehicle for innovation and experimentation in worship. Surely the offering could be made a much more dramatic expression of worship, rather than simply intermission time. The use of interpretative dance, visual aids, pantomime could be considered, along with the possibility of stressing offerings rather than money. Perhaps such offerings, or commitments, could be symbolized or verbalized by some members of the congregation as a source of encouragement to others and as an expression of dedication.

Some Additional Concerns

While perhaps not related directly to the contents of the two packets, there are some additional comments about worship that I would like to make. They are concerns or recommendations that should be kept in mind as we consider the future of worship.

1. If we are really going to be helpful in bringing about renewal in worship we must give more attention to the process by which change in worship can best take place. In the foreword of the first packet the editor wisely notes that "every congregation must find its own authentic voice and style." This is true, but congregations need more help in how to go about finding their authentic voice and style. Seeing the final results of the efforts of other congregations is helpful and inspiring, but more case studies of "how we did it," are needed. The inclusion in the second packet of the account of how University United Methodist Church in Goleta, California, moved through a process of changing its worship forms is an extremely valuable contribution.

2. As I indicated earlier in my report, I feel strongly that lay people need to be more involved than they usually are in the change and renewal of worship forms. This is stressed in the foreword to the second packet, where we are reminded that "worship is the activity of a community of faith. Participation should involve the congregation not only in the service of worship itself, but also in the planning and preparation as far as possible." I agree heartily with that statement.

In his book *Celebrations* a Dutch priest named Harry Haas shares what he calls a "diary of creative liturgy, 1953-1967."[10] Two things seem to stand out in the liturgical celebrations which he describes: (1) He always managed to involve the participants in the planning of the worship experience and the leadership of it; and (2) He emphasized the context (the contemporary milieu, as it were) in which the Mass was to take place. Thus, in an inner-city situation there developed "the skyscraper mass," while on another occasion he celebrated "the Mass of the Six Flags Over Texas."

Lay people are better educated than in centuries past and surely can take an active part in planning their own worship. The minimum participation of lay people would seem to be an active commission on worship, which then could plan for involvement of other people. For example, if an adult church school class studied the historic creeds of the church and then wrote some modern-day creeds of their own, why not incorporate some of these creeds and their authors into worship?

3. More education in worship for both clergy and laity must be provided. In a denomination which permits so much freedom in worship forms on a local level as does The United Methodist Church, the pastor must be an extremely well-informed resource person in worship. He needs to function not only as a worship leader but as a worship educator. Thus it is hoped, innovation in worship will be carried out more wisely and well.

Education in worship can be strengthened by such things as:

a. Arranging periodic consultations between the General Commission on Worship and seminary professors of worship, such as took place at Evanston in 1968.

b. Improving and enlarging course offerings in worship in the seminaries. (It is interesting to speculate whether the seminary worship practices of today will be the worship practices of the local church of tomorrow.)

c. Scheduling another national and/or some regional convocations on worship similar to the one in St. Louis in 1969.

d. Encouraging conference and district worshops and seminars on worship, carefully planned and staffed.

e. Continuing to provide resources, such as the packets and suggestions and information, about worship in the various publications of the church.

4. Too much of our traditional worship fails to give sufficient consideration to the presence of children and youth in our congregations. Our worship services have not only been very verbal, but verbal at an adult level. We need to use language, illustrations, and provide experiences that will involve children and youth in a meaningful manner.

5. We need to consider the possibility of serious polarization in a congregation if two distinctly different worship services are offered—one innovative and the other traditional. This is the direction some congregations are going, but is it the right way to go? The evidence isn't in yet. I don't know if anyone is collecting the evidence, but a word of caution needs to be spoken, it seems to me.

6. More attention needs to be given to providing suggested guidelines or criteria by which new forms of worship can be evaluted. Without taking time to elaborate upon them, I would suggest six such criteria:
   a. informed by the past
   b. theologically sound
   c. related to daily life
   d. the congregation involved
   e. understandable and meaningful to the majority present
   f. results in commitment and sense of mission
The first three are similar to three suggested by Dr. James White, although I state them in somewhat different form.[11]

7. In relationship to the last criterion listed above, let me note that the relationship between worship and mission needs to be continually explored and kept before us. The contemporary worship materials in these packets indicate creative struggle with this relationship. But there are many people whose concern for active involvement in a world in crisis allows no time or place for corporate worship. Is there any way that worship can include them? Or what about the opposite concern? How are those, who worship regularly but fail to make any direct connection between worship and the needs of the world around them, best helped to make that connection?

8. In conclusion I feel compelled to say that what we need to be most concerned about may not be forms as much as Spirit. We sometimes seem to think that if we only get the right forms, the right words, worship and people will be renewed. There is a paradox here because words and forms are essential. After all, worship is a process of communion and communication, and some form has to be used. But it is helpful to remember that the form is not the end but the means, and if we put our trust in forms *alone* we will fail to bring about genuine renewal. Like those people gathered in the upper room on the Day of Pentecost, we need to be praying for the coming of the Holy Spirit upon us so that genuine renewal can take place.

Notes

1. The institute is located on the campus of St. John's University and Abbey and the director is Father Kilian McDonnell, one of the Benedictine monks of the Abbey.
2. *The Book of Discipline* (Nashville: The Methodist Publishing House, 1968). p. 42.
3. James F. White, *The Worldiness of Worship* (New York: Oxford University Press, 1967).
4. Isaiah 6:1-8.
5. H. Grady Hardin, Joseph D. Quilian, and James F. White, *The Celebration of the Gospel* (Nashville: Abingdon Press, 1964). See chapter one especially.
6. *Ventures in Worship*, p. 12, no. 10.
7. I Corinthians 3:9.
8. *Ventures in Worship*, p. 17, no. 19.
9. *Ventures in Worship*, p. 21, no. 24.
10. Harry Haas, *Celebrations* (London: Sheed and Ward, 1969).
11. James F. White, "The Crisis in Worship." Address given at Evanston, Illinois, in 1967, at a meeting of the General Commission on Worship of The Methodist Church and professors of worship at Methodist and Evangelical United Brethren seminaries.

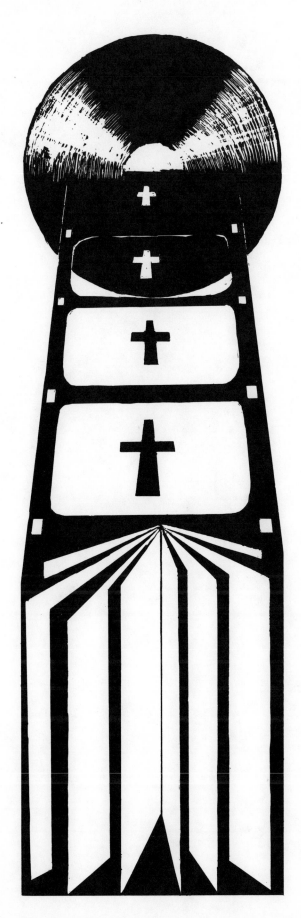

Come to Our
Liturgical Storehouse

Don M. Wardlaw
Professor of Homiletics
Columbia Theological Seminary
Decatur, Georgia

183.

Resources

Background

I Foundations for Celebration

    A. Books (chronological order)

Thompson, Bard, ed. *Liturgies of the Western Church*. New York: World Publishing Company, Meridian Books, $3.95. Historical survey of all major Western liturgies.	1961
Hageman, Howard G. *Pulpit and Table*. Richmond: John Knox Press. $3. Analysis of centrality of Word and sacrament.	1962
Shands, Alfred. *The Liturgical Movement and the Local Church*. New York: Morehouse-Barlow. $2.50.	1965
Von Allmen, Jean-Jacques. *Worship: Its Theology and Practice*. New York: Oxford University Press, $6.50. Comprehensive reflection by Reformed theologian on history, theology, and practice of worship.	1965
Verheul, A. *Introduction to the Liturgy, Towards a Theology of Worship*. Translated by Margaret Clarke. Collegeville, Minn.: Liturgical Press. $4-$5. Post-Vatican II theology of the liturgy, peculiarly sensitive to liturgy both in church and world.	1968
Brown, John. *New Ways in Worship for Youth*. Valley Forge, Pa.: Judson Press.	1969
Gallen, John, ed. *Eucharistic Liturgies*. New York: Paulist/Newman Press.	1969
Hartt, Julian N. *Theology and the Church in the University*. Philadelphia: Westminster Press. $3.25. Provocative linking of liturgy with the church's involvement in political struggle.	1969
Bloy, Myron B. *Multi-Media Worship, A Model and Nine Viewpoints*. New York: The Seabury Press. Nine reactors critique a free-flowing Episcopal liturgy at University of Michigan from their varied disciplines.	1970
Hovda, Robert. *Manual for Celebration*. Washington: Liturgical Conference, 1330 Massachusetts Ave., N.W. 20005.	1970
Stevick, Daniel B. *Language in Worship*. New York: The Seabury Press. Explores the power, place, and relative significance of language as one of the most explosive symbols in worship.	1970
Killinger, John. *Leave It to the Spirit*. New York: Harper & Row. $6.95. Lights the way for radical departure from traditional church forms to new, inventive, participatory ways of praising God.	1971
White, James. *New Forms of Worship*. Nashville: Abingdon Press. $5.75. Examines revolution in worship without losing touch with theological and historical base.	1971
Hoon, Paul W. *The Integrity of Worship*. Nashville: Abingdon Press. $8.50. A careful, comprehensive, balanced Protestant theology of worship.	1972
Hovda, Robert W., and Huck, Gabe. *There's No Place Like People*. Washington, D.C.: Liturgical Conference. Enlightened Roman Catholic viewpoint of principles involved in experimental and small-group workshop.	1972

    B. Periodicals

    Celebration, P. O. Box 281, Kansas City, Mo. Weekly supply of creative suggestions for liturgy and homily to Roman Catholic leaders of worship. Includes monthly newsletter.

Church Service Society, Edinburgh, Scotland. Annual publication of the Scottish society. Careful, scholarly.

Faith and Form, 1346 Connecticut Ave., N.W., Washington, D.C., 20036. Biannual publication of the Guild for Religious Architecture, professionally related to the American Institute of Architects. $5.

Freeing the Spirit, National Office for Black Catholics, 1325 Massachusetts Ave., N.W., Washington, D.C. 20005. A new journal for black liturgy, including services, poetry, and articles. Quarterly.

Journey, Center for Contemporary Celebration, 1400 East 53rd St., Chicago, Ill. 60615.

Life and Worship, The Rev. J. D. Crichton, The Presbytery Priest Lane, Pershore, Worcestershire, England. A Roman Catholic quarterly.

Liturgical Arts, 521 Fifth Ave., New York, N.Y. 10017. A Roman Catholic quarterly.

Liturgical Prayer, Pueblo Publishing Co., 1860 Broadway, New York, N.Y. 10023. Monthly journal with litanies, prayers for each Sunday; fresh, provocative. $10.

Liturgy, Liturgical Conference, Inc., 1330 Massachusetts Ave., N.W., Washington, D.C. 20005. $5. Monthly issue of an ecumenically minded Roman Catholic organization committed to liturgical renewal as related to social witness.

Living Worship, (same address as *Liturgy*). $10. Monthly newsletter format providing sane and sensible helps in bringing weekly worship to life at the local level.

Mass Media Bi-Weekly Newsletter, 2116 North Charles St., Baltimore, Md. 21218, or 1720 Chouteau Ave., St. Louis, Mo. 63103. Helpful, penetrating review of current cinema, television, slide packages, books on media, simulation games, short films.

Open, 116 West Washington, Madison, Wisc. 53703. Anglican quarterly.

Probe. 1800 Arrott Bldg., 401 Wood St., Pittsburgh, Pa. 15222. $5 for ten issues. A running listing by Christian Association of Southwest Pennsylvania of all sorts of liturgical resources and events.

Proclamations Productions, Orange Square, Port Jervis, N.Y. 12771. Richard Avery (pastor) and Donald Marsh (church musician) offer a regular fare of musical and liturgical songs and ceremonies on the "mod" side. Materials come out regularly, but not on stated schedule. Write for introductory packet of materials.

Reformed Liturgy and Music, Church Service Society of the U.S.A., Editorial Office, Witherspoon Bldg., Philadelphia, Pa. 19107. $6 for two publications a year. Carefully and relevantly examines current worship developments against the theological backdrop of the Reformed heritage in worship.

Response/in Worship, Music, the Arts, quarterly journal of the Lutheran Society for Worship, Music, and the Arts, Valparaiso University, Valparaiso, Ind. 46383. $5. Ecumenically oriented with Lutheran flavor; creative as well as reflective review.

Rock in Jesus, Advocate Publishing Co., Box 13504, Wichita, Kans. 67213. $3. Monthly review of Jesus-rock records, plus articles about the place of Jesus-rock and Jesus-rock artists in America.

Scan, P. O. Box 12811, Pittsburgh, Pa. 15241. $6. Bimonthly bibliography of liturgical, musical, artistic, and audiovisual materials, including reviews.

Studia Liturgica, Mathenesserlaan 301c, Rotterdam, Holland. $7. Scholarly, international liturgical journal.

This Week, World Library Publications, Inc., 5040 North Ravenswood, Chicago, Ill. 60640. Prayers, litanies, and music for each Sunday.

What's It All About? 341 Ponce de Leon Ave., N.E., Atlanta, Ga. 30308. $5. Monthly tip-sheet on what's happening in the youth-rock culture as it relates to the Christian faith.

Worship, Order of St. Benedict, Collegeville, Minn. 56321. Monthly, $6.50. Superb American liturgical journal, ecumenical in content and interest. Key articles on problems of liturgical renewal, plus exegetical and homiletical helps on the lectionary.

Yearbook of Liturgical Studies, Collegeville, Minn. 56321. Liturgical Press. Annual bibliography.

Important Single Issues of Periodicals

Austin Seminary Bulletin: Faculty Edition, 85 (November, 1969). Devoted entirely to the subject of worship. Strong biblical and theological bases in the discussions.

Chicago Theological Seminary Register, 58 (May-July 1968). The nature of celebration; how to create celebrations.

Risk, Living Liturgical Style, 5 (1969). A quarterly published by the Programme Unit on Education and Communication of the World Council of Churches, Room 439, 475 Riverside Dr., New York, N.Y. 10027. This issue explores liturgy as more than acts within sanctuaries, as central to the stuff of life itself.

II   Insight on Celebrative Creativity (chronological order)

Berdyaev, Nicolas, *The Meaning of the Creative Act*, New York: P. F. Collier. Philosophical-theological perspective on creativity, freedom, dignity in man's relationship with God.   1962

McLuhan, Marshall, *Understanding Media: The Extensions of Man*. New York: McGraw-Hill. The revolutionary new look at how human perception has altered with the advent of the electronic age.   1964

Rahner, Hugo. *Man at Play*. New York: Herder and Herder. Examines the meaning of play within human existence.   1965

Hart, Ray L. *Unfinished Man and the Imagination*. New York: Herder and Herder. Delves complicatedly but insightfully into the importance of the exercise of imagination in unfulfilled man.   1968

Cox, Harvey. *The Feast of Fools*. Cambridge, Mass.: Harvard University Press. Explores the dimension of celebration in the life of the church, revealing how important it is for us to understand the meaning of play and delight in our common life, and particularly in worship.   1969

Keen, Sam. *Apology for Wonder*. New York: Harper & Row. Delves significantly into the nature of wonder and the important role it plays today in how we perceive the world where we live. An important prelude for understanding wonder in contemporary celebration.   1969

Neale, Robert E. *In Praise of Play*. New York: Harper & Row. An account of play playfully presented.   1969

Keen, Sam. *To a Dancing God*. New York: Harper & Row. How to get ready for life to surprise you, both in mind and body.   1970

McLelland, Joseph C. *The Clown and the Crocodile*. Richmond: Knox Press. Is the dance of life worth it, despite all life's contradictions? A fine exploration of the celebrative life.   1970

Snyder, Ross. *Contemporary Celebration*. Nashville: Abingdon Press. Draws the reader quickly into the inner workings of celebration. Examines the celebrative life as communal rather than merely individual, discussing how to liberate creativity in the laity as they form their liturgies and express them.   1971

McElvaney, William K. *Cerebrations on Coming Alive*. Nashville: Abingdon Press. A book which is graphically contoured to show specific possibilities for the celebrative life.   1973

Art

I   Banners and Vestments (chronological order)

Laliberte, Norman, and McIlhany, Sterling. *Banners and Hangings, Design and Construction*. New York: Reinhold Publishing Corp.   1966

Abels, Paul and Abels, Barbara. *Discover and Create: An Arts Packet.* New 1967
York: Friendship Press. Record, drawings, songs, poems, and guide;
can be used to discover new uses of art in worship.

Anderson, Robert W., and Caemerer, Richard R. *Banners, Banners,* 1967
Banners. Chicago: Christian Art Associates, 1801 West Greenleaf Ave.,
60626 $3.

Allen, Horace T., Jr. *About Vestments.* Office of Worship and Music, 1970
Witherspoon Bldg., Philadelphia, Pa. 19107. Free. A single-page
discussion of modern and traditional vestments from the Reformed
position.

Jurack, Simone. *How Is a Banner?* Chicago: Christian Art Associates. $2. 1970
Enthusiastic description of the creative possibilities in banner-making.

Ireland, Marion P. *Textile Art in the Church.* Nashville: Abingdon Press. 1971
$27.50. Comprehensive, historical, practical survey; useful for banner
creators.

II Posters

Caring, 20 posters, incl.
"Gentle ways are best."
"Let us discover the love in each other."
Adventure, 12 posters, incl.
"Life is either a daring adventure, or nothing."
"Great things are done when men and mountains meet."
Discovery, 12 posters, incl.
"The greatest unexplored area lies under your hat."
"Fences were made for those who can't fly."
Paradox, 10 posters, incl.
"Kites rise highest against the wind."
"He who's not busy being born is busy dying."
Serenity, 13 posters, incl.
"The greatest revelation is stillness."
"Never say anything that will not improve on silence."
Wonder, 19 posters, incl.
"Who teaches birds how to fly?"
"Miracles happen only to those who believe in them."
Of Good Cheer, 23 posters, incl.
"You make my sun shine."
"Happiness is anyone or anything at all loved by you."
Becoming, 25 posters, incl.
"In the midst of winter, I finally learned that there was in me an
invincible summer."
"America is young and unfinished."
Oriental Wisdom, 13 posters, incl.
"Mind like parachute—function only when open."
"In the dew of little things the heart finds its morning and is
refreshed."
Sharing, 10 posters, incl.
"The door to happiness opens outward."
"I thank heaven someone's crazy enough to give me a daisy."
Fantasy, 12 posters, incl.
"Be the dream."
"The great man is he who does not lose his child's heart."
Festivity, 11 posters, incl.
"Start smiling and enjoy the miracle of now."
"After night there is always day and sunlight and flowers."

Commitment, 18 posters, incl.
"If there is no wind, row."
"Give me a fish and I eat for a day. Teach me to fish and I eat for a lifetime."
Insight, 22 posters, incl.
"Consistency is the last refuge of the unimaginative."
"War is much too serious a matter to be entrusted to the military."
Ecology, 13 posters, incl.
"Pollution is a dirty word."
"Where have all the flowers gone?"
Brotherhood, 13 posters, incl.
"Brother helped by brother is a fortress."
"Only those who have already experienced a revolution within themselves can..."
Values, 20 posters, incl.
"Children are the world's most valuable resource and its best hope for the future."
"If it is the truth, what does it matter who said it?"

All may be ordered from Argus Communications, 7440 North Natchez Ave., Niles, Ill. 60648; 5-10 posters $1.00 each; 11-50 posters $0.80 each, 51 or more $0.45 each.

Signs of the Seasons, 4 sets of 5 posters depicting seasons of church calendar.
The Beatitudes, each with original photo.
The Creed, 14 photovisuals depicting Apostles' Creed.
Listen Children, 7 photovisuals pleading poignantly for Christian service.
The Way of the Cross, 15 photovisuals interpret the Way of the Cross in modern context.
Church Seasons, 6 full-color posters symbols, each major season of the Christian year.
Old Testament Themes, 3 sets of 5 reflects God's plan for our salvation.
Love is . . . ., 8 giant photovisuals illustrate Paul's First Letter to the Corinthians.
Life of Christ, 15 full-color posters of Christ's life.
The Teachings of Christ, 15 full-color posters depicting key teachings of Christ.
The Miracles and Parables of Christ, 15 full-color posters.
Motivation Posters, 4 four-color visuals with motivational quotes.
God Speaks to Us in Signs, 13 photovisuals interpret symbols of our faith in contemporary terms.
They Serve . . . . *We Also Serve*, 14 photovisuals of adults and children performing community service.
God's Son on Earth, 15 four-color visuals depicting the major episodes in Christ's life.
Corporal Works of Mercy, 18 photos on 4 posters depicting need for works of mercy.
Pflaum Press, 38 West Fifth St., Dayton, Ohio 45402. Average prices on the above $4-6.

III Photography

Wells, Robert. *Celebrative Photography: A Family Reunion.* $3.25. With 22 sensitive photographs capturing celebrative instants of a family reunion, the author helps the reader/viewer approach the ordinary world with fresh vision. Encourages probing ordinary experiences with your camera.

Chicago Theological Seminary Register: Celebration II. $1.15 Reports some of the potential for awakening Christian possibility in contemporary consciousness through the making of photographs. Includes direction and theory.

Chicago Theological Seminary Register: Celebration III. $1.15. Under direction of Ross Snyder and Archie Lieberman, student photographs used as a means of humanizing ourselves. Photographs accompanied by the insights and sensings of the student photographers.

Campbell, Charles, and Husk, Gabe. *Visual and Verbal Meditations.* Slides and texts for liturgy and religious education. New Life Films, Box 2008, Kansas City, Kans. 66110. Scripture, current writings, and song lyrics accompanied by a programmed slide sequence as an assist to meditation, individually or in groups.

IV Makers of Vestments and Banners

Martha Albert, 26 Dunlap Road, Park Forest, Ill. 60466
Vienna Anderson, 1550 Cameron Crescent Drive, Reston, Va. 22070
Quequierre, 706 Broadway, New York, N.Y. 10003.
Beth Wilbanks, 51 West 94th St., New York, N.Y. 10025.

V Art Supplies for Liturgies

Christian Art Associates, 1801 West Greenleaf Ave., Chicago, Ill. 60626.
St. Benet Shop, 300 South Wabash Avenue, Chicago, Ill. 60604. Books, banners, records, posters, buttons.
St. Stephen's Church Enterprises, 3805 Warren Street, N.W., Washington, D.C. 20016. Buttons, banners, balloons, bumper stickers, records.

VI Thinking About Christian Art and Architecture

A. Books   (Chronological order)

Wetzler, Robert, and Huntington, Helen. *Seasons and Symbols.* Minneapolis: Augsburg Publishing House, $2.25 — 1962

White, James F. *Protestant Worship and Church Architecture.* New York: Oxford University Press. Much-needed examination of theological and historical considerations for building. — 1964

Bruggink, Donald J., and Droppers, Carl H. *Christ and Architecture.* Grand Rapids: Eerdmanns Publishing Co. — 1965

Disposable Forms for Worship. Youth Ministry Materials. P.O. Box 14325, St. Louis, Mo. 63178. Ideas for disposable art forms for all kinds of services. — 1970

Matthews, Wendell. *Basic Symbols and Terms of the Church.* New York: Fortress Press. Basic description of Christian symbols. — 1971

Anderson, Vienna. *Create and Celebrate.* New York: Morehouse-Barlow. $1.95. A unique guide for doing your own liturgical arts. — 1972

Rest, Friedrich. *Our Christian Symbols.* Philadelphia: United Church Press. Hardback, $3.50; paper, $1. Fundamental treatment of Christian symbols. — 1972

B. Periodicals

Christian Art, Monthly. 1801 West Greenleaf Ave., Chicago, Ill. 60626.
Faith and Art, Bimonthly. Box 408, Oak Brook, Ill. 60521. Entry subscription, $5.
   Exploring how faith and art compete and complement one another, how art
   gives meaning and expression to the human condition.

Drama

I Print Resources

Loomis, Amy Goodhue. *Guide for Drama Workshops in the Church*. National
   Council of Churches, New York, N.Y. 10027. How to prepare for, lead, and
   follow up on drama workshops in local churches.
Plays for the Church. Division of Christian Life and Mission, National Council of
   Churches. An annotated catalogue of several hundred plays. No bathrobe
   dramas, these! Plays about man's ultimate quest for reality in general, as well as
   plays about man's explicit identification with the transcendent in terms of
   Christian symbols.
Plays for Church Use. Baker's Plays, 100 Summer Street, Boston, Mass. 02110.
   Three characteristics of the host of plays listed in this catalogue: biblical,
   contemporary, and suited to production by church groups.

II Personal Resources

The Christian Society for Drama, Robert E. Seaver, President, Broadway at 120th
   St., New York, N.Y.
Dr. David Ritchey, Department of Speech and Drama, Auburn University, Auburn,
   Ala. 36830.
The Marionette Theater of the Word, c/o Roland Sylvester, 1875 East Kramer
   Drive, Carson, Calif. 90746.

Dance

Haskell, Arnold L. *The Wonderful World of Dance*. Garden City, N.Y.:   1960
   Garden City Books. A fascinating historical search into the
   development of dance from primitives to contemporary ballet. Survey
   deals with the nature of dance, and its value in expression of religious
   feeling.
Taylor, Margaret Fisk. *Creative Movement, Steps Toward Understanding*.   1965
   New York: Friendship Press. $1.50. Filmstrip and step-by-step
   guidance on how to use creative movement to resolve tensions and
   promote harmony.
————. *A Time to Dance*. Philadelphia: United Church Press. $2.95.   1967
Deiss, Lucien, and Weyman, Gloria. *Dancing for God*. Cincinnati: World   1969
   Library Publications. $4.95. Up-to-date discussions of liturgical dance,
   five choreographies, and description of five basic dance positions.
Gunther, Bernard, and Fusco, Paul. *Sense Realization: Below Your Mind*.   1968
   New York: P. F. Collier. Helps us understand the importance of
   movement and use of full-bodied sensing.

Mettler, Barbara. *Materials of Dance as a Creative Art Activity*. Mettler Studios, Box 4456, University Station, Tucson, Ariz. Handbook for students, teachers, and for anyone interested in body movement as art. To make creative dance activity easy and enjoyable for anyone who wants it.

Music

I Recordings

Abingdon • Audio Graphics

The Mission Singers

Disco-Teach. $6.95 each. Five albums of significant popular songs recorded by these young seminarians and accompanied by printed leader's guides.

Avant Garde Records, each $4.95, 250 West 57th, New York, N.Y. 10019.

Medical Mission Sisters

"Joy Is Like the Rain," contemporary/religious	AVS 101
"I Know the Secret," life/sorrow/struggle/joy	AVS 105
"Knock! Knock!" love/friendship/man/God	AV 109
"Seasons," more of same by singing nuns.	AVS 126
"In Love," joy and sorrow/bittersweet.	AVS 132
"RSVP," / "Songs of Promise" two liturgical services.	AG 4000
	AG 4001

John Ylvisaker

"Cool Livin," secular and spiritual for young.	AV 107
"Follow Me," songs on New Testament stories.	AV 111
"A Love Song," love songs scripturally set.	AV 112

Bill Comeau

"Busy Day," 13 songs for children of all ages.	AV 110
"Gentle Revolution," for alienated teen-agers.	AVS 122
"Fragments from an Unknown Gospel," poetry with musical accompaniment.	AVS 123
"Some Beautiful Day," retelling of incidents in life of Christ, set to music.	AVS 127

The Ambrosian Singers

"A Choral Tapestry," Vol. I, choral masterpieces of 16th and 17th centuries.	AVS 128
"A Choral Tapestry," Vol. II, 22 more masterpieces from 16th and 17th centuries.	AVS 129
"Jesus," the life of Jesus told in 12 contemporary songs.	AVS 130

Other Releases

"Praise the Lord in Many Voices," three records made at Carnegie Hall concert: Album I, "Mass of a Pilgrim People," featuring Medical Mission Sisters and John Ylvisaker; Album II, "Praise the Lord," solos, chorus, instruments, plus, "Psalms for the Young in Spirit," featuring Paul Quinlan, Jesuit folk psalmist; Album III, "Community Mass," interfaith chorus with organ accompaniment and "By Request," with Robert Edwin singing with instrumental trio.	AVS 102 AVS 103 AVS 104
"Keep the Rumor Going," folk music by Bob Edwin.	AV 106
"Go Tell Everyone," Sacred Heart Choir with instrumental accompaniment, "young" sound.	AV 113

"Ring Out Joy," Ed Summerlin, spiritual truth in jazz idiom. AV 114

"Holmes Sings Spirituals," Negro baritone. AV 115

"The Mass for Peace," rock mass done by Italian group in English. AVS 116

"Come to Bethlehem," Johnny Pearson, English master with chorale and orchestra. AVS 118

"Let Trumpets Sound," Chancel Choir of Second Prebyterian Church, Newark, N.J., latest church choral music. AVS 121

"Another Dawn," 12-song cycle by Frank Dumin of young man's search for truth. AVS 124

"Bubble Joy," songs by Elaine Curzio rediscovering God's presence in little things. AVS 125

"Let the Cosmos Ring," musical experience by the Cross-current Community of Toronto, Canada, a loose-knit group of youth of many faiths. AVS 131

"Becoming One," four young men sing of where unity is found in a tension-ridden world. AVS 133

"A Different Shade of Blue," songs by the religious country-folk group, Dust and Ashes. AVS 134

"The Message of Christmas," carols of many lands sung in original languages. AVS 117

"Rebirth," 5 college students sing of the "Jesus Life." AVS 135

Center for Contemporary Celebration,
$5.35. 1400 East 53rd St., Chicago, Ill. 60615

Kent Schneider
"Celebration for Modern Man," jazz arrangements with choir of young people of Lord's Prayer, Psalm 150, word-jazz sermon, new doxology.

Concordia Publishing House, each $4.95. 3558 South Jefferson Ave., St. Louis, Mo. 63118
"Hymns for Now 1: How"
"Hymns for Now 2: How"
"Hymns for Now 3: How"
10 songs from each book played folk-style, plus 10 from each book cast in hard rock and bluegrass.

G. I. A. Records, each $5. 2115 West 63rd, Chicago, Ill. 60636

Sebastian Temple
"The Universe Is Singing," 12 songs in the spirit of Teilhard de Chardin. MS 118

"And the Waters Keep on Running Through My Mind," songs for liturgical and other celebrations. MS 133

"God Is a Fire of Love," songs for liturgy in the Pentecostal spirit. MS 134

Gregory Ballerino
"Come, Let Us Worship," contemporary folk mass songs with chorus of 100 backed by guitars, bass, tambourines. MS 114

God Unlimited
"Joy and Other Sublime Aspirations," hymns in the folk idiom. MS 120
"Ride On," ten folk and folk-rock songs telling the message of salvation. MS 123

The Keyhole
"Hallelujah! Jesus Is Lord," Houston coffeehouse group sings timeless message songs. MS 130
"The Way In," contemporary messages of the faith. MS 129

The Mission

"There'll Come a Day," four seminarians working in St. Louis MS 126
    slums sing of the searching of those who despair.
"Yesterday's Gone," songs of poverty, peace, war, civil rights. MS 127
"Let's Get Together," original and familiar. MS 128

The New Prophets

"Come Follow," a trio with guitars and rhythm instruments sing MS 116
    biblically oriented songs.

Proclamation Productions, each $4.95. Orange Square, Port Jervis,
    N.Y.

Avery and Marsh

"Hymns Hot and Carols Cool," Avery and Marsh joined by two
    ladies in their church sing songs from the book by the same
    name.
"A Song for all Seasons," singers from Princeton join Avery and
    Marsh.

World Library Publications, Inc. $5.95 each, 2145 Central Parkway,
    Cincinnati, Ohio 45214

Joe Wise

"Gonna Sing, My Lord " JW-100
"Hand in Hand " LP-1002
"A New Day " 0918
"Sweet Water" FSS-7001
    songs that blend folk, blues and country styles.

Sebastian Temple

"Sing! People of God, Sing!" contemporary songs for worship SFPS-67-1
    services.
"Happy the Man," inspired by Scripture and St. Francis of SFPS-2
    Assisi.

Jack Miffleton

"Some Young Carpenter," subtle sincere Christian messages by FR-2242-SM
    composer, folk-guitarist priest.
"With Skins and Steel," vital lyrics, vigorous melodies. WLSM-33-SM

Other Releases

"Rebirth," by Lynn Haney, songs inspired by the earth-rebuild- FR-2395-SM
    ing philosophies of Chardin.
"No Time Like the Present," by Neil Blunt, folk composer and FR-1997-SM
    artist relates to the needs of our times.
"Thoughts of Time," by His People, a group of young artists FR-2104-SM
    headed by Sister Judith Bisignano, reflecting style, mood of
    youth today.
"Let All the Earth Sing His Praise," Tom Parker sings hymns in WLSM-29-SM
    folk style.
"Until He Comes," The Roamin' Collars, seminarians, sing their FR-2397-SM
    own songs.
"Selections from Young People's Folk Hymnal," Vol. II, best FR-2389-SM
    songs of the top WLSM artists.

Useful Songs by Popular Recording Artists

The following songs have enjoyed recent popularity with the public. The songs
contain the kind of insight, with implicit as well as explicit reference to the Christian
faith, that commends them for use in a liturgical setting. Consult your local record
or music store for information about album numbers and prices.

Ark 2,
"From Now On (Immortal, Invisible)," new life
Bradford, Alex
"Black Man's Lament," prejudice
"I'm All Right Now," repentance
Brewer & Shipley,
"Rock Me on the Waters," baptism
Emerson, Lake, and Palmer,
"The Only Way," commitment
Flack, Roberta, and Hathaway, Donny
"Come, Ye Disconsolate," communion
"You've Got a Friend," fellowship
Godspell
"Prepare Ye the Way of the Lord," call to worship
"Day by Day," intercession
"Light of the World," witness
"We Beseech Thee, Hear Us," intercession
Harrison, George
"My Sweet Lord," faith
"Hear Me Lord," intercession
Lighthouse
"Step Out on the Sea," faith
Newman, Randy
"He Gives Us All His Love," faith
Rivers, Johnny
"Think His Name," commitment
Royal Scots
"Amazing Grave," grace
Seatrain
"Song of Job," suffering
Simone, Nina,
"I Wish I Knew How It Would Feel To Be Free," freedom
"Why?" prejudice
Stevens, Cat
"Changes IV," new life
"Morning Has Broken," creation
"Peace Train," peace
Stookey, Paul
"Wedding Song," presence
Taylor, James
"Fire and Rain," suffering
The Who
"See Me, Feel Me," sensitivity

II Hymnals and Songbooks

Alive and Singing. Richard Avery and Donald Marsh. Port Jervis, N.Y.: Proclamation
Productions. $1. Another cycle of songs for the church year, plus fun songs both
theologically sound and biblically centered.

A Time for Singing. Geneva Press, 1970. $0.65. Mixes popular contemporary with
traditional, true folk material as well as less known contemporary folk type.

Contemporary Hymn Book. Compiled by David Yantis. David Yantis Publications,
1505 47th St., San Diego, Calif. 92102, 1971. $2. Original liturgical and worship
songs by David Yantis, plus songs by Mitchell, Temple, Blue, Strathdee, and others.
Aids to worship also. Guitar chords and melody lines.

Contemporary Worship Hymns, I. Inter-Lutheran Commission on Worship for
Provisional Use. Minneapolis: Augusburg Publishing House, 1969. $1.50. Twenty

hymns, some new, some standbys, such as, "Sons of God," "We Are One in the Spirit."

Discovery in Song. New York: Association Press. $1.50. Rock and folk-rock, texts with pictures and interpretation. No scores.

Dust and Ashes Songbook. Nashville: Abingdon Press, 1971. $1.50. Original songs on contemporary themes. Guitar chords and melody lines.

Gonna Sing My Lord. Joseph Wise. Cincinnati: World Library Publications. $0.60. Easily teachable songs, contemporary folk style, for a Mass program. Record containing all music in the book with Joe Wise singing, available for teaching.

Great Songs of the Sixties. M. Okrun, ed. Quadrangle Books, Inc. $17.50. Combines all great protest and pop songs of an activist decade. Scores for piano and guitar.

Hooray for God. Avery and Marsh. Port Jervis, N.Y.: Proclamation Productions. Vocal booklet $1.00, accompaniment book $2.95. Introits, dismissals, amens, and responses of praise. Also, "We're Here to Be Happy," "Go and Be Happy."

Hymnal for Young Christians, I & II. Chicago: F. E. L. Publications. $1.50. Ecumenical versions of an excellent selection of folk hymns with scores by composers such as Thiem, Scholtes, Blue, Rivers, Sister Marian, *et al.* Liturgical and catechetical songs, songs from Scripture done creatively, songs for children.

Hymns for Now, A Portfolio for Good, Bad, or Rotten Times. Walther League, 875 North Dearborn Street, Chicago, Ill. 60610, 1967. $0.75. Popular for its well-established hymns such as, "We Shall Overcome," "Sons of God," "O Freedom," *et al.*—26 tunes in all. Striking illustrations in collage style.

Hymns for Now II. Youth Ministry Materials, P.O. Box 14325, St. Louis, Mo. 63178, 1969. $1. Twenty-eight hymnsongs such as, "Take Our Bread," "All My Trials."

Hymns for Now III. Youth Ministry Materials, 1972. $1.50. Contemporary mood with experimental photography. Twenty-seven songs about bus rides, love, squirrels, and clowns. Songs for strumming, feasting, confessing.

Hymns Hot and Carols Cool. Avery and Marsh. Port Jervis, N.Y.: Proclamation Productions. $1. To be sung with guitar, drums, rhythm instruments, piano, or organ. Unusual pertinent, "radical" songs for church year, or anytime for a church with a developing "now" feeling.

Mission Singers Song Book. Nashville: Abingdon Press, 1971. $1.50. Original songs for our times, troubles, and triumphs. Guitar chords and piano accompaniment.

Modern Hymn Tunes. Miami Beach, Fla.: Hanson Publications. $2.50. Sixty-nine twentieth-century hymns for organ and piano. Older hymns set to modern music, sprightly, joyful, beautiful, serving as a bridge to contemporary folk-style music for those congregations that are not quite ready to move beyond traditional sounds.

More, More, More. Avery and Marsh. Port Jervis, N.Y.: Proclamation Productions. $1. Book 2 of the Hymns Hot and Carols Cool series. Liturgical as well as carefree renditions.

The Most Popular Songs from the Hymnal for Young Christians. Chicago: F. E. L. Publications. $5. Composers Repp, Mitchell, Scholtes, Germaine, Blue, and Quinlan. Such hymns as, "Shout from the Highest Mountain," "Sons of God," "Allelu!" "Clap Your Hands." Record, "Gonna Sing My Lord," can be used to teach and learn this kind of music.

New Wine, Songs for Celebration. Board of Education of the Southern California-Arizona Conference of The United Methodist Church, 5250 Santa Monica Blvd., Los Angeles, Calif., 90029. Single melody line with guitar chords. Has the virtue of containing many songs that already have or will have lasting value: "Dona Nobis Pacem," "Where Have All the Flowers Gone?" "Sons of God," "Every Star," "We Are One in the Spirit." Repp, Yantis, Strathdee, Thiem, Wise, Friedell are some of the well-known composers.

Psalms: A Singing Version. Joseph Gelineau. New York: Paulist/Newman Press. $1.45. French priest devises easily teachable versions of the psalms, the Roman Church's first hymnal. Mainly responsive and antiphonal form.

Songbook for Saints and Sinners. Carlton R. Young, ed. Chicago: Agape, 1971. Pocket size with lead line and guitar chords, $1.00. spiral accompaniment edition, $4.95. Well-known, fascinating folk hymns along with some standard traditional.

Songs for Celebration. Center for Contemporary Celebration, 1400 E. 53rd St., Chicago, Ill. 60615. $2.75. Collection of more than fifty songs, gathered and arranged by Kent Schneider, used in workshops across the country. The songs cover the church year and a variety of styles: jazz-rock, folk, organ, raga, and electronics. Bulk rates available on request.

Songs for the Easter People. Avery and Marsh. Port Jervis, N.Y.: Proclamation Productions. Book 4 in the Hymns Hot and Carols Cool series, maintaining the same level of joy, pertinence for special and non-special seasons.

Songs for the Search. Avery and Marsh. Port Jervis, N.Y.: Proclamation Productions. $1. A portfolio of songs and pages of ideas for presentation and discussion including, "Love Them Now," "Thank You, Lord," and "My Kind of Music."

Twelve Folksongs and Spirituals. Compiled and arranged by David N. Johnson. Minneapolis: Augsburg Publishing House. $1. For unison or mixed voices or guitar accompaniment. Includes "The Lone, Wild Bird," "There Is a Balm in Gilead," "Wondrous Love," "Earth and All Stars," "I've Got a Home in That Rock."

Ventures in Song. David J. Randolph, ed. Nashville: Abingdon Press, 1972. Singable, enjoyable collection of songs for both liturgical and songfest use.

Winds of God. F. H. Gere and M. H. Williams, St. Paul's Episcopal Church, P. O. Box 1363, Burlingame Calif., 94010. Choir book, $1.00; recording, $4.95; congregation's book, $0.10. A youth folk mass using some well-known numbers: "Michael, Row Your Boat," "Kum Ba Ya," "He's Got the Whole World in His Hands," plus earlier music from the "Rejoice Mass." Original composition for Nicene Creed.

The Ylvisaker Hymnerie, Part I. John Ylvisaker. Vanguard Music Corporation, 250 West 57th St., New York, N.Y. 10019. V-541, $1.25. Convenient 5x8 pew size, songs for all the church year for young in heart of all ages.

III   Music Discussion

A. Books (chronological order)

Lovelace, Austin, and Rice, William. *Music and Worship in the Church.* Nashville: Abingdon Press. — 1960

Routley, Erik. *Twentieth Century Church Music.* New York: Oxford University Press. — 1964

Miller, William Robert. *The World of Pop Music and Jazz.* St. Louis: Concordia Publishing House. Good discussion of the influence of pop and jazz in the church. — 1965

Northcott, Cecil. *Hymns in Christian Worship.* Richmond: John Knox Press. $1.95 — 1965

"Crisis in Church Music" Washington: Liturgical Conference, 1330 Massachusetts Ave., N.W. Paper discusses the nature of the changes occurring in church music. — 1967

Routley, Erik. *Words, Music, and the Church.* Nashville: Abingdon Press. $4.95. — 1968

Sydnor, James. *Music in the Life of the Church.* Convenant Life Curriculum, Presbyterian Church in the United States. — 1968

Deiss, Lucien. *Spirit and Song of the New Liturgy.* Cincinnati: World Library Publications. $7.95. Authoritative explanation of elements of philosophy of the liturgy in the Roman Catholic Mass. Profitable reading for Protestants. — 1971

DeVinney, Richard. *There's More to Church Music Than Meets the Ear.* Philadelphia: Fortress Press, $2.25. Unique discussion of how church musicians can deal with nonmusical problems, getting along with other people. Author is organist and director of music in Grand Rapids, Michigan. Much-needed discussion of the human side of church musicianship. — 1972

B. Periodicals

The American Organist, 1 Union Square West, New York, N.Y. Monthly, $3.00 a year. Stop lists and specifications on new and historic installations. Also, information on current publications in organ literature.

Choristers Guild Letters, Choristers Guild, P.O. Box 38188, Dallas, Tex. 75238. Exchange of ideas about children's choirs in churches of all denominations. Monthly (Sept. through June), membership $6.

The Diapason, 434 S. Wabash Avenue, Chicago, Ill. 60605. Formerly the AGO magazine. Monthly, $4.00 a year. Recital information and articles on performing problems and possibilities.

The Hymn, Hymn Society of America, 475 Riverside Drive, New York, N.Y. 10027. Quarterly devoted to hymnology and the publication of new texts and/or tunes. Membership, $6.50 a year.

Journal of Church Music, 2900 Queen Lane, Philadelphia, Pa. 19129. Monthly, $4.75 a year. Articles and news of church and choral music, as well as sample anthems.

Music, American Guild of Organists, 630 Fifth Ave., New York, N.Y. 10020. Monthly, $7.50 a year. Comments on performances and publishing in the organ and choral music world.

Music Ministry, The Methodist Publishing House, 201 Eighth Ave., South, Nashville, Tenn. 37202. Monthly, $5.50 a year. Related to Methodist musicians' organization. Articles on church music and anthems, reviews, good helps for local church music leaders.

Liturgi-Words

I   Books

Boyd, Malcolm. *Are You Running with Me Jesus?* New York: Avon Books. $1.25. Contemporary topical meditations by swinging Episcopal priest. — 1965

Quoist, Michel. *Prayers.* New York: Sheed & Ward. Moving and penetrating collection of very contemporary topical meditations. — 1966

McNierney, E. S. W. *The Underground Mass Book.* Baltimore: Helicon Press. $1.35. Quotations of contemporary writers and songs for use in the new liturgy in the Roman Church. Much good material for use in Protestant services. — 1968

Haven, Robert M. *Look at Us Lord.* Nashville: Abingdon Press. $4.95. Poignant prayers from pastoral experience, frank, unselfconscious. Penetrating photographs accompanying text. — 1969

Hoey, Robert F. *The Experimental Liturgy Book.* New York: Herder and Herder. $4.50. A collection of a variety of parts of the liturgy from numerous sources to give the student of liturgy examples of varieties of ways the traditional parts can be enlivened. — 1969

Kirby, John, ed. *Word and Action: New Forms of the Liturgy.* New York: The Seabury Press. $2.95. Includes most of the modern rites published by American denominations. — 1969

Rivers, Clarence. *Celebrations.* New York: Herder and Herder. Fresh presentation of the Mass with Scripture selections, readings, contemporary songs, slide projector, etc. Introductory section helpful with explanations. There follows seven complete celebrations. Lively format excites hope in traditional worship design. — 1969

Worship Resource Book. Youth Ministry Materials, P.O. Box 14325, St. Louis, Mo. 63178. $1.25. Action responses in contemporary worship forms. Songs, drama, prayers, poems, orders of worship for planning your own services. — 1969

Ahl, Anna Maria, and Rotering, Robert. *Yesterday, Today, and Tomorrow.* Winona, Minn.: St. Mary's College Press. Compilation of quota- — 1971 tions about yesterday, today, and tomorrow, gathered by Rotering, strikingly illustrated by Ahl. Useful as thought-starting quotations in the liturgy.

Balloons, Anchors, and Grapplings Hooks. Youth Ministry Materials. $1. 1971
Worship resources that break through patterns into a loving, freeing experience of Christ, life, the gathered.

Savary, Louis M. *Touch with Love, New Ways to Reach Out to the* 1971
Universe. New York: Association Press. $2.95. Uses selections from Watts, Gibran, Schutz, Fromm, Rimmer, and others to explore new ways to love and trust, to be near, to break through to each other. Can be used for places in liturgy. Sensitive photographs parallel to text.

Bimler, Richard. *Pray, Praise, and Hooray.* St. Louis: Concordia Publish- 1972
ing House. Prayers for youth and other people. Centers on fifty key words common in parlance today; words such as *advertisement, death, hunger,* etc. Language rises from experience, does not parade itself.

Brown, John P. and York, Richard L., *The Covenant of Peace: A* 1972
Liberation Prayer Book. New York: Morehouse-Barlow.

Dimensions of Decision, Selected Readings. Nashville: Graded Press. 1972
$1.50. Readings, modern and old, short and long, dramatic at points; sections on response to change, decisions and the self, political decisions. One hundred twenty-eight readings for mind-teasing in your development of liturgy.

Discovery in Word. New York: Association Press. $1.50. Ideas from 1972
contemporary writers for young people, selected by young people.

Habel, Norman C., and Misfeldt, Bruce. *Hi! Have a Nice Day.* Philadel- 1972
phia: Fortress Press. $1.95. "Fresh thoughts from fresh kids." A grab bag of expressions from young people about many Christian things, expressions that penetrate, enliven, that are brash, surprising. Words that tickle the imagination for more creative liturgical expression.

Rhymes, Douglas. *Prayer in the Secular City.* Philadelphia: Westminster 1972
Press. An easy-reading study of prayer and devotion for the modern day by an able Church of England parson.

Thurian, Max. *Moden Man and Spiritual Life.* New York: Association 1972
Press. An interesting combination of Protestant and Catholic spiri- tuality, in a modern context.

Uehling, Carl T. *Prayers for Public Worship.* Philadelphia: Fortress Press. 1972
$10.95. A primary source for contemporary prayers by those who seek to learn to create their own prayers. Vigorous language, avoids catch-phrases, is straightforward. Includes prayers on specific themes such as the family, national elections, vocations, the congregation, Christmas, etc.

Wyon, Olive. *The School of Prayer.* New York: The Macmillan Co. A great 1972
and profound English theologian guides very practically into the great Christian tradition of meditation and private prayer.

Zdenek, Marilee, and Champion, Marge. *Catch the New Wind.* Waco, Tex.: 1972
Word Books. $8.95. Compilation of nine creative and meaningful worship services, artistically blending the contemporary with the traditional. Beautifully illustrated. Combines drama, art, Scripture, liturgy, music, lighting, and literature.

II   Cassettes

Benson, Dennis. *RAP.* Nashville: Abingdon Audio·Graphics. $7.95 each. Six cassette tapes designed to grapple with contemporary crises of our age—social problems and patterns, youth and youth culture, environmental problems, etc.

_____ . *SOS (Switched-on-Scripture).* Nashville: Abingdon Audio·Graphics. $7.95 each. Action-oriented, relevant, and exciting cassette tapes for Bible study in the electronic age.